REGI

Stand and Deliver

■

Stand and Deliver

INSIDE CANADIAN COMEDY

■

Andrew Clark

Doubleday Canada Limited

Canadian Cataloguing in Publication Data

Clark, Andrew (Andrew Beatty)
    Stand and deliver: inside Canadian comedy

ISBN 0-385-25602-7

1. Comedians – Canada – Biography.   2. Canadian wit and humor (English) – History and criticism.*   3. Performing arts – Canada. I. Title.

PN2307.C52 1997   791'.092'271   C96-932239-9

Jacket photo montage by Steve Munday
Jacket design by Avril Orloff
Text design by Heidy Lawrance Associates
Printed and bound in the USA

Care has been take to trace ownership of – and secure permission for – all photographs in this book. The publishers will gladly receive any information that will enable them to rectify omissions affecting credit lines in subsequent printings.

Published in Canada by
Doubleday Canada Limited
105 Bond Street
Toronto, Ontario
M5B 1Y3

To Ella

■

Acknowledgements

Special thanks to my grandmother, Gertrude Clark, Nancy Jamieson and Bruce Anderson, without whose support this book would not have been possible. Thanks to my parents, Scott Clark and Lynn Jamieson, for their support and encouragement throughout. Thanks to David Borenstein for his couch, his friendship and for not bouncing my cheques. Thanks to my brother Matthew. Thanks to Tom and Marion Jamieson. Thanks to Judy and Brian Sally for their assistance digging up information on the Dumbells. Thanks to Doubleday Canada Limited for taking a risk on a first-time author and to all the Doubleday staff who patiently endured my neophyte foibles.

Thanks to my agent and editor Dean Cooke, who believed, before anyone else, there was a book to be written. Without his guidance, friendship and involvement there is no way this book would have made it to the shelf.

Last but not least, thanks to Alexander Jamieson for just hanging out.

■

Contents

．

INTRODUCTION

It was October 6, 1996, and I was sitting with Harland Williams, the man I was convinced would be Canada's next great comedic sensation. Williams, a thirty-three-year-old native of North York, Ontario, had paid his show business dues in Canada and America, and was in the middle of starring in his first Hollywood feature film, *Space Cadet,* being filmed on location at the Lyndon Johnson Space Center in Houston, Texas. It was a Disney film, a major offering scheduled for a summer 1997 release. After that, there was every reason to believe Harland Williams would be a household name.

The Texan weather and scenery were just as two Canadians would have imagined them. It was an idyllic eighty degrees. Beyond a line of aerospace rockets, the horizon stretched endlessly. Royal-blue sky collided with lush green pasture. Williams and I were seated under a canopy, eating our lunch during a break in shooting. I had followed Williams' career for close to five years, both as the comedy critic for the Toronto alternative newspaper *eye WEEKLY* and then for the Toronto *Star*. Comedy, by my definition, is not about funny plays, humourous writings, or cartoons. Comedy in the twentieth century means stand-up comedy or sketch (group) comedy, using material written by the performer or performers and delivered directly to the audience. Williams had entered that scene in the mid-eighties while still a student. I had accidentally fallen into writing about it in the early nineties, after a year spent running a comedy club in London, England. At that lunch in Houston, neither of us was speaking. We must both have been engrossed in some kind of minor epiphany. I was recalling a night three years before when

I had driven through a Toronto snowstorm to join an audience of about thirty people watch Williams deliver a stand-up comedy set that remains one of the most brilliant I've ever seen. Finally Harland broke the silence: "Sometimes it's hard to believe all this is happening," he said.

I knew what Harland meant: it was hard to accept that level of personal success. As a cultural phenomenon, however, Canadian comedians succeeding in the United States was as unsurprising as snow on Christmas day. Canadian comedians had been scoring successes in America since the 1920s. In the last twenty-five years, however, they had swamped Hollywood's comedy community. The line was long: Jim Carrey, *Saturday Night Live* creator Lorne Michaels, Dan Aykroyd, John Candy, and on and on. Canadians in comedy have become a cliché. Even the New York *Times* had once published a story inquiring: "What's So Funny About Canadians?" When I set about researching this book, I was determined to answer that question. My years of reporting on Canadian comedy and my heartfelt devotion to it compelled me to search for an answer. I decided early on to confine my investigations to English Canadian comedy. French Canadian comedy is a whole other story, one I was not equipped to tackle.

I discovered that many of the answers came in the form of more questions. I thought I would find the evidence in obvious places, such as the country's stand-up comedy clubs or the histories of well-known sketch troupes like CODCO and Second City. Instead I found my search led me into unexpected territory. The key to Canadian comedy was locked away in many separate mysteries. It was hidden in our history, jammed in faraway battlefields, in musty newspaper clippings, in our rugged geography, and in the cultural choices Canadians had made since Confederation — choices like loyalty to the monarchy, gun control, and medicare. It was tied to our economy and, perhaps surprisingly, to free-market principles. It led me on an odyssey that spanned the country and trickled down south to places like Los Angeles, New York City, and the state of Texas.

It was an obsessive, time-consuming trip, one for which I found myself unexpectedly free to indulge. Before committing to the project, I had led a decidedly nine-to-five existence, complete with the accompanying marital commitments. But in September 1995, less than a month after signing the book contract, my situation changed. I found myself alone and free to keep "comedian's hours." I could live a noon-to-four-in-the-morning existence.

I discovered my first clue in the eyes of the comedians. I was at Yuk Yuk's comedy club in Toronto, during a Friday night show, standing near the back of the room. It's here that the stand-ups congregate as they wait for their turn to go onstage. The boys at the back, as they are known, stare listlessly towards the stage. In their eyes there is a burning determination to go up there and "kill" (comedy-speak for perform well). Strangely, that gaze was the same one that, as a child, I had imagined my great uncle Gordon Halcrow Clark wearing as he crouched in a trench waiting to go over the top into no-man's-land. Gint, as he was called, had served in France during World War I. He had fought in such battles as the Somme and Vimy. His picture, taken in uniform as a nineteen-year-old soldier, and the pictures of his two brothers, who had also served, sat in grandfather's family album. When I myself turned nineteen, Gint's picture became the source of great interest to my family, and to my grandfather in particular, since by some miracle of genetics I had grown into Gordon Halcrow Clark's double. We were identical twins, except for our eyes. My eyes were still young. His were filled with too much knowledge. Gint's pupils seemed to break through their coloured irises like the sun breaking though the clouds. They held the look that many of his peers must also have shared. It was the look of a man staring into oblivion, bracing himself to make that mad dash into carnage.

Why comedians wore the same glare as soldiers who faced death was perplexing. It was an insight that affected me deeply. It was, however, one that I thought I would have to discard. After all, what could hip, modern Canadian comics have in common with the soldiers of World War I? What could comedy, a silly and natural pursuit, have in common with the waste and horror of world war? Then I discovered the Dumbells.

■

A Killing Joke

The gas had been meant for the Canadians. As the final Battle of Ypres raged in October of 1917, the Germans had fired the poisonous mist towards the Canadian trenches, but the winds had shifted and carried it instead towards two Irish regiments. Irish casualties had been heavy, and the Canadian 9th and 8th Field Ambulance units had been ordered to the Irish lines to help ferry the wounded back to the town. Alan Murray and Ross Hamilton, both of the 8th, were among the Canadians dispatched to give aid. The pair would drive trucks crammed with the dying and then carry the men on stretchers to a makeshift hospital, where surgeons would do what they could for them.

Ypres could no longer be called a town. Only the roads, which were broken and pocked with holes, gave evidence that it had once been a vibrant and well-populated place, that there had once been order and civilization there. The same could be said for the dying. Those who had been hit by gas blistered and coughed as their agonized lungs filled with poison. The only means of easing their suffering was to prop them on their sides and place a small tube in their mouths. They were supposed to draw their last few breaths from these cold umbilical cords.

Alan Murray worked furiously, all the while realizing that, had the winds not shifted, it would have been he who was dying. His effort was halted by the sight of one of the wounded men. He was a young Irish officer, nineteen, who lay on a stretcher outside the ruined chapel at Ypres. His head hung like the chapel's steeple, which had once leapt towards heaven but had been bowed by a steady stream of shell fire, both Allied and German. Two men held him on his side as he breathed through his rubber lifeline. Murray watched as a Canadian chaplain, about the same age as the officer, approached and told the young man that he was dying. The news stirred some fire in the dying officer's soul. The boy soldier threw the two men aside and struggled to his feet. He stood over his stretcher, then uttered these words:

> Wild regrets, and the bloody sweats,
> None knew so well as I:
> For he who lives more lives than one
> More deaths than one must die.

Then the young Irish officer dropped dead.

Murray, who had been well-educated back in Canada, recognized the verse. Those words were from Oscar Wilde's *The Ballad of the Reading Gaol*. The unbelievably dramatic scene shook Murray. As he and Hamilton returned to their unit he must have thought, 'we've got to use this in a sketch.'

Alan Murray and Ross Hamilton were both members of the 8th Ambulance Company's musical troupe and original members in the Dumbells, Canada's first, and one of its most popular, sketch comedy troupes. Many historians argue that Canada became a nation during World War I, specifically at the Battle of Vimy Ridge, when in April 1917 a Canadian force conquered a German position that both the British and the French forces had failed to take. When Canadians captured the ridge, the country achieved entrance into the nation club, and not by peacekeeping efforts but by waging war. Back home the nation rejoiced. If the victory at Vimy marked the birth of Canadian nationalism, it is fitting and more than a little ironic that it also marked the birth of the flipside of Canadian nationalism: comedy. As the battle's roar began to fade to a sorrowful echo, an army captain named Merton Plunkett was dreaming up the creation of the Dumbells.

Merton Wesley Plunkett was a twenty-six-year-old former grocer from Orillia, Ontario, who played the piano and had studied singing in Toronto. Because of these abilities the Army had assigned him to the 3rd Division and had given him the honourary rank of captain. Plunkett landed in France in 1916. Morale was, understandably, a major concern for the military establishment, and Plunkett was one of many talented soldiers assigned to boost the spirits of front-line Canadian troops. Plunkett, a pudgy man with a thick crop of blond hair, would travel to battle areas with a tent and a small piano. Working solo he would pitch the tent, steady the piano, and serenade the troops as they returned from the field. As the troops convened, he would leap onstage, flash a grin, and launch into a rendition of standard songs such as "Tipperary" or "Pack Up Your Troubles." Once his audience was warmed up, Plunkett would call for volunteers. He'd coax soldiers onstage to sing and improvise skits.

"I came out of the line and saw a big marquee," Jack Ayre, a professional pianist turned soldier, told CBC Radio producer Grace Shaw in an interview in 1964. "A fellow told us there's a fellow named Plunkett giving impromptu concerts every night. Naturally we went in, and I sat in the second row, steel helmet on and everything, and I see this little chap come out onstage and say, 'Anybody play the piano?' My pals said 'Go on, Jack.' He said, 'Who's Jack?' So they push me on, and the next thing I know I'm up there playing."

Plunkett knew there was enough talent in the Canadian forces to mount a successful revue. In fact, many divisions had their own performing troupes. The Princess Patricia's Canadian Light Infantry (PPCLI), for example, had a troupe of soldiers who put on musical revues. He idly compiled a wish list of members for a troupe of his own: Merton's brother Albert, who had lied to get into the Army and was only sixteen; Alan Murray; Murray's friend Ross Hamilton, who when properly costumed became a stunningly beautiful brunette with the falsetto voice to match; two other ambulance men, Ted Charters, a sergeant who gave a mock sermon on the Battle of the Somme entitled "No Man Knoweth When Inspection Cometh," and Private Bill Tennant, a tenor; Bert Langley; two actors, Private Frank Brayford and Corporal Leonard Young; and Corporal Jack Ayre, the pianist. Each of these men had an average of sixteen months' active service, spent in waging the worst fighting the world had ever seen. After Vimy, Plunkett got his wish. PPCLI's troupe had refused to perform for the 3rd Division because there were only three electric lights available to light their show. Major-General L. J. Lipsett then authorized Captain Plunkett to organize a 3rd Division concert party as a macabre sort of booster rally for the combat-fatigued Canadian troops. Plunkett called his gang the Dumbells, in honour of the shoulder patch worn by soldiers in the 3rd Division, two crossed red dumbbells on a French-grey background. It had been chosen to signify "silence and strength," two qualities Canadians then, as today, liked to think they had in abundance.

The show was rehearsed in July of 1917 and staged in August in a bombed-out shack at Guoy-Servins, a tiny village outside Poperinge, Belgium. It was in the heart of the Passchendaele sector, the site of the most severe fighting of the 1917 autumn campaign. During this battle, known as the Third Battle of Ypres, the Allies advanced five kilometres at a cost of three hundred thousand lives. The stage setting and effects were haphazard. Carved empty shell containers served as lights, horse-hair and rope for wigs. A cat skin was cut up to make mustaches. It is hard to imagine what the soldiers who made up the audience must have been thinking. They were on the western front, sitting front row for a music-hall production. It may just be the most surreal moment in Canadian show business.

The show was clean, fast, and full of what Plunkett saw as the basis of sure-fire material: sentiment and hokum. The Dumbells borrowed freely from the hit songs of the day. They lifted directly from British music-hall hits like "Zig Zag" and "Yes, Uncle." Ayre wrote "The Dumbell Rag" especially for the occasion. Al Plunkett had procured a top hat and tails and strutted onstage singing the U.S. hit "Those Wild Wild Women Are Making a Wild Man of Me." Hamilton, dressed as

"Marjorie," posed as a faithful girlfriend talking on the telephone with her beau (Bill Tennant) and sang "Hello My Dearie." Hamilton as Marjorie was said to be so fetching that soldiers frequently fell in love with him. One British officer later went so far as to send flowers and propose marriage.

But beneath the joviality there was a dark undercurrent. The comedic interludes pinpointed the ironic difference between the stories the troops had been told before they'd arrived in Europe — of glorious death on the battlefield, of German atrocities, of King and country — and the grim reality they'd encountered there: squalid death, disease, mud, shell-shock, and chemical warfare. Even their name, which had been based on their division's insignia, had a double meaning. Yes, Canadian troops were strong and silent, but they were also the dumbbells, the fools who had volunteered to be massacred in Europe. The Dumbells borrowed the drag element of their show from the English music hall, which in turn had brought it up from deep roots in English medieval theatre. By the early twentieth century, it was a keystone of British theatrical tradition. In the hands of the Dumbells it took on an additional, although perhaps not intentional, twist. Hamilton, as Marjorie, was adopting the persona of the flower of Canadian womanhood the soldiers had been told they were going to war to preserve. She was "Poor Belgium" before the fiendish Hun had debased her. The subtext of Hamilton's Marjorie was that this nationalist notion of what the boys were fighting for was a sham. The soldiers, the dumbbells, had been duped. The chaste girlfriend of the "Hello My Dearie" sketch wasn't a loyal maiden, she was a six-foot fellow with an Adam's apple, who needed a shave. Drag also represented a rejection of the traditional male gender role. As soldiers, the men represented the pinnacle of society's perception of manhood; a man in drag was the antithesis. He was womanly, soft, possibly attractive to other men, and most importantly, totally unfit to wage war. It's fair to assume that the Dumbells' use of drag, which was popular in all army shows during the Great War, represented a minor psychic rebellion in the audience's subconscious. Canadian newspaper journalists would later say that the Dumbells' drag element played on the soldiers' sexual frustrations, but prostitution and organized brothels were common along the western front during World War I. There was plenty of sex to be had for a soldier with money to spend. The Dumbells' drag routines were irreverent send-ups, pure and simple.

At times the Dumbells crossed the line into direct satire. Their sketch, "The Haig Co. Estate Office" (named after the Allied field marshall Douglas Haig), was an overt attack on the war effort. In the bit (a sketch), which was recreated as part of a 1979 CBC Radio documentary, a soldier enters the real estate office looking to purchase some property. "Yes, sir," he tells the salesman, who is an officer, "real estate. That's what I figure is real."

"You can't find a better investment than this," the officer says, gesturing to no-man's-land. "People are mad keen to get it, you know. They're lining up to get a crack at it."

"They are?"

"They are. They're standing in line, all right. In fact, they're fighting over it."

"Are the lots serviced?" the soldier asks.

"You bet they're serviced," the officer replies. "Gas and water. All you can take."

The show was a hit. It must have been a miraculous thing to behold. Perhaps the troops were simply so relieved to be alive, they were in the mood to laugh at anything. Regardless, they laughed and laughed big. This pleased Major-General Lipsett, who authorized Plunkett to make the Dumbells a permanent troupe. He had only one rule: the Dumbells had to be ready to perform anywhere, anytime. Plunkett enlarged the cast to sixteen and the Dumbells spent the remainder of the war entertaining the troops at the front. They performed in every possible location, from châteaux to burnt-out sugar factories to huts along the front lines. The troupe performed at least one two-and-a-half-hour show a day, often twice a day. Their crowds never numbered more than three hundred because gathering a larger group would have been unsafe; it would have drawn enemy shell fire. The troops were a tough but appreciative crowd. Murray, in the interview with Shaw, recalled: "We learned more in one year in France than we would have in ten performing for civilians. The troops had no hesitancy in letting you know if they didn't like something."

In the back of every Dumbell's mind lay the fact that he could easily be fighting instead of singing. Often their shows were disrupted by enemy fire. During the Battle of Passchendaele, some of the cast were called back to their regiments for combat duty. The Dumbells were frequently pressed into service as stretcher bearers. The war surrounded them. Al Plunkett later recalled: "Some of the men we entertained at five o'clock were dead at seven-thirty."

It's fitting that Canadian comedy was born amid a flurry of bullets and bombs. Conflict, conquest, and comedy are inseparable. It's kill or be killed. Blood must be spilled, either the comic's or the crowd's. When a comedian performs well, he says he killed. When a comedian fares poorly, he dies. If the Dumbells died on stage, and continued to do so, they'd be sent back down to the trenches where they were likely to die literally. So they played well. It's amazing what the threat of death will do for a comic's performance.

Just why we need professional comedians at all is a bit of a mystery. Laughing is as natural a function as digestion. It is a response we develop as babies and carry throughout our lives. A professional comedian brings another dimension to the equation. Laughing in bed with a lover is pleasant. It is also an isolated experience. The professional comic makes us laugh as a group. The comedian creates consensus. When the Dumbells made soldiers laugh at the thought of no-man's-land's "gas and serviced" lots, they were uniting the troops in their common fear. Each soldier knew he was not alone.

Comedy is like a set of Russian dolls. Break one doll open and you find another inside. Break comedy open and you find fear, break fear down and you find anger, break anger down and you find helplessness, break helplessness down and you find death, break death down and you find . . . life. That is the comedic paradox. The impulse to create comedy springs from a dark well, but its manifestation is exhilarating and pleasurable. Comedy is sometimes pure unadulterated fun. More often it's a tonic to cure our dreads, a way to make the incomprehensible palatable.

That's what the Dumbells did with war: they defused, however briefly, the time bomb that was each man's life on the battlefields of Europe.

We can also use tears to cope with life's troubles, but in our society tears are reserved for private moments. We cry in the car, the shower, or in the solitude of our own homes. Crying as you walk down main street will buy you a basketful of stares. Laughter, however, is acceptable. You can laugh your pain away in public.

The last half of the twentieth century has seen an explosion in the laugh business. This boom has been a direct consequence of mass media. Newspapers, radio, movies, music, and television have created enormous commonalities among people. For example, comedians can make countless Superman jokes because they know that every man, woman, and child in North America knows who Superman is. This familiarity is the cornerstone of any joke. Without it, a laugh is impossible. An audience must recognize the elements that constitute a joke, in order for that joke to work. They must be familiar with the people and institutions that comprise it. You cannot, for example, tell a joke about Lucien Bouchard to a roomful of Louisiana plumbers. They won't get it. You'd have to explain Canadian history, Quebec nationalism, Brian Mulroney, and the streptococcus B flesh-eating disease, and then they *might* laugh. Comedians are constantly searching for common ground. They start with basic shared experiences — we all have parents, we all eat, use the toilet, and grow up. It's a sure bet that most comedy club goers have sex, watch television, listen to music, and watch sports. That leaves the comedian free to make fun of targets like Madonna, the Toronto Maple Leafs' poor record, and premature ejaculation. Going just a little farther afield you find politics and professionals (lawyers, doctors), two more categories most of us (sometimes unfortunately) have experience with.

Comedians call these reference points — subjects that most people can relate to, because at some time in their lives they've had experience with them. So shortly after Bouchard lost his leg, Canadian comedian Al Rae was on sure ground when he told his Canadian audience: "Former prime minister Brian Mulroney has come down with the deadly flesh-eating disease, but surgeons are not concerned about his safety. Apparently the bacteria will not harm one of its own kind." He knew they would get the quip.

Any conversation about comedy, therefore, begins with a discussion of what we share in terms of biology, politics, history, economy, psychology, religion, nationalism, and culture. What we're laughing at tells us a lot about where we are as a country and a people. What we make the world laugh at tells us a lot about North American society. So when reporters pose the question, What makes Canadians so funny?, they're really asking, What are Canadians, as a nation, like? What is our place on the global cultural stage?

What is Canada? The most frequent answer you'd get from a Canadian is, "Not America." Canada, it is generally accepted, was formed on the negative assertion that being Canadian meant not being American. The first Europeans to settle here permanently, if you recall your high school textbook, were the French, who were conquered by the English on September 13, 1759, in the Battle of the Plains of Abraham. That mêlée had reverberations around the globe, but most importantly, it freed the American colonies of their fear of the French. Until the arrival of Montcalm, the Québécois, along with their aboriginal allies, had waged a successful terror campaign against the English colonies. With the French vanquished, the Americans no longer needed British protection, and in 1776, they declared their independence. So in a strange twist, Canada enabled the United States to assert its sovereignty. The rest is history and fast food. Following the American Revolution, those colonists who didn't wish to become part of a republic fled and settled Upper Canada (central and eastern Ontario). For the next century or so, the French and English tolerated each other, often married each other, and bickered incessantly, always realizing that without each other's aid they would suffer the most dreaded of fates. They'd become Americans.

Canada's roots, in contrast to America's, are conservative, not rebellious. Their conservatism was not the contemporary definition, which is an amalgamation of fundamentalist Christianity and free-market fervour. Those who settled Canada came for economic reasons. Their religions were the dominant religions of Europe. They hadn't lost faith in the

Pope or the Protestant Church, they'd lost faith in their chances of success in Europe. They came to Canada looking for monetary gain and a higher standard of living. The Puritans, with their grim religious attitudes, were dissidents who wanted to purify the church. They were conscientious objectors to the British ecclesiastical establishment. The Puritans, who had sided with the parliament during the English Civil War, had been cast out of the Church of England following the Restoration. They were loathed in England and fled to America in search of religious freedom. America's Declaration of Independence reflects their values. It promises life, liberty, and the pursuit of happiness. It also entrenched the Puritan notion of congregational democracy in the fabric of American politics. The Americans cherish individual freedom. They believe that if everyone works individually, it will create a common good.

Canada's history is very different. We chose our colonial status, cultivating our affiliation with Britain. We absorbed British rule and culture and by osmosis absorbed British comedic forms, from music hall in the early nineteenth century to Monty Python in the 1970s. Canadians clung to colonialism because they believed that it was better to alter an existing political system than tear it down and start over. The evidence suggests that Canadians believe that individual freedom springs from a series of collective agreements. Canada's constitution offers peace, order, and good government. This choice can be interpreted in two ways. We can surmise that Canadians are more pessimistic, that we lack faith in individuality and therefore cling to collective agreements. Canadians seem to believe that people, left to their freedom, will do wrong and as a result we choose government, not because we believe utterly in its power, but because we see it as the lesser of two evils. In this category we can file conditional free speech, big government, and high taxation. Or we can also surmise that, far from being pessimistic, Canadians are actually eternally optimistic about the capacity for individuals to find common ground and reach a mutually beneficial consensus. People, given the proper enlightenment, will achieve a greater good that in the final analysis benefits the individual more than pure self-interest. In this category we can file gun control, medicare, and the welfare state.

Our relationship with America has always been that of the younger sibling watching the bigger, stronger brother's bold experiments. From the sidelines, Canadians have seen revolution, a slave economy, a civil war, rampant individualism, capitalism beyond comprehension, and creativity and industriousness beyond anyone's dreams. We see sublime achievement and extreme failure. Although we observe, we do not feel the sting of defeat or the exhilaration of success inevitable in the myth of the American dream. We are up to our necks in American icons, but we do not participate in the American experience. What we see hasn't filled us with envy. We do not covet the Americans' crime, guns, imperialism, racism. We don't even covet their nationalism. Americans are proud to be American. Canadians are relieved to be Canadian. We look south and say, "Thank God that's not us."

Living next to America, former prime minister Pierre Trudeau once said, is like sleeping next to an elephant. We feel every twitch. I'd go farther. Living next to America is like living next to the wildest party ever held. As Canadians, we are never invited to this orgy, but we get front-row seats. The next best thing to an invitation is pointing and hooting at the lucky ones enjoying themselves — and knowing that from time to time they catch us at it. Although we may not want to live there, from time to time we dream of being included.

To us, America is the star jock in high school, loved and admired. We are the scrawny sidekick. It would be great to be responsible for the win, but instead we have to take solace in the fact that we believe deep down we're nice and hope that everybody likes us. Besides, being American means being loud and drawing attention to yourself. To a Canadian, that's social death.

Comedian Rosie Shuster, the daughter of comedic legend Frank Shuster and herself a writer for such television programs as *Saturday Night Live* and *The Larry Sanders Show,* puts it this way: "It's rude to have a big personality in Canada. Americans are allowed to be assholes. In Canada, you have to be guilty and ashamed if you like yourself too much. Canadians are more neutral and critical of each other. There is not much pie to go around, and everyone has their eyes on the other person's plate. We like to think this is being nice. When you're nice, you have to lie about your rage."

What do we do with our rage? The answer is simple: we push it down. Michael Magee, a political satirist and author of *The Golden Age of B.S.* and *The Platinum Age of B.S.,* defines Canadians as people who are lying on their backs screaming at passersby to defecate on them, adding "You might as well, everyone else does!" Canadian rage is not the rage of a conqueror, it is the rage of a victim. There are plenty of Canadian injustices, from the Westray Mine disaster to the scandal that sparked the Krever Inquiry, but as a country we refer such problems to committee and swallow our discontent.

If you are a Canadian comedian, this poses a problem. Comedians live by externalizing their discontent, by giving their anger and cynicism a public airing. They are outsiders who stand back and ridicule those on the inside, particularly those with power. Comedians live by picking on the "winners;" their favourite targets are the ruling class, whether they're rock stars, bureaucrats, or bankers. Canadians, however, have come to believe that expressing such dissatisfaction is dangerous. The comic malcontent is a corrosive force. We aren't like Americans, we've been told, we're deferential people — yet there is nothing deferential about comedy.

Obviously, Canadian comics have found ways around this obstacle. In 1917, the Dumbells discovered that comedians could display comic discontent by linking it to group survival. The release of anxieties and grumblings was joined to the collective good. For example, the "Haig Co. Estate Office" sketch was a direct bit of satire, mocking the strategy of war by attrition, which had caused so many needless deaths. By giving comic expression to the soldiers' frustration over their plight, the Dumbells were in fact stopping it from becoming open complaint. Comedy helped prevent mutiny.

Comedy in all its forms is unquestionably a survival technique. So if, as has often been argued, the Canadian identity centres on survival, the Dumbells were well equipped for comedy. The Dumbells temporarily made the war less terrifying for their audience, and not just by amusing them — other entertainers did that, too. The Dumbells' shows told the soldiers that psychic survival meant poking fun at Fate. Your destiny was not in your hands; God would decide who lived and who died. All a soldier could do was laugh and wait. That enabled the troops to return to the front. This jaunty fatalism is the particular Canadian ingredient the Dumbells added to the comedic equation. If their songs were lifted from the music-hall stage, their sketches were 100 per cent original and their presentation 100 per cent Canadian. For instance, the English soldier revues sang "Oh It's a Lovely War" to a march tempo. Red Newman, who joined the Dumbells in 1918, slowed it down and sang it like a torch song, giving it, according to Ayre, "a very sarcastic edge." The Dumbells revelled in dystopia. Life was predetermined. Once you recognized your powerlessness, you were free to enjoy it. The Dumbells used that dark side of the Canadian identity that thrives in desperate situations. The more hopeless things appear, the more likely Canadians are to send them up. This was doubly true of our wartime experiences. As a nation, we do not boast, we jest.

I recall the war stories my family shared when I was a child. They did not involve battles or fighting, but the jokes my great uncles and grandfathers told while in combat. My great uncle, and lookalike, Gordon Halcrow Clark, a nineteen-year-old soldier with the 1st Division in World War I, was wounded twice overseas (as were his two older brothers). From a hospital in France, where he was recovering from shrapnel wounds, he wrote his younger brother, my schoolboy grandfather, that the infirmary was "a good place to meet flappers." He advised my grandpa to "keep up with your studies, as it's no game over here."

My maternal grandmother Jamieson recounted a story she'd heard from the D-Day invasion in World War II. As the landing craft was pushing towards the beach, my grandfather's friend, Jack Bennett, known as Uncle Jack, had calmed his comrades by saying, "Don't worry, this ain't nothing. You should see the first day of duck hunting season on Mississippi Lake." In essence, when the going got tough, the tough got joking.

That's what the Dumbells told their audience. If you were going to die, you might as well die laughing. You could let the futility and madness drive you crazy, or you could look it in the eye and blow a raspberry. War wasn't hell on earth, it was a joke. "My boy," says a recruiting sergeant, in one Dumbells' sketch, "if you are willing to serve overseas, you will travel all over Europe, mix with the French dames, drink lots of wine in the French cafés, and all at the government's expense." "Say, Sarge," the kid replies, "that sounds a bit of all right. Put me down for overseas."

By the autumn of 1918, the war was dragging to a close. Germany was defeated, and the Dumbells were going strong. Plunkett had managed to keep the troupe active throughout the duration of the conflict. The day after the armistice was signed, the Dumbells performed *H.M.S. Pinafore* in a two-thousand-seat theatre in Mons. The Dumbells' success in the trenches had convinced Plunkett that his makeshift brood could be a money-making property. Major-General Lipsett sent the troupe on mass leave so that they could go to London for a run in the West End. British producers, however, weren't interested in a Canadian troop show. Undeterred, Plunkett booked the Dumbells into a rundown theatre called the Victoria Palace for sixty pounds a week. The show was an instant hit, spurring Mr. Johns, the manager of the prestigious Coliseum Theatre, to offer the troupe two hundred pounds a week to play the Coliseum. The Dumbells moved up in the world. They lived well — their off-hours were spent in a steam of parties and lavish dinners. The show ran four weeks. The Brits were so smitten by the Dumbells that Johns cancelled all his variety acts and put the Canadians on before his feature act, the Diaghilev Ballet. Eventually, the ballet's manager asked if his company could go on before the Dumbells — the Diaghilev was having trouble following them.

After the armistice, Plunkett immediately began making plans to extend the Dumbells' run into peacetime. He returned from France in the summer of 1919 and raised ten thousand dollars from a pair of uncles in Orillia. He gathered some original cast members, dug up another fifteen thousand dollars from his uncles, added more chorus "girls" (cross-dressing actors) and opened the show in London, Ontario. It was entitled *Biff Bing Bang*. The audience consisted of veterans, who knew them from the trenches, and their families and friends. *Biff Bing Bang* was another hit. A *Maclean's* article, published in 1952, recalled the impact that Red Newman, the Dumbells' top comic, made with his rendition of "Oh It's a Lovely War."

> When he came out in his old dirty bedraggled uniform with web gear askew, puttees undone and red wig sticking out under a battered helmet, they cheered just to see him. When he started "Up to your knees in water, up to your waist in slush," there were lumps in a few throats and when he went into that never-to-be-forgotten routine of pitching his clothes and gear on the stage as he sought an elusive cootie, it just plain stopped the show.

The Dumbells' success caught the attention of Toronto impresario Ambrose Small, owner of the Grand Theatre, who decided to back *Biff Bing Bang*. The Dumbells went on to do forty-four weeks of sold-out shows in Toronto and then toured across the country. During their first year on the road, they hit cities such as Ottawa, Hamilton, Saskatoon, and Vancouver. They discovered, as would other Canadian comedians, that touring the country was an arduous task. For the first twenty-five weeks of that tour they played only one-night engagements. The Dumbells made a profit of eighty thousand dollars. Alan Murray told a Toronto newspaper in 1955, "There were few cities in Canada capable of supporting a show for even two nights, and we were on the move almost constantly, juggling laundry, sleeping arrangements, and mail."

Broadway was the next logical step. Plunkett fine-tuned *Biff Bing Bang,* and in May of 1920 opened it in New York City. The foray, however, had almost been cancelled. During an earlier performance in Montreal, the Dumbells had made a joke at the expense of American General Douglas MacArthur's Rainbow Division, "The one," Dumbell Ben Allen quipped, "that came out after the storm was all over." The joke was particularly pointed, as it mocked the tardy arrival, in late 1917, of American support for the Allied war effort. In effect, it made the comedic point that the American troops had joined the war only after victory seemed certain.

"Although this 'killed' the Canadian ex-servicemen," the *Maclean's* article recalled, "it drew such violent and vociferous protestfrom a group of American convention wives that Ben Allen didn't dare appear again."

Word of the slight reached south. At the New York opening, two irate "wives" appeared and asked Plunkett if this was the same Canadian revue that had disgraced American soldiers. Plunkett told them the line was from "another Canadian soldiers' revue." This lie apparently appeased the patriotic Yankees and averted disaster. Said Plunkett, "If they [the wives] had ever made a fuss we would have closed that night." Instead the show ran for twelve weeks at the Ambassador Theater. A Canadian Maple Leaf decorated the proscenium arch and Canadian flags were lavishly displayed around the stage. The Canadian newspapers made big news out of the theatrical triumph. Captions like "Admits Yanks Outclassed" ran in articles dedicated to chronicling positive reviews such as this one: "No American soldier play seen in New York has *Biff Bing Bang*'s snap and vigor — nor its talent. If this be treason, make the most of it."

By the early 1920s, the Dumbells were Canada's first internationally successful comedy export. They had reached this height through hard work and good timing. The Dumbells' key selling point in both Britain and America was their ability to borrow comic forms and apply them with a uniquely Canadian style. The Dumbells, as colonials, had absorbed the dominant British culture, just as later Canadian comedians would absorb American culture. They appropriated British music-hall comedy, a theatrical genre, that in the hands of professional British music-hall performers was extremely artificial and polished. The Dumbells invigorated this comic-candy with an unabashed colonial exuberance, at the same time lacing it with dark irony. The Dumbells played up the grim aspects of the war effort to comic effect. British comedians didn't understand American audiences and could not crack the States. Canadians, however, took the best from Britain and also had a feel for the American stage. They made the music-hall style palatable for American audiences. As a result, they were the first, but certainly not the last, Canadian comedians to bridge American and British cultures.

The New York City engagement was the high-water mark for the Dumbells. More tours followed, of Canada and the United States, but there was dissension in the cast and the original crew began to disintegrate. In 1922, Murray and the entire original cast, except for Hamilton and Al Plunkett, left the Dumbells and formed their own troupe, the Originals. This off-shoot failed. The comics were not great managers. Merton Plunkett brought in new members to fill the loss, but as memories of the Great War began to fade, so too did the Dumbells. Plunkett, who had amassed almost a quarter of a million dollars through the company, went bankrupt in the stock market crash. By the time the Depression arrived, the Dumbells were history, although there were a few reunions in the forties, fifties and sixties. Cast members retired and ran shops or sold insurance. Dumbell Jack MacLaren, who had joined the troupe in 1918, founded a display advertising company in Toronto. Some adjusted poorly to civilian life. A record from The Orillia Historical Society states, "Al Plunkett married a Miss Pierce of Toronto but became increasingly fond of liquor. The last time Griff [an Orillian acquaintance] saw him was at a meeting in the Royal York Hotel about 1938 when Al sang old World War I songs for drinks."

It's interesting to note that the final undoing of the Dumbells occurred when Plunkett brought women into the troupe for the 1928 show, *Why Worry*. Until that point the Dumbells had been an exclusively all-male veteran's troupe. The inclusion of women proved that they were no longer a comedic creation that had emerged from the trenches. A New York review had praised *Biff Bing Bang* because "it is a show possessing all the romping abandon of the best variety entertainment but devoid of the mannered professional hardness." Hamilton had taken a stand against the inclusion of women. "I said: 'I'll never play in a show with the girls in it. Make your choice.' Once they brought them in it just killed the Dumbells."

The Dumbells had become just another gag show trying to push laughs and legs. They were no longer talented soldiers putting on a show; they were seasoned professionals trying to earn a buck. They had lost their sincerity. The Dumbells had been created to boost the morale of soldiers, many of whom were destined to die. As the memory of the war began to fade, they lost their reason for being. Fate had indeed decided who would return from France, and those who made it back to Canada wanted to get on with the business of living. That meant leaving the war and all its memories, both good and bad, behind.

Murray never forgot the young Irish officer in Ypres. In his 1964 radio interview, Murray recalled how he had once wanted to present the scene to troops as a straight piece of theatre. That never happened. He had tried the idea on Leonard Young, a Dumbell who had his leg blown off during combat. Young had a reputation for being a good judge of a piece of material's stage worthiness. Murray had described the moving scene to Young, who replied deadpan: "And then what do you do with the audience?"

"He was right," Murray said. "We couldn't leave them like that.

T W O

■

The Satiric Mask

Michael Magee was lecturing me on one of his favourite topics, Canadian military history and the recent denigration of once proud Canadian military traditions. It was a gloomy April day in 1995 in Toronto, and the weather matched the subject on which Magee, who never missed a Remembrance Day service at Toronto's cenotaph, was passionate. The grey-haired satirist recounted a story he had once heard from a Canadian racehorse trainer. Like the Dumbells, that trainer had served in World War I. Because of his knowledge of horses, he'd been assigned to the cavalry. One day a horse was giving him trouble. The trainer punched the animal a soft pop on the nose, which is a traditional way of disciplining a horse; the horse feels little pain and the discomfort does not linger, but the punch smartens it up. Just as he was doing this, a British officer rode by. The officer stopped and had the trainer immediately arrested for cruelty to an animal. The trainer was found guilty and sentenced to five days tied spread-eagled to a cannon wheel. Night and day, through rain and sun, defecating in his pants (as he was not allowed washroom breaks) the trainer suffered. He almost died. Like many of the stories Magee told, this one had no happy ending. The officer continued on his privileged way; the trainer held a lingering hatred for the English.

This, said Magee, was simply more proof of the malevolent nature of humanity. Waste and corruption were civilization's legacy. Good people like the trainer were wounded by bad people like the officer.

Magee and I had agreed to meet that day at the Senator restaurant to discuss the state of Canadian satire. In retrospect, the Senator, one of the city's oldest restaurants, was the ideal choice for a meeting with Magee, a man who believes Canada's best days have passed. Magee is the ultimate conservative, for whom change is a corrosive force. To Magee, Canada is a once beautiful nation that has been sold out and exploited by a wormy ruling class. It is a divine virgin violated by the grimy hands of greed and bribery. The Canadian line is "My establishment, right or wrong," Magee claims. "In a civilized country like France, they'd throw the bastards in jail. But here, all we're concerned about is keeping their names out of the papers."

After our meeting he left a message for me that said: "Andrew, I get the feeling I care more about Canada than you do. But I do. I care very much."

Magee was born in Toronto in 1930 to an affluent family. It wasn't until 1956, at age twenty-six, that he finally found his calling working in the theatre in Vancouver. As a kid he was kicked out of a series of private schools. Although he was born a card-carrying member of Toronto's establishment, Magee never felt part of it. He was caught between camps, not complacent enough to slide into affluent bliss but not removed enough to utterly reject the power structure. "The big difference between Canada and America," he says, "is that here most of the rich inherit their money. They're not self-made. The elite here is so strong they can sit back and go ho-ho-ho. If you can sustain the mediocrity, you can eke out a living as a comedian. If you want their gratuitous droppings, you can work. But if you're telling them it's all second-rate, they don't want to hear it." As a result, Magee embraces the past. He exalts noble values — honour, duty, industry, truthfulness. According to Magee, what Canada had done during World War II stood at the apex of our country's history as a nation. His patriotism was decidedly old school.

Michael Magee is a cynic, but he never fails to be outraged by the transgressions he sees perpetrated around him. Incidents like the trainer's story or the shocking murder by Canadian troops of a Somalian boy infuriate him, and Magee is not a person to turn his anger inward. He points it outward, straight at the establishment. In other words, Magee has the mind and soul of a satirist.

For my money, Magee is the most vicious satirist Canada has ever produced. After our meeting, I spent a long time trying to unravel the secret to his comic bile. Magee has the intelligence and the anger to create brilliant satire. He also employs one other device: a satiric mask. Michael Magee does not criticize as Michael Magee. When he appeared on stage or television or wrote books, as he rarely does now, he appeared as the old curmudgeon Fred C. Dobbs. I realized that was the single thread that linked Magee to his peers. In Canadian comedy from the 1940s to the 1970s, everyone wore a mask.

The first stirrings of Canadian political satire began in the spring of 1947. Canada was beginning to shake itself back into civilian life after World War II. It was little more than twenty-five years after the Dumbells had made their mark, but it was a whole world away from the trenches and cavalries the Dumbells had experienced. What counted was that after a long, six-year winter called the Second World War, which had closely followed the War to End All Wars, peace had finally come. As the snow melted, it revealed muddy green lawns that promised vibrant growth. It also exposed a sight quite familiar to Canadians, then as now: scattered beneath all that white snow lay clumps of aged dog feces. This newly exposed refuse provided a fitting metaphor for Canadian society. Beneath the cool, clean exterior lay something noxious.

The metaphor was not lost on Dora Mavor Moore, a Toronto theatrical dynamo, who that same year had formed the New Play Society, an organization dedicated to producing classics and new Canadian plays. Moore was a vivacious and imaginative woman who would go on to be one of the most influential forces in English Canadian theatre. In the spring of 1947, however, she faced a pressing practical problem. The New Play Society had promised a season of ten plays, but now their spring offering had fallen through. A replacement was urgently needed. Miraculously, with only two weeks left for rehearsal, a troupe of actors pulled together a new comedy revue. The show was a revolutionary feat. Rather than relying on stock gags and domestic humour (mother-in-law jokes) it mined laughs from Canadian politics and culture. In the past there had been loose revue parodies performed at the Toronto Arts and Letters Club and at Winnipeg's Press Club Show, but never before had Canadians turned their comic sights on themselves. By making their show a Canadian product, Moore and her cast were signalling the country's maturity as a nation. We were big enough to take a little ribbing. Inspired by the sight of dog dirt soiling the lawns outside their rehearsal hall, Andrew Allan, a maverick producer with CBC Radio, dubbed Moore's revue *Spring Thaw*.

Spring Thaw was an instant hit. Its cast was first-rate. Among the original members were Don Harron, Jane Mallet, Bob Goulet, and Barbara Hamilton. The show revelled in Canadiana. *Spring Thaw* iced icons like the Queen but never crossed the line into outright attack. It was Rosedale comedy. Their skits were high-brow, high-income-bracket stuff. For example, Mavor Moore, Dora's son and a distinguished director and critic, penned a piece called "Togetherness," in which a bishop, priest, cardinal and orthodox patriarch sang about the joys of ecumenism while physically drawing apart. In 1951, they parodied American reaction to the hit Québécois play *Ti-Coq*. The play had recently run in New York, and critics had panned its ending. *Spring Thaw* suggested various Americanized versions of the finale, including one in the vein of the musical *South Pacific*.

Spring Thaw proved that Canadians relished comedy that made fun of Canadian political life. The show ran annually for twenty-two years, each year as an original revue. Mavor was the engineer that drove the production, which he directed from 1948 to 1951 and 1953 to 1957. In 1962, he purchased the title from the New Play Society and took *Spring Thaw* into larger theatres, such as the Royal Alexandra in Toronto. During the last five years it played, the grand institution was in obvious decline. The show was revived in the early eighties but faired poorly, and then became extinct.

Spring Thaw also proved that Canadians enjoyed topical humour as long as it was delivered sideways. There were no frontal assaults.

Satirically, *Spring Thaw* was as gentle as a spring rain. Its secret, comedically, was that you, the writer or performer, did not criticize the country. You did not stand before your audience and openly attack — you created characters to do it for you. You created a comic mask that shielded you from responsibility for any inappropriate barbs or ideas. That way *Spring Thaw*'s comics and writers never broke the Canadian code of conduct. They did not call attention to themselves, they called attention to their characters. If their audience's sensibilities were offended, the characters, not the comedians, could take the blame.

This sort of satiric ventriloquism certainly was not a Canadian creation. Satirists had been employing it throughout history. Aristophanes had attacked Grecian society by creating satiric vehicles to carry his points home, and his actors literally wore masks. Restoration playwrights had put satiric words into the mouths of characters who were often little more than personifications of human foibles, the actors merely inhabiting simple, broad attitudes. The technique of the mask was, however, ideally suited to Canadian culture. Comedians, especially satirists, are critics. They question society and expose its shortcomings, but provide no answers. They make these criticisms palatable by coating them with laughter. This is an extremely subversive tactic, because it creates the awareness that society needs fixing but leaves it twisting in a vacuum. Eighteenth-century English writer Jonathan Swift had set the standard when he suggested in his masterpiece *A Modest Proposal* that the solution to Irish poverty was for the Irish to eat their babies. Comedians have been following suit ever since.

It may be more acceptable for an American to question his or her society than it is for a Canadian. Americans claim that their constitutional right to "bear arms" ensures that the population will always be ready and able to overthrow an unjust government. The United States Revolutionary war slogan was "Don't tread on me." In America, there is a history of conscientious objection. The individual's rights are to a large degree elevated above the rights and rules of the community. Americans believe that if individuals follow their own self-interest, collective good will result. In Canada, the individual's rights are subordinate to the good of the society as a whole. We are subservient to the collective good. We think it's okay for the government to intrude upon almost every aspect of our personal lives. For example, in 1996 a Metro Toronto city councillor suggested passing legislation that would make smoking a cigarette in front of a child the legal equivalent of child abuse. In Canada, individual criticism of the status quo is frowned upon because it implies a need for change. History, particularly the history we've witnessed south of the border, has demonstrated that change is often only achieved through conflict. In Canadian society, therefore, criticism, which implies a need for change, equals conflict. It threatens order, and any threat to order is better suppressed. If, however, this criticism is placed in the mouth of an imaginary character, it becomes more acceptable. Towards this end, Canadian satirists have consistently donned masks when mocking Canada.

In the fifties, two *Spring Thaw* comedians stepped out of the cast and, wearing a variety of masks, launched solo careers. Their names were Don Harron and Dave Broadfoot.

Don Harron, born in Toronto in 1924, attended the University of Toronto and then joined the cast of *Spring Thaw* in the late forties. It was there, in 1952, that he created the character Charlie Farquharson, a rustic boob from Parry Sound who hid a sharp mind under a frazzled exterior. The character had first sprung to Harron's mind during the summer of 1946, which he spent working on a relative's farm. Harron became fascinated by the accents and attitudes of the farm-hands he worked alongside. He mimicked their speech and began to etch a skilful blueprint of a rural smart-ass. The result, Charlie Farquharson, was a quick score with *Spring Thaw*'s audiences. In appearance, he was a throw-back to the Great Depression. Farquharson's clothes were weathered and torn, and he sported a jockey's cap. Satirically, Farquharson's humour advanced one step beyond that of *Spring Thaw*. His satire was concentrated in one body and had one consistent voice, rather than being diffused throughout a series of sketches, characters, and a large cast.

Farquharson derived his strength as a satiric character from his low social status. Charlie Farquharson was a hopeless hick. He was earthy, plain-spoken, prone to malapropisms, and took delight in shredding pretension. He was an instrument that an educated performer — and an urban one at that — like Harron could employ to laser-like effect. Farquharson took the "high" out of high art. When Harron, as Farquharson, rode past then prime minister Trudeau on a horse-drawn sleigh, he returned Trudeau's greeting of "Merry Christmas" with "And a preposterous New Year to you." Harron played on Farquharson's Sancho Panza appeal. The Parry Sound hayseed had a worm's-eye view of life. Since he had no stake in Canadian politics or polite society, he became a credible and palatable critic of it.

David Broadfoot was also a *Spring Thaw* alumnus who stepped out of the chorus and created a satiric character with which to pass biting comment on the nation. In 1954, Broadfoot created the Member for Kicking Horse Pass. Like Farquharson, the Member was a hick, in this case wearing a cowboy hat. He was a mishmash of various loud-mouthed Prairie politicians who had spouted venom through the fifties. Along with this creation Broadfoot added Sgt. Renfrew, a bumbling Mountie, in 1957, and in 1960, Bobby Clobber, a toothless hockey player with a trick memory. Broadfoot was a triple threat. The Member lampooned politics, Sgt. Renfrew was a Canadian Inspector Clouseau, and Bobby Clobber savaged the national pastime. Both Harron's and Broadfoot's characters were underdogs. They were low men on the totem pole, pastoral satirists from the unspoiled and frank rural regions, calling attention to all the shortcomings of the urban elite who ran the country. They were outsiders, removed from the power structures based in Ottawa and Toronto, and therefore were accepted as impartial examples of common sense. Broadfoot and Harron also liked to satirize change. They were especially adept at ridiculing fashion and the pretense that accompanies it. When Harron and Broadfoot did take shots — and they did regularly — they were aimed at politicians and other public figures. But their barbs were, by and large, delivered with a spirit of gentle merriment.

It didn't work that way for Michael Magee, who at the same time that Harron and Broadfoot were creating their satiric masks was creating one of his own. Like them, Magee used the mask of a rural hayseed. Fred C. Dobbs (inspired by a character from the movie *Treasure of the Sierra*

Madre), the honourable member from Beamsville, Ontario, a curmudgeon with a tongue of sharpened steel, was dressed in a fashion similar
to Harron's character. He wore an ill-fitting suit, which covered a full
pot-belly, and sported a fright wig of white hair and a furry moustache.
However, that was where all similarities ended. Unlike Harron and
Broadfoot, Magee got personal — so much so that some thought he was
mentally unbalanced. His attacks were pegged to specific scandals and
allegations. He was not gentle. He wanted to shame the people he
attacked with his humour, he wanted to destroy them. He wanted to tear
down hypocritical institutions. He delighted in breaking taboos, in saying the unspeakable. Where Harron and Broadfoot could be described
as middle-of-the-road politically, even liberal, Magee was pathological-
ly conservative. This did not mean he restricted his targets to the left
wing or affiliated factions. Magee, as Dobbs, railed against big business, real estate developers, media figures — anyone who held power,
money, or both. Magee was fuelled by constantly asking himself the
question, How long can these cocksuckers go on? "I quickly learned,"
Magee says, "that an old duffer could get away with saying things that
would not be accepted from a young man."

I first saw Magee as Dobbs in 1993. He was performing a lunch-
time rant at Toronto's Bistro 990, a posh watering hole for Bay Street
types and film school grads. Dobbs came out and fired off an hour's
worth of invective that decimated the house. None of his material would
have made it to television, most could not be printed in a newspaper. He
ran the scale of Canadian outrages and injustices. He cited the fact that
Canada has never, and will never, do a film on the Battle of the Plains
of Abraham as evidence of this country's "utter lack of integrity and
balls." He called for the pillory for the McKenna brothers, who had produced the CBC miniseries *The Valour and the Horror*. The series had
raked up unsavoury stories about Canada's effort in World War II, in
particular criticizing the nation's involvement in the bombing of Nazi
Germany. "As I recall," Magee said, "at the time, we weren't too sure of
the outcome." He paid special attention to Kim Campbell, who was then
poised to take the Tory leadership. "Who," he asked rhetorically, "do
these idiots think they're trying to kid?"

Dobbs was merciless. I was struck by how close the public mask of Dobbs was to the private Magee. While Harron and Broadfoot's characters were fully developed comic creations, the audience was well aware that Magee was using Dobbs to make his own arguments. Yet, incredibly, Magee had created in Dobbs a softer version of himself, unlike Harron and Broadfoot, who wildly exaggerated personal political observations to gain laughs for their outrageous comic characters. Magee's attacks had punch because, along with being a satirist, he was also an experienced political correspondent. He had covered major elections for the CBC throughout the seventies. He understood the political system and had a deep understanding of the Tory party, which made him much more dangerous than your average comedian. Magee knew where to look for dirt; he had no need to exaggerate.

Magee worked regularly for the CBC in the late sixties but had many run-ins with its supremos. He was once suspended for thirteen weeks with pay for insulting Quebec politician Gérard Pelletier on *Morningside*. In the seventies, Magee covered horse racing for the CBC and was its highest paid sports broadcaster. In 1982, he finally quit the "Corpse" in disgust over the direction CBC coverage was going.

Magee, as Dobbs, penned two books: *The Golden Age of B.S.* in 1976 and *The Platinum Age of B.S.* in 1981. These tomes articulated the Magee line. They were assaults on sacred institutions and dearly held Canadian beliefs, such as national unity and rampant government spending. Magee displayed a knack for predicting trends. In *The Golden Age of B.S.* he wrote: "When we get to 1980, the knowledge from 1970 to 1980 will equal all the knowledge up to 1970. How are we gonna deal with it, how are we gonna go with it? No wonder everyone sits bug-eyed in fronta a TV screen . . . just lulled into being a buncha slobs and consumers, a buncha people ripe for the plucking, a buncha people that pitchmen can get at any time they want, anyway they want."

In 1976, Magee tried his hand at a television series, although in this case for Ontario's arts and education channel TVO, or as Magee referred to it, "TV Zero." The result was *Magee and Company,* a fifteen-minute show aired five nights a week at 6:30 p.m. Officially, TVO executives said the educational purpose of the program was to expose the bias of news reporting. They didn't know what they were in for.

Magee used a host of satiric masks in *Magee and Company*, a one-man show fuelled by its creator's lust for satiric attack. There was J. Baunston Tudball, a fighter of all things permissive; George Blow, a veteran police officer; J. Carter Hughes, a big-business executive; Gaston de B. Hatfield, a drama critic; and the Pastor, a clergyman who headed the "Church of the Winnebago." *Magee and Company* pulled no punches. For example, this advertisement for the CBC: "If you hate talent, love mediocrity and lack the integrity to resign, there's a place for you at the CBC. CBC means jobs."

Magee and Company crossed the line of decorum on a daily basis. If Magee had kept his attacks general — for example, attacking "politicians" — he would have survived. But Magee, as ever, got personal. He named names and made reference to specific indiscretions. He wasn't making merry jests, he was calling attention to what he thought were crimes that should be punished.

A government-owned channel could only let such bile flow for so long. *Magee and Company* ran for three years and was pulled in 1978. Magee was unrepentant. "We appear to be the only boat rockers because so little is being done anywhere else. A tiny squawk appears to be a reign of terror," he says.

On the series's final episode, aired at the time of the federal election, Magee invited a group of actual pundits, from journalist Lloyd Robertson to Peter Kent, and mixed them with his own creations. It was a tough take that concluded with Fred C. Dobbs claiming that then prime minister Trudeau was "a confidence man . . . 'Separatism is dead,' he told us. We needed to hear that. Boy, it sure woke us up quick." As J. Baunston Tudball, Magee stated that the election's main issue should be "whether or not Canadians want freedom or security. Canadians may already have spoken. I think Canadians may already have said they want security, not freedom. Years ago when I worked at the post office, we used to collaborate with the opening of the mail. Now it's going to be made legal. What's the next step? If you're not doing anything wrong, who cares if somebody listens in on your telephone conversation? And what's the next step after that?"

Magee ended the show not as Dobbs but as himself. He said: "Canadians have been victims of being fair and decent people. They've gone along for a long time expecting the most, and I don't think they've had it. We've had the one-party system far too long, except for a few Diefenbaker years. In the last ten years there has been a terrific erosion of democracy in this country. If you start to think about it and begin thinking about it now, it will start to scare you, and that might be a good thing, because we might wake up."

After his series cancellation, Magee went to Hollywood, doing voice-overs for cartoon series, and remained active on the live performance circuit. He played many corporate engagements. By 1993, Magee, an expert horse player, made the majority of his income at the track. In America, he could curb his satiric tendencies, since he was not passionate about the United States. He saw it as an inferior nation when compared to Canada. In 1996, back in Ontario, he was managing a stable of thoroughbreds and going to the track at least four times a week. But his sentiments remain firm.

Magee's style of satire, or, more specifically, its content, had proven too searing for most Canadian tastes. Magee was too angry for a country that considered anger a rude and dangerous Americanism. Canadian outrage at Magee's barbs often proved nothing more than a smokescreen for apathy. Canadians didn't like to hear their country criticized, but were not willing to provide reasons to support their defence. Canadian problems were to be ignored or concealed. Once, at a corporate dinner, a heckler yelled: "Move on from this political stuff. Stop running Canada down." Others in the house supported the antagonist. Magee suggested that since they were all such fervent nationalists, the entire crowd sing the Canadian anthem. They eagerly leapt at the chance.

"When in doubt, patriotism," Magee bitterly recalls. "They tried, but they didn't even know the fucking words."

THREE

•

TV or Not TV

Shortly after meeting the angriest old man in Canadian comedy, I found myself standing before Frank Shuster, the most congenial old man in Canadian comedy. It was October 2, 1995, and I was planted on the tenth floor of CBC's new Broadcast Centre, in downtown Toronto. A gaggle of CBC employees and executives, along with columnists from Toronto's daily newspapers and assorted television crews, were all there to celebrate the unveiling of a new CBC landmark, the Wayne and Shuster Comedy Wall of Fame.

The cast of *The Royal Canadian Air Farce* was there to act as the ceremony's comic relief. Air Farce member Roger Abbott gave a sluggish speech that drew sparse laughter from the crowd. He was followed by the humourless former head of CBC entertainment, Phyllis Platt. She surprised no one by not being funny. Finally, after these tributes, Frank Shuster had a turn to speak a few words. He was the sole representative of the famous comedy duo. His partner, Johnny Wayne, the other half of Wayne and Shuster, had died in 1990. Shuster stood up and gave a lucid, lean, witty speech that was short and packed with jokes. I marvelled at the eloquence of his writing and the precision of his timing. It was nice to see an older comedian (he was seventy-eight) blow the younger generation out of the water. "Hockey gets a hall, comedy gets a wall," he noted, and then free drinks were produced and the crowd was allowed to peruse the great wall at their leisure.

The wall is in fact a corridor, which leads to the CBC's grand Studio 41, the theatre in which the Air Farce tape their shows. On either side of this corridor, photographs of the icons of Canadian comedy are hung. The CBC's researcher, Lisa Thomson, had done her homework. The Great Ones are all accounted for.

Rich Little is there. He'd begun his career at age eleven in his home town of Ottawa. He'd won a CBC talent search, *Pick the Stars,* and had gone on in 1963 to break into the American show business world via an appearance on *The Judy Garland Show.* Little's impersonations of American public figures such as Richard Nixon made him one of the world's top impersonators. There is a photo of Dinah Christie, whose satiric sketches and songs on the sixties series *This Hour Has Seven Days* won her praise. Originally from *Spring Thaw,* there is Don Harron, Dave Broadfoot, and Barbara Hamilton, the comic actress. Newfoundland comedy troupe CODCO got a picture, as did the cast of *This Hour Has 22 Minutes.* Stars like *SCTV*'s Martin Short; *Naked Gun* movie actor Leslie Nielsen; Mike Myers, creator of the hit movie *Wayne's World;* and, of course, the biggest Canadian comedian to date, Jim Carrey — are all there. And there are stand-ups like Howie Mandel, Mike MacDonald, and David Steinberg. Steinberg, who was born in Winnipeg, had contributed to the downfall of the popular American variety show *The Smothers Brothers Comedy Hour,* when his "Moses and the Burning Bush" routine so enraged CBS executives that they cancelled the whole series.

Alongside these well-known Canadian performers there are also some forgotten contributions. *Nightcap,* a sixties late-night television show that used a risky blend of slapstick and naughty references to out-draw, at one time, *The Tonight Show* in the ratings, was remembered. Broadcaster Max Ferguson got himself a picture. In the sixties, he and his sidekick Alan McFee had produced a satiric radio revue based on the day's events. There are also photos from shows that should be forgotten, such as *Party Game,* a charades show, and the eighties teen comedy *Hangin' In.*

The media milled about the wall, and as the drinks flowed the crowd gathered vigour. Toronto's entertainment community and the journalists who cover it, ignited by booze, began to speak louder and stagger with a purpose. The group looked like a casting call for extras on a zombie movie. I include myself in this esteemed company. Armed with a Molson Export I fixed myself before the wall and tried to discern some meaning from it all. Here was a wall dedicated to Canada's greatest comedy team. On it hung pictures of the business's supposed greats, and it felt a little like a morgue.

Just as I was ready to give up, three photographs grabbed my attention. In their context the wall began to make sense. Hidden there, inauspiciously displayed among the mass of comedians, was the Holy Trinity of Canadian comedy: three pioneer comedy forces that led the first raids south on stardom in America. The big three all emerged in the fifties, during Canada's golden age of television. They were Wayne and Shuster, Alan Young, and the comedy team Aylesworth and Peppiatt. This trinity represented three types of comedic talent that Canada would continue to send south: the literate, articulate jokers exemplified by David Steinberg; the physical comedians like Jim Carrey and John Candy, who played the everyman underdog; and the behind-the-scenes wizards like Lorne Michaels and Ivan Reitman. The original television triangle of the fifties could not have been more dissimilar in style and appearance. They did, however, share one common influence: radio.

By the late 1930s, radio had taken hold in Canada, and it was on radio, not on the stage, that Canada's new wave followed where the Dumbells had left off. Radio had a huge impact on comedy and shaped the art form in a number of ways. Before radio, touring comics would sometimes tailor their acts to suit the town they were playing. For example, if they were playing Winnipeg, they would insert the name of Winnipeg's mayor into their city hall sketch. Most importantly, radio forced comedians to write material that would appeal to mass audiences. If they were broadcasting nationally, as they did on the Canadian Radio Broadcasting Commission (which later became the CBC), they had to hit everyone from coast to coast. References had to have broad resonance. Obviously, comedians couldn't rely on visual gags to bag laughs. Radio demanded humour that was verbal and often incumbent on word play. Vaudeville and music-hall humour had been centred in the groin and heart. Radio was humour located above the neckline.

The pioneers of Canadian radio comedy were an unlikely pair of Calgary hardware store clerks named Art McGregor and Frank Deaville. The twosome loved to cut up on the job and took particular delight in ribbing customers. Their careers began in 1931 after a customer, a local station manager, dared them to go live on the radio. They adopted the characters Woodhouse and Hawkins, two country bumpkins with thick accents and silly minds. The broadcast was a success, and by 1933 they had won their own show. The pair played Canada's air waves until 1944. At the height of their popularity, Woodhouse and Hawkins had a weekly time slot and were producing extravagant shows that incorporated up to twenty characters per episode. Ultimately, in a move that anticipated the real future of broadcasting, they left comedy to pursue careers in advertising.

One of radio's biggest advantages over music hall was that it allowed comedians to set their sketches in fantastic locations. It also allowed a team of two to produce epic programs with enormous casts, provided, of course, that they did all the voices. Radio work freed comedians of budget constraints. They did not have to worry about set and costume costs because there were none. If you wanted to set a skit in Tahiti, or on the surface of the moon, you did, with the help of a few sound effects. On a pragmatic level, radio allowed comedians to make a decent living without too much touring. A comedian could actually lead a fairly normal life, with a family, house, dog, and mortgage. Comedy became more middle class.

But radio had its challenges. It devoured writing. Radio consumed jokes the way a famished dog would eat a raw steak. Before radio, a vaudeville comedian could use the same bits for ten or fifteen years. Touring meant you wouldn't see a performer more than once every few years. Who cared if the material was familiar, as long as it was good? Who could remember the jokes? And those who could remember came back, because they liked the jokes the first time around. Comedians were known for doing certain bits well, maybe even the same bit some other performer did only half as well, and they were expected to perform them every time they came to town.

Vaudeville comedians did have writers, generally playwrights or authors, who penned bits of stage business on the side, but most of them used routines they learned from senior performers on the circuit. Stage business was passed down through generations. Radio changed that. Comedians had to be prolific writers as well as performers, or they had to hire full-time comedy writers.

Most importantly, radio was the only game in Canada. If you were a physical comedian, you had to either adapt to radio's constraints or move south to America, where Canadian performers like Keystone Cops creator Max Sennett and actress Mary Pickford made fortunes in silent movies. In America, the talent was split between movies and radio. In Canada, the talent was all in one place. It went on the air.

The first time I met Frank Shuster, *Wayne and Shuster* had been off CBC Television for over fifteen years. It was 1993, and I met him at the CBC's Bay Street offices. He had sequestered himself away in a corner office and dove into the task of preparing a twenty-four-episode *Wayne and Shuster* retrospective. Shuster was bright and friendly. At the time, Ralph Benmergui was taking his shot at late-night talk show fame. "I told him to always surprise them," Shuster told me. "That's the key. They can never know what you're going to do next."

I met with Shuster about twice a year after that. In 1996, he invited me to his apartment, which he shared with his wife, Ruth. Shuster's apartment was done up in dramatic black, white, and red, and was decorated with modern furniture and plenty of plants. We spoke in Shuster's study, which contained a couch, desk, and television, and a wall of books that included all of S.J. Perelman's works, various histories of comedy, and several collections of plays. One of the first qualities you notice about Frank Shuster is his unabashed love of the written word. I often found it difficult to keep him on the subject of *Wayne and Shuster*. The elder comedian wanted to discuss Perelman's use of invective or the suitability of iambic pentameter (the rhyming meter that Shakespeare used) for delivering a punchline.

Johnny Wayne and Frank Shuster grew up in the same Toronto neighbourhood near Bathurst and College streets and went to the same high school, Harbord Collegiate. They were Toronto boys through and through. Wayne was a fan of the Chaps Books, pictorials that told stories of school life and military bravery. He also enjoyed a book called *1066 and All That,* an English comic book that took a humorous look at British history. Shuster, whose cousin was Joe Shuster, the creator of the *Superman* comic strip, grew up on Hollywood movies. Frank's father was a projectionist, and he and his cousin would spend hours in the cinema watching Charlie Chaplin and Buster Keaton. Later, the Marx Brothers were a significant influence. Shuster recalled that his first comic moment occurred at age seven.

"I was in a revue where we were supposed to be sea creatures in Davy Jones' Locker. We were dancing the hornpipe, a line of kids dancing, and my shoelace came untied. I spent the entire song trying to tie it up, to tie up my shoe without anyone noticing. Well, I didn't even know how to tie my own shoes — my parents did that for me. I kept hoping nobody was looking, but of course they all were. I remember the laughter and liking it. That, for me, is comedy. Everyone is in sync and one fellow is messing up. He's the comedy."

At Harbord Collegiate, Frank and Johnny engaged in amateur theatricals and school plays. Their first "professional" gig was a Boy Scout show, which the two wrote. It raised forty dollars for charity. After graduation they went on to the University of Toronto, where each studied English. There they continued to act and were involved in a series of college productions. Many were performed at the Hart House theatre. Hart House had become an important stage after World War I and had been the centre of a Canadian theatrical movement that included the likes of actor Raymond Massey and Ontario playwright Merrill Dennison, who wrote the hit *Brothers in Arms.* Wayne was news editor of the school paper, the *Varsity,* while Shuster was a copy editor. They were pretty much inseparable. They graduated in 1939 and 1940, respectively, and embarked on their master's degrees. But opportunity knocked, in the unlikely form of Javex bleach.

CFRB, a local Toronto radio station, asked Wayne and Shuster (who were not yet officially a team) to write, produce, and star in a comedy series built around household tips for women. The program would be called *The Wife Preservers,* and three times a week at 10:15 in the morning, the pair would outline household hints, ranging from how to remove stains using Javex to tips on peeling fruit without leaving a bruise. It was an early wacky version of Martha Stewart. *The Wife Preservers* went over well with listeners. CFRB decided they had hooked on to a winner with Wayne and Shuster, and asked them to produce and star in a free-form show featuring young girls. CFRB called the program *Co-eds and Cut-ups,* a title the duo loathed. Soon after, Wayne and Shuster made the jump to the CBC, when they were hired to punch up a show sponsored by Buckingham cigarettes. Unlike the practice today, in the thirties it was common for advertisers to not only sponsor radio programs but actually create them. Advertising agencies were responsible for all creative aspects of production, and the CBC provided the broadcast signal. Wayne and Shuster's program was called *Blended Rhythm,* a pun on the alleged quality of Buckingham cigarettes. It featured announcer Herb May, musical co-ordinator Burt Austin, and a pair of singers called the Campbell Sisters. Meanwhile Wayne and Shuster continued to perform live, raising money for charities such as the *Star* Fresh Air Fund, which helped underprivileged children.

When World War II broke out, both enlisted. Johnny was called first and then Frank, but they both ended up in entertainment. The days of the Dumbells' combat revues were gone. The military had learned the value of entertainment during the previous war and put great effort into presenting professional-quality shows. Wayne and Shuster became part of the *Army Show,* which had two branches, a radio show broadcast from Toronto, and a live touring show that played overseas. They were part of the live show and took their act on the road. These wartime efforts were extremely productive. For the first time, Wayne and Shuster played to a cross-section of Canadians. This allowed them to experience in person what made Canadians laugh. On radio, they had been removed from their audience. The *Army Show* put them front and centre. The show also brought the two Toronto boys in direct contact with American show business. Many big-name entertainers played for the troops, and performers from various countries often shared the same stage. Wayne and Shuster once worked with Jack Benny in a skit in which Benny tried to join the Canadian Army. Wayne and Shuster tried to dissuade him, but a disgruntled Benny produced his draft notice, signed by the Queen herself. After some deliberation, the comedians discovered that while Benny's notice was legitimate, it was a draft call for the Boer War.

The *Army Show* played for thousands of troops, stationed both in Europe and in Canada. Over four years it earned three million dollars, which was funnelled back into the Army's coffers. By the show's close, the duo were writing the entire production and starring in most scenes. After peace was declared, they continued their Army-related work, producing a series called *Johnny Home*. It was a comic take on the trials and tribulations of servicemen returning from war. The pair's reputation was growing daily. "If there is any single comedian or group of comedians in Canada today who are more likely to hit the really big time across the line quicker than Wayne and Shuster," journalist Thomas Price wrote in a 1947 issue of the magazine *Jewish Life,* "I for one would like to meet them."

Wayne and Shuster returned to radio in Canada and stayed there until 1950, when they were given a shot at television. As continues to be true for many of Canada's best, the team's big break did not come from those at home who knew their work best, but instead from broadcasters in the United States. Johnny and Frank were off to appear on TV in New York and the *Tony Twin Time* show, which was sponsored by Tony Home Permanent. The host was a young unknown actor named Jack Lemmon. Early in the run of the show, the producers asked the Canadians to take over as hosts: "They weren't too pleased with Jack Lemmon," recalls Shuster. However, the duo turned down that offer. In 1952, after seeing the two Canadians on American TV, the CBC decided to offer them a series. But Wayne and Shuster weren't convinced that TV would last, let alone replace radio. At first they declined, but eventually, Shuster says, they " saw the writing on the wall." They accepted CBC Television's offer; their first show aired in 1954.

Wayne and Shuster ran until 1967 in black-and-white, from 1967 to 1989 in colour. The shows were not typical comedy programs. Their bits were often set in historical times or far-off places. They used large casts — as many as thirty-five actors at a time — and demanded elaborate sets. They once had the CBC construct a life-size replica of the Trojan horse, all to set up one punchline: "Is there a doctor in the horse?"

This was typical of their material, which ran along this pun and parody line. Wayne and Shuster revelled in word play, even writing an entire sketch in iambic pentameter. They often employed this kind of classical reference in their humour, managing to combine elevated themes with mainstream references. Many sketches put a contemporary spin on standard routines:

> SHERIFF: Doc, the Ringo Kid's in town! The Ringo Kid
> — the dirtiest, rottenest killer west of the Rio Grande.
> He's a murderin' outlaw!
> DOCTOR: Sheriff, sheriff. How many times do I have to
> tell you? There are no such things as outlaws. Just
> problem cowboys."

In 1957, the pair went to England and shot a special for British television. While performing there, Ed Sullivan, the king of variety television, caught their act. He liked what he saw. Sullivan offered the duo $176,000 to appear on twenty-six episodes of his show. They took the offer and fled the CBC, but instead of moving to New York, kept their homes in Toronto and flew down for tapings. Before their first show, May 4, 1958, they spent twenty-five hours rehearsing for their sketch "Rinse the Blood Off My Toga," a fourteen-minute skit that followed a private eye, one Flavius Maximus, as he investigated the death of Julius Caesar. It contained two bits that became instant history: "If I told him once, I told him a million times. I said Julie, don't go." It also included this famous exchange, which may be the only joke told in Latin on American television:

JOHNNY: I'll have a martinus.
BARTENDER: You mean a martini?
JOHNNY: If I want two, I'll ask for them.

Wayne and Shuster's first appearance drew raves from the American press, who called them "unqualified hits" and "one of the best comedy teams to be seen around here for a long time." The day after the broadcast, bars all over Manhattan were offering their customers "martinus." In an interview with Walter Harris, of *Saturday Night* magazine, Ed Sullivan explained what he believed was Wayne and Shuster's appeal. "They are literate. Unlike most American comedians, they have a fresh, satirical approach. I want them to stay in Canada and commute to New York, so that they don't get contaminated by our people. So many of our writers seem to foregather at Lindy's and Reuben's and hash out their jokes together. The result is an unoriginal, flat series of scripts, in which the same jokes constantly appear with few variations. I want Wayne and Shuster to go on writing as they've always done and to be themselves."

Wayne and Shuster went on to appear on fifty-eight episodes of *The Ed Sullivan Show*, from 1958 to 1970, giving the duo the all-time record for number of appearances by any performer. Sullivan gave them *carte blanche*. He encouraged their predilection for elaborate sets and extravaganzas. Sullivan told his staff, "If Wayne and Shuster want elephants, give them elephants." Sullivan awarded Wayne with a silver dollar on which the words "Do It Your Way" were stamped. Whenever Sullivan's crew would argue about a set change or line reading, Wayne would slap it on the table.

The New York–Toronto commute suited the Canadians perfectly. Since their days travelling during the war, they had avoided what Shuster calls "the gypsy life" of show business. There were many offers to play casino showrooms like the Copacabana. They turned them all down. Once they told an agent from MCA that they weren't interested in going on the road because they "were happy." To which the agent replied, "There's more to life than happiness."

The American press quickly dubbed their comedy "literate slapstick," which pleased the comedians. There was plenty of truth in the analysis. On the slapstick side, Wayne and Shuster had been raised on the same cultural diet as any American kid: movies and comic books. They were also influenced by burlesque, which had been born in the 1860s. Originally a poor cousin to vaudeville, burlesque shows were divided into three parts. The first was a series of songs and comedic bits. The second, a series of dancers and acrobats. Finally, a third act featured elements of the first two, a chorus line, and comedy bits in a parody of a current hit play. In the 1920s, striptease was introduced as the fourth act. Johnny and Frank were well acquainted with the form. In university they had spent more than one afternoon at the Casino Theatre, a Toronto burlesque hall, watching the comedians and the strip acts, and their physical style reflected these influences.

The duo's presentation was as brazen and zany as that of any American team. But as American TV critic Hal Humphreys observed, Wayne and Shuster were university educated. This gave them their literate edge. Most American comics, like Jimmy Durante, never got past the fourth grade, and worked their way up through burlesque houses. Wayne and Shuster combined a burlesque style with their literary backgrounds. They gave audiences broad fun that had an intellectual core. The pair kept this core pure by excluding outside influences. Wayne and Shuster did their own writing. They did not use hired guns. The literary references were a fresh element that scored with the critics.

This was the key to Wayne and Shuster's winning formula: a University of Toronto education, honed on Canadian radio, seasoned by four years of performing for military audiences, delivered with a Borsch Belt sensibility. Their literate slapstick worked well into the sixties. Wayne and Shuster were a fixture at the CBC throughout that decade. By 1970, however, the darlings of Canadian comedy were falling out of favour. In the mid-sixties they'd tried their hand at sitcoms, doing *Holiday Lodge* in the States. The show had scored well on American television but was, using Shuster's word, "awful."

A new brand of comedy arose in the late sixties that was angry, lewd, and edgy. Its backers, many of whom were in the media, lambasted Wayne and Shuster, complaining that they had failed to keep up with the times. Barry Westgate of the Edmonton *Journal* called them "a couple of tattered has-beens who have let the world of comedy entertainment leave them far, far behind." And in a 1968 *Globe and Mail* review of the first of "a threatened half-dozen Wayne and Shuster comedy hours," Leslie Millin wrote: "This is not Canadian humour at all. It is the rattling of two skeletons in an old musty Canadian closet and we have been listening to it for too long."

It's true that Wayne and Shuster chose not to jettison their own brand of comedy in favour of something more modish. They were established veterans with more than thirty years in the business, and they knew what they wanted from their careers. The new wave did not excite them, so they passed on it, just as they'd chosen to pass up the opportunity to move to New York, or work the casinos. But the familiarity of their "literate slapstick" had bred contempt, and even accusations that their comedy was "not Canadian." How ironic, when the distinctively Canadian style of their sketch comedy was what had made them so popular with Canadian and American audiences for so long. Still, it wasn't until the early 1990s that they received the proper recognition for their achievements. Wayne and Shuster got their wall.

The media is often quick to herald the arrival of genius and just as eager to pronounce its passing. The Canadian media is especially insecure about being a step behind or out of sync. That's why so much of our best talent goes undiscovered until it appears on American television, or is alternately condemned for hiding out north of the border or selling out by "going south." The phrase itself, once only a geographical description, now bears connotations of betrayal. The reasons for this insecurity are complex. The reality it presents to Canadian comedians is simple. As Jim Carrey told me in 1992, "People up in Canada need to know you've been validated down here." Even the CBC, which out of self-interest might attempt to discourage such sentiments, seems prone to dismiss the value of their home-grown content. Some of the CBC's mistakes have grown to legend. For example, one CBC producer told Canadian sketch comedian Mike Myers that "Wayne's World," his spoof on the suburban teenage heavy metal music scene, could never be more than a three-minute sketch. Myers' character, Wayne Campbell, and his signature refrain "Excellent," have since gone on to become a multimillion-dollar franchise. Many of the best and brightest have been ignored by the broadcast system that most needs them and have eventually fled south.

Their patron saint, although many of them don't know it, was the first Canadian comedian to fly south solo: Alan Young. During the forties, fifties, and sixties, Young set the pace for every Canadian who would carve his or her own niche in America. Before there were Jim Carrey and Howie Mandel, there was Alan Young. Young had two forces at work for him — his tremendous gift for physical comedy and his knack for creating lovable, comic figures from life's bottom rungs. They were traits that every solo Canadian comedian who followed him would possess to varying degrees. If you judged him solely by his picture on the Comedy Wall of Fame, Young would not score well. In it, he stands beside the actor with whom he became a household name during the sixties: Mister Ed, the talking horse.

Young was born in Northern England and moved with his family to Vancouver when he was six. Technically an Englishman, Young was, in spirit, a Scotsman through and through. His given name was Angus. Young was a descendant of William Wallace, a famous Highlander and member of the clan Cathgart. His parents were both working class and harboured theatrical aspirations. His father, a shipbuilder, tap danced as a hobby. Young played his first professional gig when he was thirteen, earning two dollars for performing a monologue for the Caledonian Society of Vancouver. "When a Scotsman puts out two dollars for entertainment," Young later said, "it's got to be good." He decided to become an actor at age fourteen.

As a teenager, Young toured Canada and the northern United States steadily. He acted as master of ceremonies, gave monologues, and played the saxophone and drums with dance bands. Unlike Wayne and Shuster, Young was not university educated. He worked his way up through the ranks. No one would call his style literate. It was smart but not high-brow. You would not find too many Shakespearean references in his material. Young's greatest strength was his physical comedy, which he modelled after silent movie comedians such as Charlie Chaplin and Harold Lloyd. He was gifted with a sixth sense when it came to delivering a visual punchline. He could draw a huge laugh with a slight lift of the eyebrow or turn of the head.

At age seventeen, Young began work at CJOR, a Vancouver radio station. He wrote scripts and acted in sketches, making fifteen dollars a week. After a stint acting in a play, Young went to Toronto and began writing for a radio program called *Stag Party,* in which he invited various guests to appear and trade quips and skits. By 1939, he was the foremost comic in Canada. Like many of his generation, Young's career was interrupted by World War II. He enlisted in the Canadian Navy and served as an officer until 1943, when he was discharged. Young returned to Toronto and resumed acting. He soon landed his own program on CBC Radio, *The Alan Young Show,* which became popular across the country. Young began to receive attention from American producers but turned down a number of offers to go south. Then he began to hear a refrain that has become all too familiar to Canadian comedians. Listeners would tell him: "My, you're funny. You're good enough to be in the States. If you're good enough, why aren't you in America?" Young used to reply, "But aren't I good enough to stay in Canada?" He wanted to stay in Toronto, but it seemed that the greatest compliment a Canadian artist could get was, "You're good enough to go to the States."

In 1943, Frank Cooper, a New York talent agent, heard Young's program while dialling through the Toronto stations. He liked what he heard and made an offer. This time Young did not refuse. The following year, Cooper booked the Canadian comedian as a summer replacement for the radio series *The Eddie Cantor Show,* at $550 per week. While Young was the first Canadian comedian to go solo in America, he was also the first to bomb. His mild-mannered speech didn't go over with American listeners. They were used to broad, loud comedians who had emerged from burlesque and vaudeville — guys like Phil Silvers and Sid Caesar. On radio, Young and his meek Canadian persona languished, but not before Twentieth Century Fox had signed him to act in two feature films at thirty-five thousand dollars each. The films, *Margie* and *Mr. Belvedere Goes to College,* were worse than Young's radio work. By 1947, at age twenty-nine, it seemed that he was finished.

Disheartened, Young planned a tour of Canada ostensibly to see old friends, but mainly to make some money. His plans were foiled by a traffic accident that left him with a broken vertebra and put him in a cast for six months. It was probably one of the best breaks of his life. He stayed in the United States and in 1949 married Virginia McCurdy, an American singer who had worked on his radio show. At the same time he entered the American vaudeville circuit. This earned Young his second shot at the American market. The Columbia Broadcasting System (CBS) decided that Twentieth Century Fox had erred in their handling of Young. They signed the Canadian comic to a five-year television deal and built a show around him. *The Alan Young Show* debuted, from Los Angeles, in 1949. It was the second biggest budget production to come out of Hollywood. Young had begun his career in Vancouver making fifteen dollars a week. Now he was making nine thousand.

The virgin television industry was the ideal vehicle for Young. His talent for physical comedy had been wasted on radio, but on television, viewers could pick up on every subtle gesture. On television, he excelled playing low-key, lovable losers. There was a lighthouse keeper annoyed by the arrival of a beautiful shipwrecked damsel; a man who fell in love with a store mannequin; a Scoutmaster who learned the fundamentals of the birds and bees from his own Scout troop; and a nervous first-time airplane traveller. Young's comedic appeal was that of the average guy stuck in crazy circumstances. A critic described him as "an everyday bloke slightly confused with the fast moving world." Young's jokes used domestic settings, shops, kitchens, and living rooms. He was everyone's goofy next-door neighbour. This formula worked with American audiences, who were happy to invite such a good-natured comic into their homes. Mastering this persona came naturally to a comedian who hailed from a country where deference and self-deprecation are considered national treasures. Other comedians, like French film star Jacques Tati, adopted an similar mild-mannered approach, but only Young found acceptance in the American market, because he looked and sounded like an American.

"TV is something I've had in mind for years," he told *Saturday Night* magazine in 1950. "I've always thought visually and actually felt handicapped trying to portray the character I was trying to establish on radio. Now I show visually the pixy gent who is never quite sure what it is he's doing or how to do it."

Young's show won two Emmy awards in 1951. John Crosby of the New York *Herald Tribune* wrote, "For my money television has only produced two young comedians who look as if they are going to stick around for a while — Sid Caesar and Alan Young." Crosby was half right. Caesar's *Show of Shows* had a long run, but Young's vehicle lasted a mere two seasons. He was out of luck once again. Young left North America for England and spent two years producing and directing television specials. He made a handful of films — *Androcles, Time Machine,* and *Tom Thumb* — and then, in 1962, Young was back at CBS for a third try. This time he was working opposite a formidable co-star, the talking horse, Mister Ed. Young played Wilbur Post, an architect who moves to the country with his wife and is befriended by a palomino with a gift for the gab. Ed, a troublemaker with a big ego (so far as horses go), spoke only to Wilbur. The humour sprung from this bizarre concept. The series was Young's biggest success. *Mister Ed* made Alan Young, for the third time, an overnight sensation. This time fame also made Young rich, since he had arranged to be a part owner of the series. *Mister Ed* ran for six seasons and later went into syndication.

In 1966, Young appeared on Broadway in a play entitled *The Girl in the Freudian Slip*. It was savaged by the critics. This set-back proved one too many. The critical thrashing Young received changed the course of his life. He left show business to become a Christian Science practitioner. He cut all ties to the entertainment industry, with the exception of his involvement in the Ebony Showcase Theater, an all-black theatre company based in Los Angeles that he had helped to organize and backed financially for twenty years. In 1971, Young moved to Boston to become a director and producer at the Christian Science Center, where he wrote and produced church training films. "I haven't left show business," he told the magazine *Canadian Panorama* in an article entitled "Whatever Became of Alan Young?" "Now I'm in bigtime show business — the kind of show business that's really worthwhile." On the topic of *Mister Ed,* Young showed impressive objectivity. He remarked,

"It's not the greatest show in the world, no message there, but it's brought a lot of happiness to children." Alan Young died in 1973.

Young's had been a bumpy ride to commercial success, one that ultimately came on Hollywood's terms. He had chosen to let Hollywood control his creative destiny by choosing his projects for him and by having teams of writers script his gags. Wayne and Shuster, by contrast, had found moderate success in America by remaining in Canada and by controlling the writing of their shows. They didn't want to go Hollywood, and Hollywood reciprocated by leaving them alone. Wayne and Shuster were happy to be the most popular comedians in Canada. If there *was* more to life than happiness, it appears they never knew it.

Another comedy duo, about ten years younger than Wayne and Shuster, took an altogether different route, although it ran through many of the same locations. Their Wall of Fame picture shows them dressed as college boys from the Roaring Twenties, with raccoon-skin jackets, straw hats, and canes. The twosome are hamming it up and obviously delivering a high-energy punchline. Looking at their photo, I found it hard to believe that two such outrageous comedians ultimately became renowned for their ability to disappear into the background. Frank Peppiatt and John Aylesworth were behind-the-scenes wizards. Starting in the early fifties, they were among the first comedians to perfect, and in many ways define, the role of the television comedy writer.

Like Johnny Wayne and Frank Shuster, Frank Peppiatt and John Aylesworth were both Toronto boys, although Peppiatt spent some time in Montreal. They had grown up listening to the radio. Both kids loved serial programs and the comedy of George Burns, Fred Allen, and Alan Young. Aylesworth had always harboured ambitions to become a writer. As a high school student, he had written for the *Canadian High News* and after graduation had done a short stint as a radio personality on a small station, CFPX, in Port Arthur, Ontario. Aylesworth loved to joke and in his social circles was a recognized cut-up. Peppiatt was also an extrovert, who loved sports. He was a basketball all-star and played football in high school and later at the University of Toronto. Peppiatt cultivated a mischievous streak throughout his adolescence, which earned him a reputation for cracking up the locker room. He graduated with a bachelor of arts in English and psychology. Frank and John met in 1950 at the MacLaren Advertising Company, founded by Jack MacLaren — the same Jack MacLaren who had performed in and written sketches for the Dumbells.

The pairing of Peppiatt and Aylesworth was like thunder finally meeting lightning. Both men were relentlessly irreverent and had a near-pathological need to buck authority. This impulse manifested itself in creative and rather diabolical ways. For example, Frank and John were not fond of their supervisor, who was, Peppiatt recalls, a mean, tyrannical man prone to giving employees verbal lashings. One day the fellow came into the office wearing a prize possession, a brand-new hat, complete with his initials stitched inside the brim. He beamed with pride. Peppiatt and Aylesworth saw their opportunity. That afternoon they spent the equivalent of a week's salary each and purchased two identical hats, one a size larger than their boss's and one a size smaller.

The following day, their boss appeared with his hat. The pranksters waited until he went to the washroom and then switched his hat for the larger version. The office at MacLaren Advertising was laid out with a border of glass-walled offices enclosing a bull pen for the secretaries and copy writers. After the supervisor returned, the entire office watched in muffled hilarity at lunch-time as their leader placed the hat on his head, and it dropped to his ears. The boss then stuffed tissue in the hat and replaced it, heading out for lunch. Later that afternoon, Frank and John switched the large hat for the smaller version and placed the tissue paper back in the crown. Again the office watched as the tyrant donned his new hat, only to find that now it was too small. This comic torture went on for a week.

I interviewed Frank Peppiatt at his Toronto home in the fall of 1996. He is a tall man, over six feet, with a crop of white hair and a trim white moustache. We spoke in his study, which is lined with Emmy awards and other pieces of show business memorabilia. Peppiatt still had the same devilish streak in him. "The office would go berserk," he recalled of their prank. "Then someone took me aside and said, 'He thinks his head is expanding. I think he's going insane.' So we let him in on the joke, and he thanked us. He said he was really starting to worry. And you know, he was a lot nicer after that."

Frank and John started their comedy careers with the birth of CBC Television in November 1952. Peter MacFarlane, one of the producers, asked them to write an hour's worth of comedy for a proposed comedy show that CBC had commissioned. MacFarlane had worked with Peppiatt and Aylesworth at MacLaren's and knew all about their practical jokes. The duo had written comedy commercials for MacLaren's, using humour to sell everything from cigarettes to dishwashing liquid. Peppiatt had first-hand professional comedy experience, having spent two years as the agency representative on the Wayne and Shuster radio series. Occasionally, both he and Aylesworth would do walk-on parts, speaking lines such as, "Here's your hat, Mr. Shuster." MacFarlane was green. He had got his spot at the CBC by virtue of the fact he had spent two months at a television arts school in New York, and, according to John Aylesworth, "he knew what a television camera looked like."

Peppiatt and Aylesworth scripted two skits, a commercial parody and a border-crossing bit. The commercial spoof was a pitch for "Frig" refrigerators. In it, Frank opened the Frig to reveal John crouched inside. He then espoused the great benefits of a life lived in the Frig. You never had to worry about the heat, shirts stayed crisp, the Frig did everything but turn out the light. The bit displayed the duo's talent for off-beat comedy. Peppiatt and Aylesworth also liked satire. Their early sketches favoured targets such as television commercials and authority figures. The second of their first two sketches was a piece in which a mild-mannered Canadian (Aylesworth) tries to re-enter the country after an afternoon in Buffalo, and is grilled by a combative customs official (Peppiatt), who accuses Aylesworth of smuggling an American cigarette across the border.

MacFarlane loved Aylesworth and Peppiatt's script but couldn't find anyone to perform it. Television then was not attractive to Canada's top entertainers. Radio was still king, and no one believed a box with a grainy black-and-white screen was going to topple it. "No one would quit radio," explains Peppiatt. "They didn't take television seriously. [But] we could see what was happening in the States. When Milton Berle was on, there were no customers in any of the restaurants. Life stood still." Desperate, MacFarlane asked Peppiatt and Aylesworth if they would screen-test for the show. Their audition would be the following day at six in the morning. The duo stayed up all night and, powered by adrenaline, aced the audition. The CBC made them an offer. They would get fifty dollars each to write the show and another fifty-three for performing. The show would run for an hour each week. "So," recalls Aylesworth, "like idiots, we said yes. We had no idea of what we were getting into."

The CBC gave the team a month to work up their first show. Frank hired a Toronto actress, Jill Foster, to round out the cast. On January 2, 1953, they were on the air. The show, *After Hours,* was inspired lunacy. Frank and John were fearless, trying everything and anything to get a laugh. One bit had the pair ambushing their announcer with a water pistol. "You hold him," Peppiatt told his partner, "and I'll *shrink* him to death." Television had no rules, so they were not concerned about breaking any. They dressed up as the Marx Brothers, cowboys, knights, and space cadets, threw ketchup and mud, rode each other piggyback. The pair parodied the American serials that they had grown up listening to on radio. This was an important shift in Canadian comedy. It demonstrated that the strongest cultural influences in Canada were no longer British, but American. Canadian kids were growing up listening to and watching American entertainment. When they became adults, they reached back to their childhood influences and turned them into satire.

After Hours' entire production budget was one hundred dollars per show. The band leader, Jack Kane, led a three-man band that played in front of a backdrop that suggested a full-strength orchestra. There was no money for sets or costumes. The performers borrowed props and sets from the CBC's stock room. Peppiatt's mother sewed his Superman costume for a parody of the comic-book hero. To cut costs, Peppiatt dressed as Clark Kent simply by putting on a hat and a pair of glasses. The rest of the actors pretended not to recognize him. John and Frank's solutions were purely pragmatic, but they also packed the absurdist punch they liked. The duo serialized their successful sketches, including many Superman skits. In one, Superman returns home to his alcoholic father and shrewish mother. He sleeps in a horizontal phone booth. His parents quarrel incessantly, and when he asks them to clam up, they scold him with "You think you're big time because you can fly."

One of Peppiatt and Aylesworth's ground-breaking inventions was the inclusion of mini-films, shot on sixteen-millimetre stock, with the live action. Frank and John would hit Toronto's streets with a few comic ideas and film zany short flicks. These films used surreal effects, like reverse motion, to create off-the-wall comedy. For example, they shot a parody of marathon swimmer Marilyn Bell's crossing of Lake Ontario. In the Peppiatt and Aylesworth version, Bell (played by Aylesworth) is swimming across the lake when she is stopped by a customs official (Peppiatt), who pops out from underwater. After frisking her, he allows her to continue. *After Hours* received its share of negative reviews. Toronto's literati thought it too brazen and raw for audiences. It was uncouth. The Toronto *Star* later called it an "unspectacular." High-brow critics objected to the show's low-rent production values. They were most likely irritated by the fact that Peppiatt and Aylesworth were unapologetic about their minimal resources. But these attacks played on the team's fear that television would not last. On the side, they continued working at the advertising agency.

The CBC cancelled *After Hours* at the end of July 1953, but they kept Frank and John on. In 1954, the duo was given control of the CBC's variety hour *The Big Revue*. The program was the broadcaster's variety spectacular and ran every two weeks. *The Big Revue* had a larger cast, a six-member dance troupe, a twenty-eight member orchestra, a vocal coach, choreographer, and dialogue coach. It was a tough grind for Peppiatt and Aylesworth, who did three to four sketches per show. *The Big Revue,* to use the fifties term, was square. It was starched and mainstream. Peppiatt and Aylesworth were the epitome of hip fifties television — young, brash, creative whirlwinds who thrived under the pressure of live broadcasts. The mix did not last. They hosted *The Big Revue* for only one year. The CBC was not supportive of their work. The press material promoting the show, for example, stated: "Their efforts were more generally acceptable, viewers taking them, leaving them as they wished, without getting worked up about them." Not exactly gushing praise, coming from their publicist.

In 1955, the team was awarded another show, entitled *On Stage*. Like their previous projects, this one ran for just one season. From 1955 to 1957, Peppiatt and Aylesworth worked independently on separate CBC projects. Peppiatt worked on *Here's Duff, Hit Parade*, and *The Jackie Rae Show*. Aylesworth created *Front Page Challenge*, the famous quiz show that became the longest running program in Canadian television history. Then, in the late spring of 1957, Canada's public broadcaster made what would become a patented CBC move. By then, Wayne and Shuster were working on television, and at the CBC there was only room for one comedy team. So in 1957, the corporation let Peppiatt and Aylesworth slip away. Says Peppiatt: "They came to us and said, 'We have no idea what you're going to do next year.' Next year was four months away. John and I both had families to worry about. There was no security. We were upset."

American producers were more than happy to help calm their nerves. Peppiatt moved to New York and began working on *The Steve Lawrence and Eydie Gorme Show* and then on to *The Steve Allen Show*. Aylesworth went to write for the CBS variety show *Hit Parade*, joining director Norman Jewison, who had directed all of their work for CBC-TV and had left for America a few years earlier. Peppiatt says that CBC executives were surprised by their departure. "They asked us why we were leaving. We said, 'You didn't ask us to do anything.' They were shocked. They expected us to just sit in Toronto, with families to support and no guarantee of work, and wait for them to make up their minds."

For Steve Allen, Peppiatt wrote bits like "The Question Man," a gag in which a straight man would read questions to Allen in reverse order, giving the answer, to which Allen would provide the question:

> ANSWER: Tomato Paste.
> QUESTION: How do you keep tomatoes from
> falling apart?

The bit lives on to the present, its most recent and famous incarnation being Johnny Carson's "Great Carnac."

The Steve Allen Show had eight writers. The American writers liked to tease their Canadian co-worker. They drew a border through the office, dividing Peppiatt from the rest of them, and called him a "snowback," a play on the derogatory term used to describe Mexican immigrants. The ribbing was all in good fun, and even if it had been serious, it would have been worth the aggravation, says Peppiatt. Working conditions in America were far superior to those at the CBC, and the money was fabulous. Peppiatt and Aylesworth each made ten times what they had earned in Canada.

"There was much more respect for writers in America," maintains Peppiatt. "They needed writers, and they knew they needed writers. They realized that they needed new ideas, and anyone who could get them would make them a winner."

Peppiatt and Aylesworth worked separately until the summer of 1958, when they teamed up again and became two of four writers scripting *The Andy Williams Show*. The program was directed by the duo's old friend Norman Jewison. In 1959, they moved to *The Perry Como Show* and stayed for five years. It was their longest contract. That job proved a good education in the more subtle points of surviving in television comedy. The golden rule was solidarity. The show's head writer, Goodman Ace, told his staff that when Como asked them, "Who does the most? Whose idea was it to do this?" they were to reply, "We all do it." Frank and John learned that the key to survival lay in a passive resistance to authority. On *The Steve Lawrence and Eydie Gorme Show,* Peppiatt had encountered an incompetent and abrasive head writer. He would call his writers to his house for 10 P.M. meetings and then leave to have dinner with his wife. He took credit for others' ideas at production meetings. The situation worsened until the writers were on the verge of quitting. Peppiatt then suggested that they write a sketch set in the 1920s. "But Steve Lawrence hates the twenties," one writer piped up. "Yeah, I know," Peppiatt replied. "That's the idea." They wrote the twenties sketch, which the head writer, who was unaware of his star's views, presented. He claimed, "I wrote it myself." Lawrence was furious, yelling, "I hate this stuff." After a few more such gambits the head writer was gone.

From 1965 to 1968, Peppiatt and Aylesworth worked on a variety of projects, including writing for some of the biggest stars in American TV, such as Dean Martin, Frank Sinatra, Dinah Shore, Julie Andrews, Bing Crosby, and Johnny Carson. *Maclean's* magazine dubbed them the "one hundred thousand dollar men." In 1969, Frank picked up a copy of *Newsweek* and saw country singer Loretta Lynn on the cover. John checked the television ratings and discovered that many of the top ten shows were CBS country sitcoms, like *The Beverly Hillbillies.* The series they were working on at the time, starring comic Jonathan Winters, had been cancelled. They were still, however, responsible for producing thirteen more episodes, either with Winters or some other star. Peppiatt and Aylesworth decided the solution was to combine country music and comedy. *Hee Haw,* a country-music comedy hour, was born. Peppiatt and Aylesworth sold the show to CBS, which bought thirteen episodes, and the network ran them as a summer replacement for *The Smothers Brothers Comedy Hour.* With only a month to shoot the first few episodes, Frank and John flew to Nashville and signed some talent. Looking north, they brought in Don Harron, to portray rural bumpkin Charlie Farquharson. They also brought in Canadian entertainer Gordy Tapp.

Neither writer had any knowledge of country music. They based their ideas solely on a Canadian stereotypical notion of what the American South was like. *Hee Haw* was a product of a Canadian conception of what American country music meant. According to Aylesworth, the Canadian writers agreed "to make it a real hick fest. Plenty of clichés. We'll have a corn field for corny jokes, and a barber shop, and a fishing pond. *The Beverly Hillbillies* was just a bunch of hicks fishing in a swimming pool. We'd make *Hee Haw* all about what the hicks did before they got to Hollywood."

Hee Haw was an instant hit, but after six shows, it was cancelled. The head man at CBS, Bob Wood, wanted to "urbanize" the network and was dumping country shows such as *Hee Haw* and *The Beverly Hillbillies*. The cancellation did not stop Frank and John. They telexed every television station in America announcing that *Hee Haw* was available in syndication. A syndicated show is one that has no network affiliation and no national broadcast slot. It is produced independently and sold directly to individual stations. Lawrence Welk had been the first producer to syndicate his show, when it had lost network support because executives felt his audience was too old. Peppiatt and Aylesworth were the second. They poured every cent they had into the production. The first three episodes were aired with little support from advertisers. By the fourth week, the ratings came through. *Hee Haw* was on top. The money followed. *Hee Haw* was signed by 216 stations. The profits from the series, which went on to run for twenty years until 1991, made Peppiatt and Aylesworth wealthy men. "Put it this way," says Frank. "We realized why the networks didn't want anyone to get into syndication."

Aylesworth and Peppiatt and their American peers helped create the system that exists today. Ironically, virtually no one outside the business knew who they were. That's probably the biggest compliment you could give Frank Peppiatt and John Aylesworth. The role of the television writer is to put words in the mouths of stars in such a way as to sound totally natural. Peppiatt and Aylesworth were chameleonlike in their ability to write for anyone, from Sinatra to Judy Garland. Los Angeles and New York now have roomsful of their descendants toiling for today's stars. Frank Peppiatt and John Aylesworth were trail-blazers of television comedy, two of the medium's first comedy writers and producers. Today it is common for a network show to have a writing staff of ten to twenty. Many writing staffs in America will have at least one Canadian writer among them. Canucks are so commonplace, they aren't even noticed. The bottom line is, can you do the job?

Peppiatt and Aylesworth had an edge on their American competition. Many American writers had strictly writing backgrounds. By getting their start in Canada, the land of snow and limited budgets, Frank and John learned to understand and "write" for every aspect of production.

Even in the fifties, CBC shows had little or no budget, and writers were expected to carry many extra burdens. They had to understand television lighting, set design, and costume, and know how to create them with little money. This grass-roots, cash-strapped Canadian experience helped Aylesworth and Peppiatt become successful down south. *Hee Haw,* for example, was shot in two two-week taping sessions down in Nashville. The show was structured around a series of recurring locations, in each of which Frank and John would shoot every line of dialogue in one long shoot, assembly-line fashion. It was efficient and cheap. Hollywood loved it.

They were also the first writer-producers to learn the golden rule of Canadian comedy: "In Canada you reach a point where you have nowhere to go but down," says Aylesworth, "to the States, which is up."

F O U R

■

Continuous Entertainment

Gary David had always said that he'd quit stand-up the day he couldn't do it anymore. Well, that day had arrived. It was July 18, 1996, and David had given his last performance. He had died of cardiac arrest in his sleep two days earlier. Things just don't get more permanent than that. Now Toronto's comedy community was massed in a Mississauga cemetery, patiently waiting for workers from the Ridley Funeral Home to lower David's corpse into the earth. The funeral brought together stand-ups who on any other day would not even talk to each other. It also brought forth from the sixty in attendance a solemn respect they were unaccustomed to bestowing. The comedians had brushed off their suits and put on their good shoes. Normally most would not have been caught in anything more elaborate than jeans and a sweatshirt. The cut of their cloth was crass. With their white socks and black shoes, they looked like fourteen-year-old boys en route to a school dance. Fashion savvy is not something normally associated with the laugh trade. Only Mark Breslin, the founder and owner of Yuk Yuk's, Canada's large and powerful comedy chain, wore a designer suit. That's Mark Breslin for you. He would rather starve than look bad. The most glaring difference between the comics on any working day and their behaviour at David's grave side was their silence. You could not hear a peep. They stood mutely in honour of a comedian for whom each one held a kind thought and a large portion of respect.

Gary David had been in the business for twenty-eight years. At his wake, which was held the night of his death, his fellow comedians had paid homage to him, especially to his comic timing. They said he was the best there had been; he was a surgeon. I had never seen a wake like it before. Yes, there was the obligatory drinking, but David's peers also took turns standing at a microphone telling jokes. Some mocked him. Some became maudlin. Some, like close friend Mike Bullard, found it too difficult and after standing briefly, sat back down again. Paul Smith, a professional Yuk Yuk's comic, told the room that David had gone because "God must have needed a headliner." This drew a gasp of disgust from comedian Boyd Banks. "God needed a headliner?" he scoffed. "Are you kidding me? *God needed a headliner!* The guy's fucking dead, for Christ's sake. You say God needed a headliner? Fuck!" The outburst drew an avalanche of laughs, especially from Smith.

At the funeral, I stood three rows back as the funeral assistants lowered Gary's casket, and scanned the gathering. The mourners were sombre, some teary. I directed my attention towards two of the eldest members of the crowd — Rummy Bishop and Frenchie McFarlane steadying themselves to my right. David's death would hit them in a unique way. Bishop, McFarlane, David, and a comedian named Harry Russell, who because of his chronic bronchitis had not made the interment, had been a special brotherhood. These four men were the original seeds. There had been other comedians — like Doug Romaine, Canada's answer to Red Skelton, and Joe Murphy, who had also worked Toronto's Casino and Roxy burlesque houses — but Gary David and company had been the first four real stand-up comedians in Canada. Now they were three.

The Fearsome Foursome had formed in 1973, back when dinosaurs roamed the earth. In Toronto around that time, the comedy situation was simple: there were no comedy clubs. There were folk bars where people sang and the occasional hip young singer/comedian did a set, and there were theatres where headliners like Red Buttons played. Full-time comedy clubs, featuring a stream of comedians and a headline act, were not even a dream. They were still a little under a decade away. Stand-up comedy did, however, have a home, although not a particularly welcoming one. If you wanted to earn a living as a comic, you could do so by telling jokes during the dead air left between the performances of exotic dancers. In 1973, stand-up comedy did not mean adoring audiences and television deals, it meant naked women and unruly crowds. It meant burlesque. In Toronto, it meant specifically Starvin' Marvin's on Yonge Street and the Victory Theatre on Spadina Avenue.

Young comedians talk of those days in hushed amazement. It is as inconceivable for them to imagine a world without comedy clubs as it would be for an English professor to imagine a world without universities. I took a special interest in the period as I grew to know the comedy scene. To me, it was a piece of missing history. In the winter of 1996, I finally began to track it down. I met Gary David for a drink and a chat, and he gave me telephone numbers for his three peers. One by one I interviewed them.

I found seventy-seven-year-old Rummy Bishop living in an artists' retirement residence down on Toronto's lakeshore. His apartment was small, well kept, and decorated with photographs of Bishop in various show business venues. One had him shaking hands with John F. Kennedy.

"When Starvin' Marvin's opened up, they had me pegged as the host," he recalled. "We couldn't agree on money. I was working the 500 Club in Atlantic City and I said, 'I'll take seven-fifty a week.' Then Marvin himself gets on the phone and says, 'Do you want to gamble? We'll give you three-fifty a week and an extra fifty dollars each week we stay open.' After two days he came and said, 'How about taking the seven-fifty? If we have to keep giving you a raise, it'll break us.'"

Starvin' Marvin's became instantly popular because it offered sexually desperate men the opportunity to see full nudity. Toronto in the early seventies was a sexually repressed place. In fact, most forms of pleasure were frowned upon. Drinking laws were strict, films and magazines were censored. The population was still predominantly white,

Protestant, and up-tight. Some of Toronto's neighbourhoods still prohibited liquor. Although a youth faction of hippies, artists, and university students experimented with sex, drugs, and free love, most of Toronto clung steadfastly to puritanical values. Burlesque had survived in Toronto through the first half of the century, but by the seventies it was competing with massage parlours. In its time, the full frontal nudity at Starvin' Marvin's was a first. Before Starvin' Marvin's there had been only partial exposure. To give these skin revues a little dignity, comedians were brought in as an extra bonus.

While the city of Toronto remained morally rigid, politically Canada was swinging left with vigour. Trudeau and the Liberal party were running the country, and an era of public spending boiled at full heat. Artists were big beneficiaries of this federal and provincial largesse. During the 1950s and then on into the 1960s, Canadian governments, perhaps inspired by the British example of public funding for the arts, seized upon the idea that the best way to create a flourishing artistic community was to supply money. If you wanted sublime theatre, dance, film, television, painting, and poetry, all you had to do was cut the artists a cheque, the theory went. Once the artists had money, or at least a middle-class income, art would flow like beer at a legion hall. Funding bodies such as the Canada Council, the Ontario Arts Council and the Saskatchewan Arts Fund sprang up and sprinkled government money on the arts community like fertilizer. After repeated doses of currency, they assumed, all that was left to do was sit back and watch the flowers grow.

Comedy was absent from the list of arts considered socially redeeming enough to warrant a squeeze of cash. All comedy — by its very nature ugly, overtly sexual, offensive, and politically explosive — was left out in the cold. Comedians criticize society but offer no solutions. This makes them dangerous. Politically, funding comedy would have been suicidal because it risks offending too many constituents. The most innocuous joke can still raise the ire of at least one audience member. The CBC circumnavigated this danger by programming low-risk acts, like Wayne and Shuster, and by providing a limited amount of time for contentious comedians, like Max Ferguson. Those out for blood, like Michael Magee, were chastised and rooted out. At the entry level, where so much funding was being given out in other arts fields, comedians were excluded, their trade considered low-rent and sleazy. Ironically, the fact that comedy was looked on by critics and bureaucrats not as art at all but rather as cheap entertainment resulted in its being left alone to develop as a healthy art. And comedy is an art, there is no mistaking that. The demands placed on a sketch comedian or stand-up easily equal those placed on an actor or singer. Done right, comedy reaches sublime artistic heights.

In Toronto during the early seventies, stand-up comedy fell lower than sketch comedy, which was linked to theatre. Stand-up sprang from American vaudeville and burlesque. Its three core ingredients were its use of a single comic voice, reliance on the spoken word, and a brash, confrontational nature. Artistically, stand-up was a comedic expression of the American belief in free speech and an individual's right to question his or her society. In practice, those who exerted this right suffered. Lenny Bruce, the quintessential comedic conscientious objector, endured such a severe backlash against his comedy that it eventually killed him. Bruce died of a drug overdose. In Canada, stand up's American overtones, in part, kept it out of the funding game. Its elevation of the individual and the individual's right to criticize society was decidedly un-Canadian in the eyes of funding bureaucrats. It had no theatrical ties and, worse, epitomized all the American qualities that our national cultural thinkers like to claim don't exist in the Canadian character.

Ironically, there was no ill will in the comedy community. In fact, I have found no evidence of a comedian even asking the government for money. This is not surprising. There are few generalizations that hold true of all comics. Only one sticks down the line: comedians despise authority. Comedians are willing to put up with poverty-level wages in exchange for being part of a profession in which they have only five minutes of contact with their employers a week. The big attraction of the comic lifestyle is its independence. No nine-to-five job, no boss looking over your shoulder, no forms to fill out. The concept of asking the government for money was, and remains, unthinkable to comedians. If you want funding from the government, you have to explain why you are worthy of it. You have to submit yourself and your art not to the scrutiny of an audience but to the scrutiny of a roomful of bureaucrats. I can honestly say that I have never met a comedian who would subject him or herself to such treatment. It's not that they wouldn't want the free money — hey, who wouldn't like the cash? To the comedians, however, kneeling before the government is a sign of failure. They'd rather starve in dignified silence than grow fat in loud obsequiousness.

In the world of comedy, life is simple. That's one of comedy's charms. No explanation is necessary, ever. You do your act and you get paid. If the audience laughs you're untouchable — until they stop laughing. If they don't laugh, you don't work. There is no bargaining in stand-up, no selling. The comedian delivers his or her act, and if the audience laughs they have, in effect, bought the goods. That has always been the deal, and that will always be the deal.

That was the deal back in 1973, when Rummy Bishop, an American, first graced Starvin' Marvin's' stage. Born and raised in Philadelphia, Rummy did not get his name from drinking; he acquired it as a child during a snowball fight. Bishop had taken a few ice balls to the nose and was dubbed "Rummy" because of his beet-red snout. The name stuck. He came to Toronto a seasoned stand-up comedian. At age fifteen, back in 1938, Bishop had formed the Bishop Brothers trio with his cousin Joey and a myriad of third parties. Each "extra Bishop" brought something to the act — free clothes, a little money, perhaps some talent. But the driving force behind the act was definitely the Bishop cousins. The Bishop Brothers played their first gig at the Rathskella in Philadelphia, opening for a musical act called the Three Peppers. They made seventy-five dollars a week. When they asked for ninety a week and top billing, the owner told them to "get the hell out." The firing didn't hurt. Rummy and his partners had been booked to play Buffalo and a few casinos and showrooms. In six months they were making $300 a week and were signed by the William Morris Agency. They also began playing Mafia-run clubs, specifically the Nut Clubs in Philadelphia and Miami. Bishop liked working mob rooms. "I never got screwed [around]," he says. "We never even had a contract. We always got paid. The hoods liked me — they figured I'd never fuck them. It was when I started working with so-called legitimate businessmen that I got ripped off."

Still, there were occasional moments of terror. One evening a few goons came into a club the trio was playing and lined the patrons up against the wall while, with machine guns in hand, they searched for the owner. "They wanted to kill him," Bishop recalls. "They didn't find him — that night."

It wasn't uncommon for a mob leader and his soldiers to commandeer a venue for the evening. They'd simply enter, secure the club, and then announce that no one was coming or going until the boss and his crowd had finished enjoying themselves. Once in a while one of the Bishops would come close to getting killed. In 1941, after spending an evening in Miami dancing with a couple of young ladies they picked up at the Nut Club, Joey and Rummy took the stage to find a surprise sitting in the front row.

"There was a guy looking at us," Rummy recalls, "and I looked at him, and he looked down at the table, and I noticed that underneath the table he was pointing a gun at us. Then I noticed the guy was Ralph Capone, Al Capone's brother. Well, he doesn't shoot us. He smiles and we start improvising with him about his gun. The audience loves it. After the show he calls me over, and it turns out he knows about the girls. He asks me questions about the women we were out with the night before, one of whom, I find out, is his wife. Nothing had happened, although Joey had tried to go home with what turned out to be Ralph Capone's wife. Joey had asked if he could come up, and she had said she had a baby in the room. He had said, 'Don't worry, I'll be quiet.' I remember Joey being puzzled she told him, 'It would be better for you if I didn't.' Well, Ralph Capone wants to know who was with who — you see? I told him nobody was with nobody. He says, when two men and two women go out, *somebody* has to be with *somebody*. Then he asks me if Joey can take a joke. He walks over to the bar, which was separate from the stage, and grabs Joey by the collar and pushes him against the wall. The entire place went quiet. Then he says, 'You son of a bitch, you went out with my wife.' So everybody figured there was going to be a killing. He pulls out the gun he'd showed me and says, 'I ought to let you have it right here.' Joey turned white. He was shaking.

Capone kept banging him against the wall. He was trying to get Joey to admit he was sorry, so he could do something about it. Joey just kept saying he didn't know Capone's wife. You could see Capone wasn't acting — he got madder every time he slammed Joey against the wall. But the maitre d' broke it up and everyone sat down."

Shortly before the end of World War II, Rummy Bishop was drafted and the Bishop Brothers broke up. The split was inevitable; there had been plenty of acrimony and quarreling. The cousins weren't exactly kissing. "Joey was not easy," says Rummy. "He loved me as much as he loved anybody, and that ain't saying much." After the military, Rummy went solo and put together a revue called *Burly Q. Capers*. It was a mock burlesque show complete with showgirls and acrobats but no actual strippers. The revue had a successful two-year run across North America. Rummy continued to work live, appeared on *The Tonight Show* — a highlight of his career — and his cousin's television show. Joey had become rich and famous and had occasionally thrown Rummy a bone. He had a role in the movie *Ocean's Eleven,* which starred members of the fabled "Rat Pack," a glitzy group that included Frank Sinatra, Dean Martin, and Joey Bishop, among others. But Rummy, who had a wife and kids to support, needed steady work. So in 1973, he and his family packed up and came north to Toronto and Starvin' Marvin's. Why Rummy chose a city in which there was little work and no exposure to American show business poses a puzzling question. He says it was simply a matter of money.

Soon after he started at Starvin' Marvin's, Bishop opted to work only nights. The strip club's management had given him the power to hire new comedians, and he quickly signed two stand-ups to work the day shifts, Gary David and Harry Russell. David was an American out of San Francisco. He was an ex-marine who'd served combat duty in the Korean War. After his tour he'd joined the merchant marines, left, bummed around Montreal, and been generally aimless. Finally, at age thirty-nine and married, David had decided to become a professional comedian. "My friends thought I was funny," he said, "so I gave it a try."

Harry Russell was a Toronto-born comedian who hailed from a show biz family. His father was Stan Russell, the first man, according to

Russell, to play a sax in a dance band. His uncle was a choirmaster and his mother was a music teacher. Russell performed his first show at age six and as a boy learned piano, sax, vibraphone, and the drums. He left show business and got married in 1951 but couldn't stay out of the game. Russell began to sneak out on his job to work the burlesque houses. "It was either kill somebody, have a heart attack, or quit my day job." He quit the day job. His marriage ended too, leaving Russell free to join extensive tours as part of a musical comedy act, hitting places such as Vietnam, Japan, New Zealand, and the Philippines. He left the group and returned to Toronto and straight stand-up comedy in the early seventies. His bread-and-butter gig, along with the odd Shriners' show, was at the run-down, six-hundred-seat Victory Theatre. For five shows a day he made $175 a week, "if I was lucky," and told people who asked where he was working that he was appearing at the "Old Vic," referring to the respected London venue. The Victory Theatre offered a band, the odd B movie, and an average of four naked women an hour. The dilapidated theatre had a reputation for sleaze. Enthusiastic patrons masturbated while sitting in back rows. Comics referred to these individuals as the "*Globe and Mail* Set" due to the fact that they shielded their self-manipulation by placing copies of the newspaper over their laps.

Russell hated the work and found himself wondering, Who do I have to screw to get out of here? The Victory Theatre was taking its toll. He began to lose his grasp of reality. He knew it was time to leave when, during one show, he convinced himself that a stripper who lifted her leg back over her shoulder as part of the act was readying to "piss all over the band." When, in 1974, Rummy Bishop offered him a place on Starvin' Marvin's' stage, it actually seemed like a step up.

Not long afterwards, twenty-nine-year-old comedian Frenchie McFarlane entered the picture. McFarlane had grown up in Montreal, where as a child, his mother once told the Toronto *Sun,* "he was a real little bugger." In his previous careers, McFarlane had been a pitch man for a dubious oil company known as Gulf American. He had also sold "land in Florida." His real name was Craig, but "that sounded like an accountant" so he switched to Frenchie. McFarlane started working as a comedian in Montreal in 1972. Performing before audiences that were half French and half English meant that at any given time, half the crowd didn't understand his jokes. To bridge the language gap McFarlane developed a very physical style.

That suited Starvin' Marvin's, which was a very physical place.

If a patron of today's skin palaces had walked into Starvin' Marvin's between 1974 and 1976, he would not have realized he was in a strip club. Today's strip bars are just that, bars where women strip off their clothes and occasionally perform sexual acts. By today's standards Starvin' Marvin's was the Royal Alexandra. The stage was laid out like a fashion runway. Lined along it were five rows of seating. As a dancer gyrated her way down the stage, a series of coloured lights marked her path. In the foyer, there was a snack bar that served popcorn, chips, hot dogs, coffee, and soft drinks. Starvin' Marvin's was a no-alcohol establishment. There was also no physical contact with the dancers.

The women used elaborate costumes, some costing as much as two thousand dollars. Each "girl" was required to do twelve minutes of striptease per show. In the early days, they danced to a live band. Bishop recalls their routines. There was "Vampira," who emerged from a coffin, had a trickle of blood running down her cheek, and sported a stake, which she incorporated into her routine. There was a nun, a schoolgirl, a hooker — all the stereotypical teasers. The best of the lot, according to Bishop, was "Princess Lily." She was a deaf mute from Vancouver who danced by feeling the vibrations off the stage. "Believe it or not, she drew a deaf crowd," says Bishop. "Whenever she played, there would be a lot of deaf guys." Sex with the dancers was frowned upon by the management and since three of the four comics were married, inadvisable from a domestic standpoint.

Says McFarlane, "People thought we fraternized. Never. They were crazy, crazy women. Think about it. If you take your clothes off in front of two hundred and fifty men for a living — that's a hard thing to do." Backstage things could get rough. "Once I introduced a girl, and she didn't come out," remembers Bishop. "I went back to see what was happening. Jerri King, another stripper, had this girl by the throat and I mean hard. I seen blood coming out of the girl's neck and she was slowly sinking down. I gave Jerri a karate chop on the hand and said, 'What the hell are you doing?' Jerri just said, 'She was sitting in my spot, in my chair. She knows it's my chair. I told her to get off. She didn't. That's where the fight started.'"

Patrons of Starvin' Marvin's paid for a single show that lasted 105 minutes. Of that time, the comic was to do a minimum of thirty-five minutes of talking, most of which was spent introducing dancers. He did an average of five minutes of material between each girl with ten minutes off the top of the show to warm up the audience.

The material was deep in the gutter. When I asked Gary David to repeat a few jokes for me, he told me they were uniformly unprintable. High-brow it was not. Bishop would do impressions of various ethnic stereotypes as he introduced the strippers. For example, there would be a Japanese man bringing on "Cockasuckiwucki." He would also promise the crowd that the next stripper was going to "come out, do two cart-wheels, the splits, and pick up a watermelon," or "do something really different. She's gonna come out and shit on the stage. Right on you, sir."

The favoured means of bringing a stripper on was by insult. "Put an ugly girl onstage and introduce her as ugly and you're a prick," Russell says, explaining his logic. "Put a beautiful girl onstage and introduce her as ugly and you're laughing. I would say: 'I want you to be kind to this girl. She's an old-time stripper, she's been around for forty-five years. She has only one tooth and it's broken and chipped. She's an organ grinder. Her tits are like the leather soles off two old army boots. Her ass is falling down to her ankles. But she needs the money, man. She's got five kids she's supporting, and her husband's left her. So let's be kind.' Well, out would come this beautiful woman."

The four comedians also practised stock humour. Stock jokes are time-tested gags with straightforward set-ups and punchlines. The set-up is a sentence or thought that establishes a joke's context, subject, and rhythm. The punchline is the thought, which generally arrives in the form of a surprise, that twists the set-up and creates the laugh. A typical construction might be:

> SET-UP: A guy goes to the doctor and says, "I don't
> know what's wrong with me. Every time I get up

and look in the mirror, I throw up."

PUNCHLINE: "I don't know what's wrong with you, either, but your eyesight's perfect."

Russell's routines leaned towards ethnic humour, doctor jokes, and wife jokes:

> A guy's wife comes home and says to her husband, "I met a man today and he started complimenting me." Her husband says, "Oh, yeah?" She says, "He told me I had beautiful eyes. The most gorgeous hair he'd ever seen. The fairest complexion. The most exquisite breasts." "Oh, yeah?" her husband says. "Did he mention your big fat ass?" "No," the wife says, "your name didn't come up once in the conversation."

"Guys don't go to strip clubs to see comics," Gary David said in 1995. "The comedians were there to fill time. You were there to stop the show from being a meat market." No technique was good enough to solve the problem that Bishop and the boys faced every show. In the words of Harry Russell, "How do you compete with a naked woman?"

The answer lay in the timing and delivery these burlesque comics adopted. Bishop, Russell, David, and McFarlane all used a very emphatic style. They drove set-ups and punchlines down their audience's throats. This style was epitomized by American comic Phil Silvers of *Sergeant Bilko* television series fame. Silvers was the top burlesque comic of his day before going to television. His measured set-ups, in which all the elements are clearly laid out for the audience, allowed him to crack punchlines with split-second delivery. It's an approach that worked for the fearsome foursome. "You have to be a bully," says Russell. "That's the secret of being a burlesque comic. You have to take over. You don't pay attention to the audience."

Starvin' Marvin's' crew was also vindictive. Hecklers were handled with a sharp and fast tongue and, when necessary, a show of force. During one show, when a fight broke out in the audience, Bishop stopped it by sports-announcing the conflict. Both pugilists started laughing so hard they couldn't punch. McFarlane was known to get physical. "When I walked onstage one night, a guy looks at me and says, 'You're a fucking asshole.' I just turned around and I kicked him right in the face. Bad thing to do. I'm sorry about it today. He waited outside with nine of his friends. I had to go and get some security, some heavy-duty guys from upstairs. They scared them away. There was another guy I kicked right in the nuts. He came at me with a bottle."

For their trouble, David, McFarlane, and Russell each made $250 a week for their eighteen shows, around $13 a show. The strippers made around $200 a week.

By 1975, the club was on a downward spiral. The new owner had opened the Neptune Body Rub parlour above the club. Bishop, Russell, and McFarlane claim he was pressuring them to encourage audience members to go upstairs after the show to "relax." During shows, girls from the body-rub parlour would sit in the audience and come on to customers. "The body-rub joint was like having a whorehouse above your head," says Russell. Unfortunately for the comics, some of the girls working upstairs were more attractive than the strippers, McFarlane says. "They'd walk into the theatre during a show and every head would turn. You'd lost the set. But I knew I had to do it, because it was the only game in town."

Eventually the game grew unbearable. The Body Rub ruined Starvin' Marvin's. Bishop was the first to leave in 1977. The remaining comics fought to get his evening slot, but they too soon left. "Starvin' Marvin's was the beginning of the end of burlesque," says Russell. "It was a big flash before the star fades. It's probably a good thing. The kids today wouldn't be interested in doing the burlesque approach to comedy, much to my chagrin. It's the fastest learning curve there is. A year in burlesque is worth five anywhere else. In the old days, the new acts paid the top banana a percentage of their salary, in exchange for learning. Frenchie, Gary, and I learned from Rummy for free."

In fact, Starvin' Marvin's was not the beginning of the end of burlesque, it was the last gasp. Burlesque had begun to disappear long before Starvin' Marvin's first exposed female genitalia in 1973.

As Starvin' Marvin's died, a new stand-up comedy arena was being constructed. A kid named Mark Breslin, along with some renegade Toronto comedians such as Paul Mandel and Chas Lawther, was trying to get a stand-up cabaret off the ground. These comics would go on to revolutionize Canadian comedy. They owed a lot to the gang at Starvin' Marvin's. The birth of stand-up comedy in Canada had not been pretty, nor had it been easy. Burlesque comedy was a rough business that left little time for esoteric analysis or development. Gary David epitomized the life.

Following David's death, his friends began to discover a few truths about that life. In his closet, beneath some photographs and letters, they found his birth certificate. His real name was not Gary David but Gary Tomlinson. The elder comic had always implied that he'd been born in San Francisco, spent time in the merchant marines and Marine Corps, and then moved to Canada. In fact, Gary Tomlinson had been born in Birmingham, England. Russell told me he'd always had his suspicions about his friend. "Gary always said 'parm-tree.' Nobody from California says 'parm-tree.' I used to kid him about it. But I figured it was his business, and he was a lovely guy and that's what counted. We talked a bit about his history once. It was a depressing story. Gary had a horrible childhood. He came from a very abusive home. His father would tell him, from a very young age, You're useless, you're never going to amount to anything,' and Gary suffered a lot of physical abuse. So far as the stories he made up for people about his youth, he only made up the good stuff."

At age fourteen, David had run away from home and joined the British merchant marines. He jumped ship when he reached America and spent a year homeless. David slept in abandoned cars on the outskirts of Chicago. He won a green card by joining the Marine Corps and signing on for active duty in Korea. During the war, David participated in or witnessed a lot of killing, which left scars. He moved to Montreal, drove a cab, married, and finally tried comedy while tending bar at a men's social club after a move to Toronto. His life had been a struggle. In the smoky, raw world of burlesque and then later in stand-up, he found a sense of belonging.

If you apply the logic of Canadian arts funding — that Canadian art

can only flourish if it enjoys financial support from the government —
stand-up and sketch comedy in Canada should have died with burlesque's
last wheezes onstage at Starvin' Marvin's. In fact, the opposite has
occurred. Even today, most comedians have been forced to scratch their
way up from the bottom and have worked in conditions that would make
the average Stratford Festival actor grow faint. The absence of artificial
supports means that only the best comedians can survive. The result?
Jim Carrey, Lorne Michaels, John Candy, Martin Short, Dan
Aykroyd, and a host of other international comedy stars.

The Burlesque boys left a solid foundation upon which the new club
scene would flourish. But, as often happens to pioneers, Bishop and his
peers, with the exception of Gary David, were unable to continue in the
business they helped to create. They never made it into the new breed of
comedy clubs. Bishop went on to work in Canadian television, on series
such as *Snow Job*. Russell worked cruise ships and liked the gig.
McFarlane worked one-night gigs in bars and plenty of corporate shows
for business meetings and dinners. Their best days, it appeared, had
passed. The Starvin' Marvin's crew had slugged it out, doing their five
minutes between dancers, and then they blipped from the horizon.
"Nobody finishes with show business," Russell told me. "Show business
finishes with you."

Gary David was one exception to that rule. "He finished with show
business in the only way he knew how," one comedian remarked to me
at the cemetery. "That's probably the only time Gary ever died."

Bishop and McFarlane took a few extra moments at David's grave
side. A few of those moments were for Gary and a few were for business. Ever the hustlers, the pair were trading work notes. Was
McFarlane going to the reception, Bishop wondered. No, McFarlane
replied. "I've got to be at a gig in a couple of hours."

FIVE

■

The Yuk Yuk's Experience

The elevation of Canadian stand-up comedy from strip-club diversion to lively art form began in June of 1976 with the creation of Yuk Yuk's in Toronto in a Church Street basement. The stand-up club's attraction was a mystery, even to those responsible for it. In August of that year, only months after Yuk Yuk's was born, Mark Breslin, the twenty-four-year-old maverick who created the club, told Jack Kapica, the books editor of the *Globe and Mail*, "One of the problems of Yuk Yuk's is that everybody is having fun and we don't know why. I see it as a professional show, maybe of dubious standards." Kapica agreed, citing as an example "Beaford Seaman's Flabby Thighs and Butter," a sketch act about a Professor Sphincter "discovering his new muscle." However, these very dubious standards turned out to be Yuk Yuk's biggest selling point.

Stinker acts received cruel treatment at Yuk Yuk's. That was at least half the fun. The management had a tape recording, which they played frequently at high volume, of the "Crucify Him" chorus from the Andrew Lloyd Webber musical *Jesus Christ Superstar*. They used a cardboard hook to drag bombing acts off the stage. Poor comedians would receive a "two-minute penalty for boring the audience!" Breslin had a girlfriend dress up in a French maid's outfit and walk the aisles selling rotten tomatoes to throw at the acts. Yuk Yuk's was a grimy circus. The single thread that tied its acts together was that they were all a little crazy, and at the same time often displayed flashes of pure genius.

In this respect, Yuk Yuk's was a mirror image of its creator. To understand Mark Breslin — no easy feat — is to understand the growth of Canadian stand-up comedy. The two forces are woven together, each having played a part in the creation of the other. Mark Breslin influenced the growth of stand-up comedy in Canada, and stand-up comedy influenced the growth of Mark Breslin. Examining this phenomenon is not for the meek. Breslin is without a doubt the most controversial man Canadian comedy had produced. For starters, Breslin would make the case that he produced Canadian comedy. Mark Breslin is not afraid of being hated. If anything, he fears apathy.

My first brush with Breslin occurred in 1992 when I was writing for the Toronto alternative newspaper *eye WEEKLY* (now *eye*). I was a young punk, all of twenty-four years old, who had the bright idea that Toronto needed a weekly column dedicated to covering the machinations of the comedy business. I knew little about the Hogtown scene, having acquired most my experience in London, running a comedy club on the British circuit. I didn't let this deter me. In one of my first columns I covered a weekly Sunday night gig at a Queen Street West bar called Chicago's. It was a comics' collective, in which stand-ups booked the show and kept it running to provide a place to experiment with new material and hang out. It was what's known in the comedy business as an inside gig, where the audience is made up largely of stand-ups and other people hooked into the scene. Most of the stand-ups working at Chicago's had worked for Yuk Yuk's, which by that time had grown into a chain of comedy clubs. The Chicago's crowd had left on bad terms, claiming Breslin had blacklisted them for demanding the right to play non–Yuk Yuk's clubs. The Chicago's show was disorganized, a little edgy, and the emphasis was on content over form. It reminded me of the London alternative scene, so it was easy for me to get my head around comics' night at Chicago's. I wrote a story called "The Comics United Cannot Be Defeated."

The afternoon the story ran I received a call from Ron Vaudry, a veteran comic. Vaudry is short, stocky, has the manners of a drill sergeant and the heart to match. He also possesses a keen insight into comedy. Vaudry has seen many comedians surpass him commercially (Jim Carrey, Mike MacDonald, Howie Mandel) and many more fall by the wayside. Vaudry had done a free set at Chicago's and I'd mentioned his act in my piece. Now he told me that because I had reported the free gig, he had lost five thousand dollars' worth of Yuk Yuk's work. Vaudry said Breslin had called him every name in the book. Vaudry had denied doing the show. Ron Vaudry is a tough guy, but I thought I could hear him tearing up on the other end of the line. He begged me to agree to keep quiet about any letter that Yuk Yuk's would force him to write to the paper calling me a "lying sack of shit." I told him I wouldn't guarantee anything. I hadn't made his performance up; he had been there. I said if they blackballed him I'd be certain to report that story, too. Vaudry never wrote a letter, and Yuk Yuk's eventually let him back in the door. The incident established Mark Breslin in my mind as a man who wasn't afraid to attack.

My next Breslin experience occurred later that year, in June. I wrote an article stating that Canadian comedians didn't get enough profile at the Toronto People's Comedy Festival, a one-week annual event (from 1992 to 1994) sponsored by Molson and organized by Breslin and Yuk Yuk's. (In previous years it had run under the name Molson's Comedy Releaf.) The festival showcased big-name Americans and high-profile Canadians, and I implied that the Canadians weren't too happy, quoting Yuk Yuk's stand-up Lou Eisen. Apparently, Breslin hit the roof. To make things worse, I was told Yuk Yuk's staff had to physically restrain Breslin in order to stop him from going to *eye WEEKLY* and demanding my dismissal. Yuk Yuk's publicist Mary Arsenault asked me, "Do you have something against Mark Breslin?" I said no. She went on, "You have been warned." I asked if that was a threat. She repeated the warning. After that, I figured I was not Mark Breslin's favourite person.

Which made the fact that, four years later, I was meeting Mark Breslin for high tea at the posh Four Seasons Hotel extremely ironic. It was a bitterly cold afternoon in February, and as I walked to the hotel rain pelted down like a million icy pins. It froze on contact, making the roads and cars glow like neon under the street lights. The interior of the Four Seasons, by contrast, was a rococo sanctuary. The furniture had *faux*-gold finish, giving the dining room a vaguely aristocratic ambience. The waiters were starched and prim. At any moment I expected some powder-faced damsel with a two-foot wig to pop out and stick a mole on my cheek. When I arrived, a hostess said, "You're Mister Breslin's guest," and shuttled me to his table.

Mark Breslin has a cobra's charm. He is hypnotic, measured, graceful, calculated, sleek, and at any minute you know he might strike. Then again he might just as easily offer you a cup of tea. He was wearing a black leather jacket cut as a waistcoat, on top of a conservative sweater. It was a typical look for him: Forest Hill elite with a dash of Sex Pistols. Breslin smelled of cologne but I couldn't make out what type. Everything about the event was vintage Breslin down to the last detail, and I knew this was no accident. He had orchestrated everything in order to create an aura fitting a man of his importance. I was on his turf and he wanted me to know it. I might as well have been in his bedroom. Two hours later he was making the kind of confession you might expect to hear across a pillow.

"The fact that I've avoided suicide for the past twenty years — and I've had enough grounds for it — is the biggest victory of all," he told me. "I've actually managed to keep alive." It was an admission that would surprise many who know Breslin and shock those who hate him. He is the founder of and majority shareholder in Yuk Yuk's, the only chain of comedy clubs in Canada. His image for his critics in the stand-up community is that of inhuman tyrant. To them, Breslin has no feelings and no weak moments. He is a machine obsessed with his vision and his empire. He is constantly manoeuvring to amass more power so he can use it to impose his will. Breslin is the godfather of comedy. Yet there is no comic in the country who did not once feel tremendous attachment to Breslin. He has moments of extreme generosity. He looks out for his brood. If it weren't for him, they would all be out of work, or worse. To Harland Williams, Breslin is not only a professional influence, he is a friend. "If I make it, I'd like to go back to Yuk Yuk's and play a week at Mark's club," the stand-up says. "At the end of the week I'd just let him keep all the money and spend it on whatever he wanted." Breslin's name has come to mean many things in the comedy business, all of them contradictory.

Mark Breslin was born in Toronto in 1952. He was a late baby, his mother forty-three and his father fifty-five the day he was born. He had two sisters, one nineteen years older and the other twenty-three. As a result he grew up receiving all the attention of an only child as well as the advantages of a kid with siblings. On the down side, Breslin was picked on relentlessly as a child. He was a small, shy kid and as such was a magnet for abuse. Breslin remembers being eight years old and coming home from school in tears every day. Things were worse in high school. Years later, when patrons would try to get into Yuk Yuk's with the line, "I'm a friend of Mark's from high school," Breslin instructed his doormen to reply, "Mark Breslin had no friends in high school."

When Breslin was fifteen, the younger of his two sisters was struck with multiple sclerosis. The family moved to Forest Hill into a larger house where they could take care of her more easily. Watching his sister suffer from such a cruel and debilitating disease had a profound effect on Breslin, instilling in him a sense of bitter rage. He never got over it. At a young age, he became convinced that the world was an unjust place.

Breslin attended Forest Hill Collegiate and was exposed to the well-heeled and sheltered world of Toronto's upper class. There he met Joel Axler, who would become his closest friend and eventually play the role of Sancho Panza to Breslin's Don Quixote. After graduation Breslin took an arts degree at York University and briefly entertained thoughts of pursuing a career in literary criticism. In the summer of 1975 he scored a job handing out leaflets at Harbourfront Theatre, a city-run venue on the edge of Lake Ontario. "I met these wild, crazy, bohemian artists and I exploded," he recalls. After that, he says, "there was no way I was getting a graduate degree."

Breslin rose through the ranks and became Harbourfront's musical director. The theatre's director at the time was Don Cullen, a Toronto actor who in the mid-sixties had run the Bohemian Embassy, a café that showcased every type of artist from writers like Margaret Atwood to comics such as Dave Broadfoot. Cullen had a well-honed artistic sensibility. As an actor he had worked for Wayne and Shuster and appeared in the North American touring company of *Beyond the Fringe,* the British sketch troupe that starred Dudley Moore and Peter Cook. Cullen encouraged Breslin's wild side, and the kid from Forest Hill quickly became infatuated with the theatre's comedy nights. He began to book acts like La Troupe Grotesque, a cabaret act performed by Paul K. Willis and Michael Bonacoeur. Rick Moranis was doing spots as a solo act. It was a very seventies experience. There were plenty of drugs and sex to go around. The Harbourfront gig lasted a year and a half. Then in the spring of 1976, Breslin and most of the other staff at Harbourfront were let go. Axler, and a stand-up named Paul Mandel (no relation to Howie) who had been hanging out at Harbourfront, suggested that Breslin join them in starting their own venue, limiting it to comedy. It took a while to convince him, but when Breslin finally agreed, he became the driving force behind the new venture.

In 1976, there was no comedy venue in town. Starvin' Marvin's had closed, as had the only other previous comedy showcase, the Improv at Friar's Tavern. Starting in 1974, the Improv had hosted a six nights a week variety show that presented musicians, jugglers, and comedians such as Larry Horowitz and Johnny London. It also had its own collection of freaks, like Phil the Poet, who read prose off a pizza box. The club managed to hang on for a year and a half, but closed in 1975. Horowitz tried comedy at a Wellington Street restaurant, but this too eventually tanked. Sketch comedy was available at a new theatre called the Second City, which had attracted a pool of gifted performers such as Ottawa sketch comics Dan Aykroyd and Valri Bromfield. It would later be recognized as a gold mine of Canadian sketch talent, but, at that time the cast and its producer, Andrew Alexander, were struggling to keep the show alive. The city was still Toronto the Good. There was, however, a pent-up demand for comedy and a segment of the population that was interested in stand-up. This interest was due in part to television.

Breslin and his peers had grown up watching TV and had been exposed to stand-up on *The Tonight Show*. They knew stand-up existed but had never seen any live. So they decided to create their own version.

After losing his Harbourfront job, Breslin tried sharing a night with a folk club at the Church Street Community Centre located at 519 Church Street. The venue was an old bowling alley located in the basement. The experiment failed. Breslin's comedians were sharing the stage with folk singers. It was a battle of energies. The "folkies" were positive and loving; the comedians were angry, chain-smoking cynics. To be frank, they were trouble-making bastards. Breslin and Axler negotiated with the centre's board of directors to book a night of their own. A deal was reached: for thirty-eight dollars a night, Breslin and his new club, "Yuk Yuk's," could play every Wednesday between 8:30 and 11 P.M. On June 2, 1976, they opened. Yuk Yuk's' Church Street home was a dingy rectangular room lined with tables, each one surrounded by a cluster of chairs. The stage was small, and behind it was painted a grotesque pair of red lips with the club's name written on them. There were two floodlights, a stool, and a microphone. Patrons could purchase coffee or soft drinks. There was no liquor licence. Admission was two bucks.

Breslin pulled his comics from across the city and across the country. Roughly half of Yuk Yuk's' stand-ups were from out of town. It was as if every Canadian kid who'd conned his parents into letting him stay up late to watch Johnny Carson's monologue had migrated to Toronto. (Fledgling stand-ups then were almost all males.) The shows had a very anti-establishment attitude. Breslin's motto was "Good is good, and bad is as funny as good." Nothing could stop the show. Once, a tramp wandered drunkenly onstage, peered around, and left. The comedian did not even notice him. "Mark encouraged the madness," recalls Paul Mandel. "We were telling the burghers of Toronto they were full of shit, and then we'd take money from them. Mark, Joel, and I would crash Rosedale parties and cause trouble. It was psychic violence."

When a Yuk Yuk's comedian was good, however, it was often a revelation. Paul Mandel once became enraged by a table of philosophy stu-

dents and presented a version of *Hamlet* that was high fibre. "Alas, poor
Bran Muffin, I knew him well," Mandel intoned, then proceeded to hurl
bran muffins at the audience while reading from his divorce papers and
crying. He was visibly teetering on the edge of a breakdown. It floored
his audience. The performance was ground-breaking because it flouted
the rules of conventional comedy. Mandel didn't tell stock strip-club
jokes or adhere to an objective notion of "funny." He used stand-up as
a completely personal, subjective expression. "We were dumbfounded,"
says Axler. "We couldn't believe it. It was like, yes, *yes*. That's it. That's
what it's all about!"

Breslin led the rude wave. He was the evening's host, and he intentionally set out to offend and shock his audience. He was a rude ring-
master who trashed his customers a second after he'd taken their cash.
He was a vicious imp, insulting and happily degrading his targets. Breslin
hand-picked taboo subjects and rolled in them like a pig wallowing in
mud. Breslin selected macho members of the audience and engaged
them in discussion of the minutiae of homosexual practices. When
angry patrons walked out during a show, Breslin would chase them to
the door screaming, "Go fuck yourselves! The Jew has your money!
The Jew has your money! And there's nothing you can do about it!"

Artistically, one of Breslin's earliest contributions to stand-up was
his elevation of the role of host. In the United States, the host or emcee
is the lowest man on the roster. He is either an inexperienced rookie or
a friend of the owner who needs some extra cash. The American host
does ten minutes of "Where you from?" material at the beginning and
then spends the rest of the show introducing the acts. This did not appeal
to Breslin. After all, he wanted a larger role for himself. Breslin wasn't
about to play some stooge bringing out the real acts; he wanted to be a
top comedian in a coveted position. In Canadian clubs, the host will do
fifteen to twenty minutes of material off the top, five to ten minutes
between each act, and finally round off the show with five closing minutes. American shows tend to run like cattle calls. The Canadian system
clearly makes for a better show. The host is a refreshing lift from bad
acts and a compliment to the good ones.

Yuk Yuk's became an instant hip ticket. Toronto's upper class was into slumming, and the mink-coat crowd lined up every Wednesday. They adored Yuk Yuk's degenerate quality. To Breslin, it was a terrific joke. His attitude was, I'm going to make you stand outside in the cold, then I'm going to make you pay, then I'm going to serve you a coke and charge you a dollar-fifty when it only costs me a nickel to buy, and then I'm going to come onstage and insult you and call you a fag. And guess what? There're no refunds.

Talented comedians began to gravitate to Yuk Yuk's by spring of 1977. After years without a legitimate outlet, stand-up comedy finally had a home. The star line-up included the trio Nip and Tuck Tub Rag, Steve Brinder, Steve Shuster (Frank Shuster's son), Chas Lawther, who'd written for CBC Radio and who later became "Chuck the Security Guard" on CITY-TV, Don Cullen, and Gerry Bednob, the country's first East Indian comic. The Starvin' Marvin's crew tried to crack Yuk Yuk's, but none were able to swing the hip crowd. Frenchie McFarlane says Breslin and his cohorts felt that the Starvin' Marvin's guys were too sleazy. Only Gary David would ultimately make it, and it would take him three years of reworking his act. Business at Yuk Yuk's continued to boom. For two years the crowds kept pouring in. By 1978, it had become apparent that the joke was verging on a serious pay-off. It was time to make Yuk Yuk's a full-time proposition.

Breslin threw himself into the project with typical abandon. He raised money from "rich friends" and scouted for venues. He found another basement, on Bay Street. It was in the heart of Yorkville, which at the time was a trendy hangout for Toronto's bon vivants. Yorkville had been folk bars and drug dens in the sixties. In the late seventies it was boutiques and sushi bars. Yuk Yuk's would be an intrusive bit of nastiness. With a loan from the Bank of Nova Scotia, two thousand dollars of his own money, and twenty-two thousand raised from his friends, Breslin closed the Church Street club, opened the Bay Street club, and ran it six nights a week. Suddenly there were six times the spots to fill. Comedians began to get the stage time they needed to improve rapidly. The Bay Street club, which became known as "the Downtown," altered

Yuk Yuk's audience. The Downtown brought in a middle-of-the-road clientele. There were still plenty of walk-outs. Each night at least a third of the audience was so offended they left in disgust. Says Breslin, "And I'm proud to say I think I'm the one who chased them out."

A pecking order grew up among the comedians. Although there were more spots available, there were also more people trying to get them. In 1973, there had been four stand-up comics in Toronto. In 1979, there were at least forty trying to be stand-ups. Ralph Benmergui, an actor and pal of Breslin's from Forest Hill Collegiate, and Michael Rappaport, a Canadian with Los Angeles experience, joined the stable. A wunderkind from Ottawa named Mike MacDonald moved to Toronto and began destroying crowds on a regular basis with his vicious tirades. The talent pool was unbelievably strong. On any given night a crowd might see eight or nine stand-ups, all of whom would eventually become headliners. A boot camp mentality took hold. MacDonald and his crew stood on top; the amateurs below were treated like dirt. They weren't spoken to. They were ignored. MacDonald and his clique, which included Benmergui, came down hard on those who were trying to break in.

The notion of "breaking in" was a new one. The fact that Canada actually had a stand-up comedy community and that aspiring comics would have to *earn* their way into it marked a major step up for the business. A burlesque stand-up was measured by his toughness and his timing. Comedy club comedians were also measured by those qualities, but in addition were marked for their material. It was not just a question of being funny; it was a question of offering something special or new.

To solve the problem of finding new talent, Breslin borrowed a concept from the United States. The answer was simple: you held an amateur night and let the talent find you. This method has remained unchanged for the last twenty years. Amateur nights are, in Breslin's own words, "a necessary evil." Jokes lose value each time they're told. Comedians lose value each time they're seen in a comedy club. The result is that club owners need new comedians, *ipso facto* they need amateur nights. They live and die on their supply of new blood.

Blood is a constant in comedy. It comes in many forms, representing

Marjorie (Ross Hamilton), *left,* and Marie (Alan Murray), *right,* with the Dumbells' creator Captain Merton Plunkett, 1917. Drag was an essential and subversive ingredient in their comedy. Hamilton's Marjorie was said to be so fetching that one British officer proposed marriage.

The Dumbells in khaki, 1917. They were soldiers first, comedians second. Most of the troupe had seen an average of sixteen months' active service during World War I. Said cast member Al Plunkett, "Some of the men we enter- tained at five o'clock were dead at seven-thirty."

At age twenty-six, Michael Magee adopted Fred C. Dobbs as his acerbic and aged alter- ego. Magee used the satiric mask of a rural hayseed to puncture Canadian society's pre- tensions. "I quickly learned that an old duffer could get away with saying things that would not be acceptable from a young man."

In the sketch "Frig," John Aylesworth, *left*, espouses the glories of life in his refrigerator. "No heat worries, and shirts stay crisp." The sketch typified the duo's talent for commercial parodies.

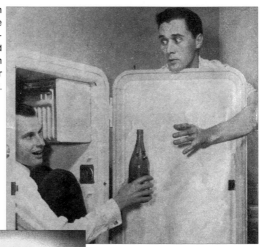

Frank Peppiatt, *right*, and John Aylesworth. In 1952, the newly-formed CBC Television network asked the pair to produce one hour's worth of live comedy each week. "Like idiots," recalls Aylesworth, "we said yes." The result was the innovative series *After Hours*.

Aylesworth and Peppiatt were chameleon like in their ability to write for anyone, from Frank Sinatra to Judy Garland. For American TV star Steve Allen, Peppiatt wrote the routine "Question Man," a gag in which a question is answered in reverse order. Answer: Tomato paste. Question: How do you keep tomatoes from falling apart?

Johnny Wayne, *left,* and Frank Shuster in 1935. They grew up in the same Toronto neighbourhood. In 1939, they got their break writing and starring in a Javex bleach household tips radio program called *The Wife Preservers.*

In 1995, the CBC unveiled The Wayne and Shuster Comedy Wall of Fame at the CBC Broadcast Centre. Ever the polished comic, Shuster quipped, "Hockey gets a hall, comedy gets a wall."

In this sketch, Wayne, *left,* as bumbling TV detective Frank Columbo, attempts to deduce how poor Yorrick came to such a grim end.

Don Harron as Charlie Farquharson. An accomplished Shakespearean actor, Harron started his career in the *Spring Thaw* revue and made Charlie a much-loved comic character who was prone to malapropisms and ironic observations.

In the early 1970s, The Royal Canadian Air Farce continued the satiric tradition begun by *Spring Thaw. From left to right:* Dave Broadfoot, Don Ferguson, John Morgan, Roger Abbott, and Luba Goy. Their 1993 television show was to become the CBC's most popular program, pulling an average of one million viewers an episode.

The Bishop brothers at the Nut Club in Miami, Joey Bishop, *centre*, Rummy Bishop, *right*. Rummy recalls Al Capone's brother Ralph pulling a gun on Joey and saying, "I ought to let you have it right here." Joey's offence? The comedian had spent the previous evening dancing with Ralph's wife.

(Below) The Bishop brothers at the Nut Club in Pittsburgh, Rummy (seated on the piano), Joey (in bra and skirt). They brought an emphatic burlesque cadence to their comedy, driving home jokes in an unbridled, forceful style.

After Joey's success, the Bishops gained access to high society. Here, Joey and Rummy meet John F. Kennedy.

Rummy Bishop gained celebrity as the host of Starvin' Marvin's strip club. Here, he hams it up with Canadian prize fighter George Chuvalo.

Three-quarters of the Fearsome Foursome. *From left to right:* Gary David, Rummy Bishop, and Frenchie McFarlane along with Rummy's wife. The comedians delivered their jokes in the time left between the strippers' dances. Crowds were tough. "Guys don't go to strip clubs to see comics," David said in 1995. "The comedians were there to fill time and stop the show from becoming a meat market."

The Bishop brothers got their start in American burlesque houses, like the Troc. Patrons of contemporary strip clubs would not recognize these shows, which featured exotic costumes and theatrical effects.

Mike MacDonald and Leatrice Spevack. In Yuk Yuk's early days, MacDonald was the preeminent comedian. He was the host of many parties, at which the comedians would drop acid, party all night and turn up the next evening for their sets. MacDonald later quit drugs, and found religion. "No withdrawal, no nothing."

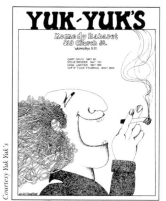

In 1976, Yuk Yuk's Church Street club was a bastion of guerilla comedy. Admission was two dollars, coffee and soft drinks were served. The spot quickly became *the* ticket for Toronto hipsters. "Mark (Breslin) encouraged the madness," recalls Yuk Yuk's comic Paul Mandel.

Joel Axler idolized Mike MacDonald's comedy, but MacDonald's drug use soon crushed Axler's faith in the industry. "The comedy business is so ugly I couldn't stand it."

A brotherhood formed among Yuk Yuk's comedians. Weekly road hockey games were a staple of comedy life. Norm Macdonald, *upper row, far left,* Harland Williams, *second from left, upper row,* Mark Farrell, *third from right, upper row,* Harry Doupe, *lower row, centre, in Yuk Yuk's shirt,* Larry Horowitz, *on Doupe's left.*

Left, Yuk Yuk's stand-up Colin Campbell in 1984 at Punchlines in Vancouver. Campbell was one of the most promising comedians to come out of Canada in the early eighties. When he drank, he was prone to violence and blacking out.

Campbell's closest ally on the circuit, Harry Doupe. "The demons that made him drink are the same ones that made him funny," Doupe says of his troubled friend.

Memorial held for 'best' B.C. comedian

CAMPBELL:
prolific writer

A memorial service was held Friday at Qualicum Beach for Colin Campbell, a writer and performer judged by many of his peers to be the best comedian to come out of Western Canada.

Campbell's body was found Jan. 1 in heavy brush about 1½ kilometres from his home at Qualicum Beach. The 33-year-old comedian had been reported missing Sept. 24 when he went for a walk and failed to return.

At the time of his disappearance he was taking medication for a chronic back ailment, friends said.

The coroner's office said cause of death couldn't be determined, but there is no suspicion of foul play.

Campbell was a fixture at Punchlines comedy club in Vancouver for many years and is remembered for his standup routines as an opening act for the Pointer Sisters and Reba McEntire. He was also a prolific writer and worked on a number of CBC comedy and variety shows. Earlier this month, Punchlines held a benefit in his memory.

Harry Doupe, who returned from San Francisco to take part in the benefit, said Campbell was "the best comic to come out of Western Canada." Doupe, who covered the West Coast comedy circuit with Campbell in 1985, called him "the biggest influence on my comedy style."

Rich Elwood, manager of Punchlines, said Campbell had "the gift of comedy. Many comedians learn their comedic skill as they go, but Colin had a bright, broad observational humor from the start. He was funny most of the time."

Campbell is survived by his wife, Beverly.

Campbell went missing in September 1991. His remains were found three months later a kilometre and a half from his home in Qualicum Beach, British Columbia. Cause of death has never been determined.

MISSING MAN: Police are asking for public assistance in locating Colin Campbell who went missing from his Qualicum Beach home this week.

Man disappears from QB home, search started

Police are asking for public assistance in the search for a Qualicum Beach man, missing from his home since 5 a.m. Tuesday (Sept. 24).

Colin Alexander Campbell, 33, was last seen walking away from his residence on 241 Elizabeth Ave.

He is described as 5' 10", 200 lbs. with a husky build, brown, wavy, shoulder-length hair and hazel eyes.

Campbell was last seen wearing a white sweat shirt with the logo 'Punch Lines', blue, knee-length baggy shorts, running shoes and sport socks.

RCMP Const. Dean Bruyckere noted Campbell is on medication and may appear disoriented. He may be unable to remember his address or telephone number, said Bruyckere, explaining that Campbell and his wife, Beverly, are new to the area.

Anyone who has seen Campbell or knows of his whereabouts is asked to contact local RCMP, at 248-6111.

both new and vibrant talent and what is left onstage after someone "dies." Amateur night is a blood bath. I call it the "Night of the Living Unprofessionals." It's a little joke I tell myself to bolster my resolve to observe these massacres. Because the first thing to understand about amateur nights is that no one really looks forward to them.

Club owners don't look forward to them because they are scheduled on off-nights (Mondays or Tuesdays), few drinks are sold, and often to a very few people, creating some belligerent drunks. The acts often stink. The professionals who host them don't look forward to them because they are nauseated by the calibre of the comedy. Only the odd member of the audience looks forward to them, and *odd* is the operative word. These are people like "Roberto," who never misses a Yuk Yuk's amateur night and who spends the evening drinking seven or eight glasses of water with lime and making seven or eight trips to the washroom.

Certainly the amateurs who perform don't look forward to amateur nights because they are scared to the point of mortification. At the same time, they live for the five minutes of attention they receive. This is enough to bring perhaps one or two thousand of them each year to amateur nights across the country. Those who are "lucky" enough to land a spot endure a baptism by fire. Each "comic" gets five minutes to try to get a few laughs. Most do not. They are humiliated, booed, and basically shredded by the crowd. It is an evening when aspiring comedians lay it on the line before a roomful of surly drunks.

Without a doubt the harshest of Toronto's amateur nights — perhaps the most cruel amateur night in the country — was Yuk Yuk's "Crash and Burn Monday," implemented in 1995. Ron Vaudry created it because he wanted amateur nights to return to their raison d'être, which he has described as the chance to "watch freaks die." Vaudry has hosted more "new talent nights" (the politically correct term) than he cares to remember. Before the Crash and Burn concept was put in place, Yuk Yuk's was pulling maybe twenty people to an amateur night. Afterwards, they were getting one hundred. Pain sold. At least other people's pain sold.

"There are basically two categories of amateur comics," Vaudry maintained at the time, "the totally insane delusional and the pathetically inept. Once in a while there's one with some potential. I tell the amateurs who work my night, 'A thousand turtles go out and one comes back.'"

The scene of this slaughter is Yuk Yuk's Superclub, formerly known as "the Uptown" because of its location near Yonge and Eglinton in north Toronto. In 1993, Breslin closed the Downtown because he felt the club was no longer financially viable due to high rents and wrong demographics. The closure made a lot of comedians unhappy. The Downtown had been the most beloved club in the country. According to one stand-up, it had "seen more booze, drugs, sex, whores, violence, smokes, and brilliance" than any other club in North America. It was hallowed ground. After deep-sixing the Downtown, Breslin renovated the Uptown and renamed it the Superclub. It immediately earned the nicknames "the Supper Club" and "the Stupor Club."

The Superclub, like all Yuk Yuk's, is a black box of a room with a small stage and a brick wall. Right behind the microphone stand is a large glowing sign that reads "Mark Breslin's Yuk Yuk's." It seats about 450 people and is suitable for TV and radio tapings. Its walls are covered with pictures of Yuk Yuk's comedians. What's funny about the comedians' portraits is that they were all taken at the outsets of their careers. The stand-ups are all young and fresh and sporting eighties haircuts. In this respect they have the opposite effect as the picture of Dorian Gray. The portraits remain clean and pure and full of the hope their subjects possessed when they started out in the business, while the comedians themselves deteriorate. Sometimes, if a comic is standing by his photo, I swing my head back and forth quickly and get a haunting before-and-after effect.

When I go to the Superclub I like to sit at the back. This goes double for amateur night. It gives me a better view of the snake pit. In November 1995, I decided to record one night of fun with the amateurs, and headed down to the Superclub for some Crash and Burn. Upon arrival I learned that Ron Vaudry had quit and wouldn't be on. Vaudry had walked because Yuk Yuk's brass had told him he could play their clubs but would no longer be booked by their management agency, Funny Business. This was nothing new for Vaudry, who was constantly at odds with Yuk Yuk's management. As a host, Vaudry had been especially hard on the comics, lambasting each one as he or she got off the stage. He loved to watch them bleed. He was a comic Darwinian, resolved to drive the weak out of comedy's halls. "I'm not like other comics," Vaudry would tell hecklers. "I'll shoot you in the head and fuck the wound."

Lou Eisen was Vaudry's replacement, and when it came to torture of the amateurs he proved no slouch. Eisen began the evening with, "Hello everybody and welcome to the Clarke Institute Mental Hospital's Outpatient Program." He then explained that amateur night ran "something like the Rodney King video." He polled the crowd to see if anyone had been to amateur night before and advised those who raised their hands to "get a life." (Breslin liked to say of some of his amateur night comics that if they hadn't been up on stage holding a microphone, they'd likely be at the local 7-Eleven holding a gun.)

The onslaught continued with a first-timer named Shawn Hutchings. He was stocky and tall, with a shaved skull and a mad look on his face. Hutchings stalked the stage, punctuating his march with grunts and yelps. He rubbed his close-cropped head frequently.

"A bit of a buzz." (Pause.) "Crack, that's my drug of choice. Robbing and stealing from your family." (Pause.) "He's on the rock!" (Pause.) *"I'm bombing. Easy on your bomb!" (Pause.) "You ever done rock?* Makes you go broke. Crackheads, pipe, weed!"

Needless to say these subtle musings did not rake in the laughs. Only the boys at the back of the room (Eisen, myself, and a stand-up named Harry Doupe) were laughing. I was in hysterics. Doupe, who had more than ten years of experience as a professional, kept staring at the stage in disbelief and then cracking up. Hutchings' psyche was just hanging out there on a clothesline. It was either laugh or puke.

Hutchings stopped a moment and scratched his bald head. We were unaware at the time, but he was preparing to launch his worst line to date: "Have you been following that Paul Bernardo thing?" he asked the audience. "Something about him raping a bunch of women? He pleaded *no contest* for rape." Hutchings paused. "There's a *contest* for rape?"

Hutchings' time had elapsed and he was brought off stage by the sound of a Yuk Yuk's employee yelling, "Get off! Get off!" Eisen returned with a perplexed expression and deadpanned to the crowd, "Shawn Hutchings, ladies and gentlemen. As my rabbi would say, *'That's one fucked-up white guy.'*"

Next up was Victor Osorno, a teenager in rapper attire. Osorno got two minutes into his set before being kicked off for doing some Robin Williams material. This rip off was by no means rare. Amateurs often used jokes they'd culled from tapes and CDs. The sound guy at the back yelled, "That's Robin Williams' joke. Get the fuck off the stage." Osorno froze. "I said get the fuck off." Osorno left.

Eisen came back and riffed on Osorno's performance. "Kind of makes you miss Shawn Hutchings."

Then came Warren Brown, a homely trucker in a cowboy hat. Brown did his impression of being raped by Hells Angels on the highway. "It's amazing what you'll do with a gun to your head. You want that sucked? No problem. I do shoes while I'm down there." Brown's act was followed by video clips from the movie *Full Metal Jacket,* in which a soldier blows his head off with a shotgun. Then up scurried Chris Howl, a young man with red hair done in a bowl cut. He had a canine face that was blotched and pale. It was a nice reflection of his personality. Howl made a half-hearted attempt to do some material and then simply began to insult the audience in a way that was in no manner humorous.

"I don't need you to fucking tell me," he screamed at a woman for some imaginary slight. Howl tried to compose himself and get back to his prepared material. "There are too many diseases out there. AIDS? Who would fuck a green monkey?" Someone in the audience continued to talk. "Pipe down!" Howl yelled. "I don't get it," the heckler returned. This bit of constructive criticism did not go over well with the young comedian. "I *know* you don't get, lady! I *know* your husband isn't fucking you enough. Don't *tell* everybody!"

Howl's face screwed up into a red ball. His lips twisted into a jack-o'-lantern grimace. He jammed his eyes shut and then flashed them open, "Leave me alone," he wheezed, "I'm not well." Howl then stormed offstage, throwing the microphone stand down in despair. His heckler gently caught it and carefully stood it upright. Eisen reappeared with the same stunned expression he'd had after the Hutchings fiasco. "Have you ever," he asked the crowd, "seen anything like that in your life? Talk about a lack of lithium." Around this time I stopped making notes and began to fantasize about sex, food and television.

It is not impossible for an amateur to kill. There are those rare times when an amateur delivers a knock-out set. Norm MacDonald, who had gone on to fame on the television program *Saturday Night Live,* is said to have done the best amateur set in the history of Canadian stand-up. It happened in Ottawa back in the mid-eighties. Howie Wagman, who runs the Ottawa Yuk Yuk's, says MacDonald blew the crowd away. Ironically, MacDonald was unaware of this fact. Wagman had to beg him to return. "I told him, I am not letting you not perform again," Wagman recalls.

My night at the Toronto Crash and Burn, however, was not one of those miraculous times. At the end, Eisen came up and insulted all the amateurs who had been on the show and thanked the crowd for its patience. Then the technical guy played a tape of the end of the Steve McQueen movie *Papillon,* in which Papillon, the prisoner, escapes from Devil's Island on a raft of coconuts. He decides to risk his life, to chance being eaten by sharks or drowned by raging currents, rather than suffer another minute of wretchedness. It was a sentiment to which each member of the audience could no doubt relate.

I staggered out into the night, reeling not from alcohol (I had not had a drop), but from the tidal wave of psychological dysfunction that is amateur night. You can't learn much about the art of stand-up comedy from amateur night, except, perhaps, how incredibly difficult it is. You can, however, learn a great deal about why people entangle themselves in the stand-up web. It is all ego and need. Many stand-up comedians are the sort of people who are unwilling to live without the world revolving around them at least once a week. That's what amateur night gives those who play it. For five minutes they are the centre of the universe, even if they only serve as sideshow diversions, there to amuse the audience with their mental cuts and bruises.

And yet, out of this skewed morass real talent emerges. Every working stand-up has started out at amateur night. In 1976, at age fourteen, Jim Carrey performed his first amateur night at Yuk Yuk's Church Street basement. Carrey's father had brought him to the show and put him onstage. The younger Carrey bombed, and didn't return to Yuk Yuk's for two years. Once he did, however, he quickly established himself. Even the naturals have to serve their time as amateurs. "That was my in," Carrey says of his amateur days in 1979. "That's where it started for me. I used to drive a hundred miles a night to work free at Yuk Yuk's for a year before I started making money at it. I used to drive from Jackson's Point and back every night."

One duo, Al Rae and George Westerholm, had a particularly fast rise from amateur night around that time. They were two punk kids in their early twenties who prepared for gigs by drinking a case of wine. After imbibing, George would cut Al's hair. The pair were a new-wave version of Martin and Lewis. George played the slick straight man to Al's brain-damaged maniac. They met in a high school cinema appreciation class and found they shared the same nihilistic bent, as well as a love of alcohol. When they later travelled on the road, they insisted on being paid in cash. They split the money by throwing it in the air and then scrambling to pluck up the bills. Whatever you got was yours. It made little difference — it all went to booze anyway. When they appeared on amateur night and played their song "When Are You Going to Die, George Burns?" they became a big hit, especially with Breslin.

"You wanted to kill, to leave them a laughing hulk," says Rae. "No one talked to you. There was no mingling. You couldn't get a free pop. You were lower than dirt. It made you hungry. The top guys would go to Meyers Deli across the street [from the Downtown] and hang out after the show. To be invited was a big privilege. If you went and you weren't invited, you would not be allowed to sit with them. You had to sit at your own table. It was entirely based on your comedy. It had nothing to do with your personality. To get paid twenty bucks to do a set was the greatest thing in the world. No one ever thought they were going to get paid."

"We were a group of edgy, mildly terrified twenty-ish men, standing at the back of the room blowing joints and waiting to do the bits you'd been working on all week," says Benmergui. "There was a real electricity. We were all terrified together."

By this time, however, Mark Breslin was too filled with ambition to be scared. In the beginning, no one had thought Yuk Yuk's would be anything more than a good time. Says Axler, "The idea of comedy clubs making money, that was so far out we didn't even contemplate it. I remember one night, my father, who had run the Yiddish Theatre when it was at the Victory [the theatre that later became a strip club], said to me, 'I saw your show. I was impressed. You better get a liquor licence.' I thought, Yeah, he's right. Why hasn't that ever occurred to us?" It hadn't because they'd been driven by a deep psychological need, claims Breslin. "We'd been brought up on sixties sex, drugs, and rock and roll. Toronto was so puritanical and Victorian. We wanted a centre for the punk point of view. It was never a business."

By 1980, that attitude was changing dramatically. It became evident that stand-up was not only a business but a business that was going to boom. Clubs were beginning to pop up across the country. A comedian named Rich Elwood had opened Punchlines in Vancouver. In Montreal, Ernie Butler had opened the Comedy Nest. Breslin decided he would go one better. He had the name, which was well-known, and he had the comics, which he'd gathered over the previous three years and watched develop. The mechanics of a stand-up club were simple: you needed tables, chairs, booze, a stage, a few lights, a microphone, and someone to take tickets.

Breslin had toured the Yuk Yuk's headliners through western Canada in 1979 and 1980. That trip convinced him that stand-up was not strictly a Toronto phenomenon. The decision, for him, was simple. He'd build a chain; he'd start a Yuk Yuk's empire. It was a remarkable insight and indicative of the business acumen that Breslin has shown in his domination of stand-up comedy in Canada. He has always been able to predict the public's appetite for comedy. He saw a chain of comedy clubs when such a notion was unheard of. In this respect, Breslin is a pioneer in not only Canadian but North American comedy.

Breslin decided that Yuk Yuk's first satellite would be in Montreal. In March 1980, the Montreal club opened at the corner of Drummond Street and Maisonneuve Boulevard with a champagne-fuelled party. The show featured the top rung of Yuk Yuk's Toronto regulars. On the bill were stand-ups Mike MacDonald, Larry Horowitz, Marla Lukofsky, who had learned her craft playing Toronto coffee houses, Steve Shuster, Jim McAleese, Howard Busgang, Lawrence Morgenstern, and sketch group La Troupe Grotesque. Breslin came on as the emcee. The Montreal *Gazette* called the evening "a sparkling sample of Canadian talent."

Breslin didn't know it, but this show would be the high-water mark for the Montreal club. Vaudry says that by using an all-Toronto lineup, Breslin alienated the Montreal community. "They came in and tried to rub Montreal's face in it. That was a big mistake. You don't wear your Maple Leafs jersey in Montreal." The impresario had also misjudged the market. The English community was not large enough to support the club and its costs. Montreal's Anglo population shrank after the 1980 referendum. In 1981, a recession hit. Yuk Yuk's Montreal began to bleed losses. Eventually it would lose $50,000. Things weren't much better in Toronto. The revenue raised from the Downtown, which had no liquour licence, was slim. A Yuk Yuk's TV pilot for Global Television cost another $30,000. In 1982, the Bank of Nova Scotia called in Breslin's debt. Yuk Yuk's was on the brink of being repossessed lock, stock, and barrel. In a foolhardy attempt to keep things going, Larry Horowitz and club manager Howie Wagman slept in the Downtown club. If the bailiffs changed the locks in the dead of night, they reasoned, they could simply open the doors from the inside. But Breslin and his club avoided destruction. He closed the Montreal club and took the loss. The Toronto Dominion Bank ponied up the cash to bail him out.

This near-death experience taught Breslin a valuable lesson: Keep start-up costs low. During the eighties, when most nightclubs cost six figures to open, Yuk Yuk's spent an average of $30,000 to $50,000 to start a club. Breslin next opened a club in Ottawa and the Toronto Uptown club. The Montreal set-back had also taught him that the key to staying alive in the stand-up market, was to control the talent. His three clubs gave him clout. He could now give comedians enough work to provide a full-time living. He had the carrot (his clubs) and he had the stick (barring a comic from playing those clubs). Breslin had the makings of "the deal."

The deal, which had unofficially been in place since the Downtown opened, was that Yuk Yuk's comedians played Yuk Yuk's clubs and one-nighters exclusively. A "one-nighter" is any comedy show that takes place in a non-comedy venue, for example bars, hotels, or restaurants. According to the deal, if a comedian played an outside or "independent" gig, he or she was out. That comic would no longer be allowed to play Yuk Yuk's clubs or one-night shows. All stand-ups who worked Yuk Yuk's clubs were also required to be represented by Yuk Yuk's management company, Funny Business. "The deal is, and always was," says Breslin, "I'll protect your market if you protect mine. It would be so easy for me to cave in and book American acts. I could get them for less and I could score points in America. All I say is, don't play my competition unless I can't give you the work."

It was a marked change from Breslin's initial attitude. In 1976, he had complained to the *Globe and Mail,* "One of the things that bothers me about Yuk Yuk's is that it operates in a vacuum. There's nowhere else in the city for a comic to go." The deal reflected a rise of what some comedians call the "Bad Mark." The Bad Mark is the bully his comics fear, the man who deals in business with an uncompromising dedication to his own purposes and the bottom line. In Breslin's view the deal was a matter of pure survival. Without it his chain would fold. Canada, he was quick to point out, could not compete with the American economy of scale. The only way for him to keep stand-up Canadian was for labour and capital to make a deal.

Not everyone saw things his way. The deal has produced friction since its inception. Howie Mandel, the first Yuk Yuk's comic to leave and make it big in the States, on the television series *St. Elsewhere,* refused to obey the deal and fell out with Breslin. Mandel had been with Yuk Yuk's since its early days on Bay Street. Jim Carrey caused grief by taking a rival gig in 1981 at a comedy club in Montreal called Stitches. Carrey was supporting his father, mother, and sisters through comedy and had taken the gig because it paid a large whack of much-needed cash. In retaliation, Breslin threw him out. Carrey found refuge at a Barrie, Ontario, club then run by a comedian named Wayne Flemming. He eventually returned to Yuk Yuk's, according to Leatrice Spevack, a former Yuk Yuk's office employee who managed him during the early eighties, by agreeing to play the Yuk Yuk's Montreal club for free. It was a humiliation he did not easily forget. Simon Rakoff and Howard Nemetz, two Montreal stand-ups who had moved to Toronto after Yuk Yuk's left their city, tried on several occasions to start a comedians' union. They wanted the right to book their own work on the outside. They failed each time but succeeded in raising Breslin's wrath. He loathed them for their efforts and banished them from his stand-up kingdom. No one followed them. By 1982, the deal was receiving little resistance. The comedy boom was bursting. Stand-ups went along with Breslin and made good money. "In this business, you find that if you make somebody money, you're a great guy," says Breslin. "And if you don't make somebody money, you're a terrible guy."

Stand-up comedy continued to rise in popularity. It seemed as if every bar that had once housed rock bands or a disco ball was giving stand-up a shot. By 1983, stand-up comedy, which only seven years earlier had not been considered a profession, was now producing headline Canadian comics earning as much as fifty thousand dollars a year. Breslin's empire mushroomed to fourteen clubs with openings in Hamilton, London, Edmonton, Calgary, Buffalo, Rochester, Victoria, Mississauga, Halifax, and Vancouver. In 1985, Yuk Yuk's got its own television show on the CBC, which ran for a year before being cancelled. The expansion had a downside. It ended the golden age of

Toronto's Downtown club. When there had only been one club, all the talent had been based there. More clubs meant that the Downtown gang was broken up and sent touring around the country. Before expansion, the comics would meet almost every night at the Downtown to bounce jokes off one another. It was a catalyst to creativity. Now, a stand-up could go three months without seeing a peer. The magic, says Al Rae, had gone.

Survival for a comedian in the Yuk Yuk's chain rested on the comic's ability to play Breslin's system. In 1986, Breslin described his position to the *Globe and Mail* as having "market pre-eminence." More or less, he had a monopoly. He became the godfather of comedy. Like all god-fathers, he demanded loyalty. "Loyalty means a tremendous amount to me," says Breslin. "You can say, for better or worse, anybody who ever helped me on the way up, I helped out, even if I don't believe in them."

Stand-up continued to run on an utterly free-market principle. Comedians were paid solely what Breslin thought he could make back from them. "I realized what it was all about one night when Mike MacDonald asked George and I how much we got," remembers Al Rae. "We said $300. He laughed at us and then he said, 'The other features get $800 for a weekend set. I get $1,800. Why? *Because I can.*' Right then, I knew it had nothing to do with unions or business or anything. Mike got a grand more than everyone else because Breslin knew Mike MacDonald would sell-out. He knew that he would still make money, even if he had to pay Mike more. So we approached Mark and asked for extra, because we were getting, as a duo, what a single comic was getting. We appealed to his sense of fair play. He agreed. That was how you got things done at Yuk Yuk's. You approached Mark, and if he agreed, great. If not, you were out of luck. We got the money and we didn't care if the other guys got it. We weren't there to fight for the other guy. We were out for ourselves. If they wanted more, let *them* talk to Mark."

In the meantime, the first wave of Yuk Yuk's–bred Canadian stand-ups had headed south. Jim Carrey hop-scotched through three managers before going to Hollywood in 1984. Leatrice Spevack says Carrey was driven to succeed. He did not let his ego run wild, even though he was

recognized in Toronto as a formidable talent. Carrey also eschewed the
stand-up night life. He did not drink heavily nor indulge in drugs. Carrey
did, however, take a dispassionate approach to relationships. All decisions
were made according to what they would do for his career. When Carrey
dumped Spevack for a new manager, she was stunned by the cool manner in which he engineered the shift.

In 1986, Breslin got a break of his own. Joan Rivers was starting a
show on Australian media mogul Rupert Murdoch's newly formed Fox
Broadcasting Network. *The Late Show with Joan Rivers* was set to run
a half-hour before the *Tonight Show*. It was a direct challenge to Johnny
Carson, and as a result of the deal Rivers, who had been groomed to
replace him, was on the outs everywhere in Hollywood. No one would
risk angering Johnny by working with Joan. So when she was shopping
for a comedy co-ordinator, Rivers went outside the United States and
found Breslin. The one-time Forest Hill brat began booking all the comedy acts for Rivers' show, flying back twice a month to oversee Yuk
Yuk's business. Breslin had finally hit the really big time. The Yuk Yuk's
chain, which then numbered nine clubs, was worth an estimated six million dollars in Canada and he was lined up for stardom in the U.S.A.
After watching others go down and strike it rich, it was at long last Mark
Breslin's turn. He bought a Rolls Royce and drove it around Toronto.
Then he moved to Los Angeles and drove it around there. His ambition,
he informed the *Canadian Jewish News,* was "to rule an even bigger
big-time comedy empire and dynasty."

"Finally," Breslin told Hana Gartner of the CTV television news
magazine *W5,* who profiled him in a segment entitled "Yuk's Bucks,"
"somebody from the outside said, 'You are the best; we want you here.'
I feel vindicated."

A year later it was Breslin's enemies who were feeling vindicated.
Breslin had tied his fortunes to a loser. Rivers was dumped by Fox and
replaced by stand-up comedian Arsenio Hall, who went on to several
highly successful seasons. Just as Fox was finally climbing up from the
ratings basement, Breslin was being cut loose. The chance to play in
Hollywood, one Breslin had always dreamed of, was gone. Yuk Yuk's'

founder returned to Canada, only to discover that his chain had deteriorated. The stand-up comedy boom was beginning to bust in North
America. Demand was declining. Television shows, such as *Evening at
the Improv,* had saturated the airwaves with mediocre stand-up. Televised
comedy was safe and boring. The comedians were forced to use broad
reference points to score with millions of viewers. Appearing on these
programs became known as "jury duty." The deplorable state of televised stand-up inevitably affected the live stand-up market. Patrons were
turned off.

By 1989, the bubble had burst completely. The clubs were still oper-
ating, but they weren't turning the same kind of margins. The real pain
came in the decline of the one-nighters. These gigs had been the comedians' money work. Club comedy paid, but not well. A stand-up would
earn forty dollars for a set when he wasn't headlining. On some week-
nights he worked for free. The bust was more severe in America. Stand-
up had been allowed to grow uncontrolled down south, and consequently
many marginal clubs had sprung up. One-nighters, for which a comic
could make anywhere from one hundred to one thousand dollars, broke
out all over the country like acne on a teenager. Club owners offering
one-nighters weren't concerned with quality; they cared about quantity,
as in the quantity of alcohol drunk. In Canada, Breslin had controlled
the spread. His ego had worked to his country's advantage. Thanks to
his near monopoly of stand-up, it had not oversaturated the market.
According to Brian Ainsworth, who from 1985 to 1994 acted as Breslin's
creative partner and orchestrated all Yuk Yuk's forays into television,
that was always Breslin's intent: to preserve the integrity of stand-up by
controlling its supply. "His attitude was, if you don't control where the
comics play, the business will get diluted, and it will just degenerate into
bar bands. The talent pool would disintegrate. He sees himself as the
commissioner of the league rather than an owner. He always believed he
was doing the best for comedy."

Besides the North American comedy bust, which was beyond his
control, Breslin faced a log-jam at the top of the Yuk Yuk's hierarchy.
Many of the original players were still there. Comedians like Ron Vaudry,

Lawrence Morgenstern, and Larry Horowitz stood at the front of a stable of talented and not-so-talented "middles." A middle comic is someone who can do twenty minutes of good material before the headliner comes on. Middles are one step above opening acts. They are either young comedians on their way to becoming headliners, or mediocre comics destined to middle for the rest of their lives. These comedians felt they weren't getting the opportunities they deserved. "Breslin was telling everyone to quit their jobs and move to Toronto," says stand-up Steve Levine, one of the disgruntled. "He was like a drug dealer. He'd get you here, get you hooked, and then there'd be no work. You'd beg for work."

By the summer of 1990, a band of unhappy comedians had formed and festered. The disenchanted, about thirty of them, most of whom were young and from the middle ranks, began to meet secretly to discuss their options. A new club had opened in Toronto called The Laugh Resort. It was a single venue, but it offered headline opportunities and was in desperate need of comedians. The club had a few old pros, all ex-Yuk Yuk's guys such as Simon Rakoff and Evan Carter, but it was low on depth. The rebels held a series of meetings with Breslin and his associates, Yuk Yuk's president Jeff Silverman and Brian Ainsworth. Both men had joined the chain during the boom years to help run the financial side of things. A showdown was arranged. Dissident stand-ups Steve Levine, Mark Farrell, Brian Hartt (who was beginning to write for the CBC Television series *The Kids in the Hall*), Eric Tunney, and Brent Butt met at Yuk Yuk's head office while the rest of the rebels waited down the street at the Pilot Tavern. The meeting was tense and filled with acrimony. The stand-ups were combative and Breslin's henchmen were defensive. The comics said they wanted permission to work the outside. Breslin said he'd think about it.

The rebel comedians' hopes were encouraged by the arrival of the Bureau of Competition at Mr. Breslin's front door. The federal body had begun an investigation into Breslin and his chain in the spring of 1990. They were searching for evidence that Breslin and his deal broke federal competitiveness regulations. If the bureau found evidence that

Breslin was running a monopoly, it could order him to change the deal. The bureau began to meet with comedians individually. Breslin countered by organizing his comedians and pushing them, or at least encouraging them strongly, to fight the bureau. Ultimately, they accepted Breslin's promise not to impede competition. He called it a victory for his system.

Says Levine, "We thought if all the comics could pull together there would be a revolution." All the comics, however, did not pull together. Around two thirds of the disgruntled returned to Yuk Yuk's. The deal held. What was he worried about, stand-up Tim Steeves had asked Breslin during the fracas, "it's small potatoes." "So what?" Breslin countered. "Big potatoes or small potatoes, they're *my* potatoes!" Levine and eight other comedians moved to The Laugh Resort. The rebellion, which had been brewing since Breslin's deal first took shape, had finally occurred, but it had occurred on a small scale.

Says Breslin, "All the people who say they left because they were morally opposed to the deal, don't believe them for a second. Nobody ever leaves anybody for moral reasons in this business. They just didn't get the jobs that they felt they deserved, but I felt they didn't."

Yuk Yuk's, like Gary David and the burlesque comedians, continued to benefit from an absence of government funding. Yuk Yuk's was a profit-making enterprise. Thanks to Breslin's deal, hiring — and some might say exploiting — Canadian talent became economically viable. As a result, Yuk Yuk's showcased and continues to showcase Canadians to Canadians. The company rarely books American acts. Things could have been otherwise. Catch a Rising Star, an American comedy chain, made numerous attempts to establish a foothold in Canada. Yuk Yuk's fought them off and, to ensure another American stand-up giant didn't muscle in, Breslin copyrighted the name "Improv." That said, it should be noted that Breslin was prepared to sell to Catch a Rising Star in 1987, when the Joan Rivers show was launching. It should also be noted that by using Canadians, Breslin maintains control. He can boss them around and dictate terms. If they don't like it, they can leave.

Ironically, despite its dedication to capitalist business practises, Yuk

Yuk's operates on the inside as a very socialist institution. Yuk Yuk's does the comedians' thinking for them. The company plays mother and takes care of the grimy details. Comedians are told where to work, and when they are on the road they're told where to stay and where to eat. Their lives are laid out for them. All the stand-up has to do is show up at his gig. In exchange for this stability, comedians trade a slice of their independence. Yuk Yuk's is a paradox: ferociously free-market on the outside, socialist on the inside.

After the rebellion had been quelled, a small war of attrition began. Breslin sent friends, like his right-hand man Jeff Silverman, to The Laugh Resort to check the size of the crowd. These comics would then be blacklisted. Tim Rykert, a Yuk Yuk's doorman with stand-up aspirations, acted as an observer. He would go to Laugh Resort shows and sit in the audience, making note of how many customers were there and who was performing. Rykert later turned coat and joined the blacklisted set.

In January 1990, the war continued to heat up. Boyd Banks, one of Breslin's exiles, was quoted in an Edmonton alternative paper saying that Breslin had made death threats against blacklisted comedians. Claimed Banks, "He was talking to another comic and he said, I quote, 'If this was New Jersey, they'd be floating in a river' . . . It's basically death threats and innuendo. He's just playing hardball." As to Breslin's reaction to the allegation at the time, some say he went ballistic. Breslin says he was mildly offended. He admits he did make the statement, but it was meant to imply generosity and understanding, as in, "If this was New Jersey they'd be floating in the river, but we're not stooping to that level. We're being reasonable."

"I never get mad when someone makes a business decision to leave Yuk Yuk's and all its Byzantine and complicated rules for somewhere else," Breslin says. "But you don't have to try and drag me down at the same time, because you wouldn't even be able to leave if it wasn't for my organization. The way you walk away is, you take me out for dinner, you tell me you can no longer do business with me and that you're sorry, and then you pick up the check. And then we remain friendly, at least."

According to stand-up Harry Doupe, Banks was not content to let the incident drop. He telephoned Breslin and left messages daring him to sue. Breslin eventually did. He filed a slander action against Banks and demanded one million dollars in damages. Although Banks had no money for Breslin to take, the thought that he would have to go to court and face a judge was unnerving. At the same time, his loathing for Breslin was limitless. He routinely railed against him and worked himself into delirious frenzies describing how low he felt Breslin was. Banks held out for nine months and then obliged Breslin by agreeing not to repeat his accusation and not to discuss the particulars of the settlement.

It was the "Bad Mark" who got most of the attention between 1989 and 1992. The rebellion and the investigation had hurt Breslin personally. He believed that the comedians who had migrated from Yuk Yuk's were out to destroy him and the company he had built. To a man who valued loyalty, it was a bitter twist of fate. Breslin saw comedians like Steve Levine, whom he felt he'd given their starts, turning on him and trying to ruin him. His temper tantrums became legendary, although that side is never shown to the media; he is far too measured for that. According to eye-witnesses, seeing Breslin lose his cool is an embarrassing and unnerving experience. Ainsworth remembers one such episode, which occurred backstage at a Molson Comedy Releaf show in Massey Hall. A roving cameraman was taping the crowd, getting footage of comedians and technical staff. Breslin felt he was not getting his fair share. He became agitated. He kept pulling Ainsworth aside and insisting, "I'm not getting filmed. Tell that guy to tape me. He's taping everyone else." Ainsworth was busy running the actual performance and gave Breslin's pleas little regard. The mini-mogul finally blew his lid and began to upbraid Ainsworth before the entire backstage crew. "I don't care if you're fucking busy. You get that fucking camera on me! Do you understand, you fucking asshole? I want that fucking camera taping me!"

Ainsworth claims he picked Breslin up under the arms and held him a foot above the ground. He told Breslin, "I don't have time for this shit," set him down, and went back to work. "After that he settled down," says Ainsworth. "He was like a kid who needed to be put in line."

By 1993, Breslin was in line for his second shot at television. The timing was good for him. He'd cornered the stand-up market and was in desperate need of a new challenge. Breslin's shot was the job of executive producer for CBC's variety show *Friday Night with Ralph Benmergui.* The former Yuk Yuk's stand-up had left the game in the late eighties and joined CBC Radio as a host. Benmergui had quickly risen through the ranks to find success on CBC Television's lunch-time public affairs chat show, *Midday.* After Benmergui's stint at the podium for the Gemini Awards, Canadian television's awards ceremony, Ivan Fecan, who was then head of CBC programming, felt Benmergui could be Canada's answer to Arsenio Hall. In the new Broadcast Building an enormous studio was built, ready to house Benmergui's new show. It would be a mix of talent, music and comedy with the likable Ralph Benmergui at centre stage. It would be *really Canadian* and appeal to viewers from age ten to ninety.

And so the stage was set for a massacre.

Almost within seconds after Benmergui's first broadcast in 1992, critics were screaming for his blood. Benmergui exacerbated the situation by taking their abuse badly. This whining, from a former journalist, made them redouble their attacks. John Haslett Cuff, of the *Globe and Mail,* relentlessly hammered Benmergui. The show was too American, it was too Canadian. By the end of its first season, many thought Benmergui and his show were history. The CBC opted to give it another shot. They brought in Mark Breslin to save their souls. Breslin fired all the writers and brought in his people: Larry Horowitz, Joel Axler, a writer named Martin Waxman, stand-ups Steve Shuster and Frank Van Keeken, and a journalist and former Yuk Yuk's waitress, Donna Lypchuck. Breslin reshaped the show to appeal to a young, hip audience. He stuck up a reproduction of a mural from the ruins of Pompeii as a backdrop. The show featured such strange segments as "Communist in a Box," a bit in which Frank Van Keeken, dressed as a Marxist rebel and locked in a cage, would lambaste the audience for decadence. Shortly before Christmas in 1993, *Friday Night with Ralph Benmergui* was axed. Breslin took the blame. See? his detractors said, he can't do television. He is the kiss of death.

By then, Bad Mark's twin, the "Good Mark," was getting more pro-file. I met "Good Mark" in December 1993 while standing in line for an Andrew Dice Clay concert. Clay, an American comedian who was infa-mous for his often offensive racially motivated and sexually biased material, was playing Massey Hall in Toronto. To many he represented everything that was odious about stand-up comedy. The Toronto police were obviously expecting trouble. They had shown up in force, both mounted officers and constables on foot. They were there to stop any rioting. Breslin was excited by the fact that a comedian could stir up such controversy. He saw Andrew Dice Clay's profanity as an ironic device: Clay was presenting and exposing America's ugly side. Breslin talked animatedly about the prospects of Benmergui's show. It had not yet been cancelled, and he talked about booking edgy acts and shaking the CBC up. He was intelligent and well-mannered. He was the Good Mark I had heard of but until then had never met. As we spoke, I recalled what all the comedians had said was Breslin's greatest quality: his artis-tic conviction. It could win over the worst enemy. For instance, in 1996, Boyd Banks returned to Yuk Yuk's, because he felt The Laugh Resort was censoring his act. Says Steve Shuster, "Mark is the only club owner who will get your Sylvia Plath references."

Breslin champions the misfits. He figures the straight-ahead comics will get approval anyway. In 1983, for example, Breslin brought up a Californian stand-up named Sam Kinison. He was a former evangelist, survivor of two divorces, and without question one of the most influen-tial talents to come out of the market over the last fifteen years. Onstage Kinison was a nihilist and misogynist. He coined the tag line "Any man who understands a woman is one." Due to his controversial material he could not get work in the States. In his early days in Los Angeles, Kinison slept in a car in the Comedy Store parking lot and lived on drugs and hand-outs. His 1983 late December run at the Downtown has become mythologized for both its artistic power and its substance abuse. Kinison would do three or four lines of cocaine, smoke a few joints, and drink six double-vodkas. Then it was showtime. Tight-assed Toronto didn't exactly embrace his act. On opening night, with lines like "I don't have an act. I don't have a car. I didn't eat yesterday. I had to borrow these clothes . . . SHE TOOK IT ALL!" Kinison all but cleared the room. Breslin approached the he-devil after the show and handed him one hundred dollars. Kinison figured he was being given the kiss-off, once again, and would not be asked back for the following night. "I'm really sorry, Mark," he said. Breslin replied, "That's a bonus. Every time you clear the room, I'll give you an extra hundred bucks."

Like him or hate him, everyone will admit that Mark Breslin was what was required at the time. "The comics would have been little Canadian niggers slaving away as middles or openers for American acts that would get flown up," says Axler. Only someone with Breslin's almost pathological ambition, cunning, insecurity, and primitive urges could have built this industry out of nothing. When it comes to Breslin, it is love-hate. Credit his madness. Breslin is an off-centre individual, and admittedly so. "I feel I am mentally ill," he told me at the Four Seasons. "I have been under the care of psychiatrists most of my life, for various narcissistic disorders and manic episodes. If anyone has a positive view of mental illness, it's comedians, because a lot of the language and iconography is the same for the mentally ill and a comic. Instead of thinking, A, B, C, they think, A, B, green, three. Comedians idolize the concept of madness because it represents the ultimate mental freedom."

When I first dealt with Mark Breslin, I saw a monster, something out of *The Twilight Zone*. He was a short demon terrorizing a whole community, myself included. I've come to see him in less black-and-white terms. Breslin can indeed be vicious. I get the feeling, however, that he is trying to get back at people who are long gone. The two defining aspects of his personality appear to be the bullying he endured as a kid and the pain he felt watching his sister suffer from MS. They infused Mark Breslin with two essential elements for comedy: powerlessness and rage. Comedy is the art form of the impotent. Comedians are valiant cowards who love a lost cause. If they thought things could change, they'd be activists or politicians, not comedians. But in their heart of hearts they know the world will always be out of order, so they remind us that Rome is burning but never reach for a bucket of water.

"You either succumb and every single incident becomes large, or you ignore it all and repress it and you become the coldest guy on the planet," Breslin had said of his own experience that day at the Four Seasons. "There have been moments when I felt like I was drowning, and there was nobody there with a life preserver. People were actually standing on the dock laughing as I was going down. My whole life I've been falling apart, and the pieces burst into flames as they're hitting the ground. I see the comedian and comedy as a way of extinguishing those flames. I expect it to save me, and that has caused me a lot of grief over the years.

Breslin added ruefully, "If you're not mentally ill when you get into this business, you'll be mentally ill when you get out."

S I X

■

The Road Warriors

*In regards to the shows on the one nighters, please leave your artistic
license at home and bring along your dick jokes. As much as we try to
educate these owners, the majority of them just want entertainment. We
hate to say it but they look at comedy like they look at bands. They want
to fill their rooms with people drinking. Remember: You are doing this
for the money, not to be discovered. Letterman's people aren't looking
for talent in Taber, Alberta. Keep* YOUR *sense of humor.*
— *from* Welcome to Yuk Yuk's Alberta: The Comedian's Bible

At age twenty-one, David Merry never had less than $1,500 (U.S.) in his
pocket. He golfed, womanized, and relaxed in the hot Nevada sunshine.
Merry was a professional blackjack player in Las Vegas, and life was
good. He was a card counter and used what's known as the "High Op
One" method to win big. Merry counted the deck on his toes and used
a scale of probabilities, which he had memorized, to determine the opti-
mum time for betting. He did not work alone. For two years, Merry
played on a five-player team. This team worked anywhere from twenty
minutes to two hours a day. The gamblers pooled their money to
bankroll big bets. Typically, they played a casino thus: Two members

acted as counters. They watched a table and waited for the "high op" (high opportunity — the moment when the odds were greatest that the hand could be won). When the "op" arrived, they would signal to two players who were standing near the table. These players would sit down, and then the counters secretly gave them the count. In this way the players knew exactly what cards were coming up. The remaining member of the team, the "bank," would circle and wait for the golden opportunity. When the time was right for a clean-up bet, the players would signal him. He would then sit down and bet thousands of dollars. It was a very effective and completely illegal way to earn a living that netted Merry two to five thousand dollars a day.

The team members never used the word gambling. "The casino had our money and we were going to get it," Merry explains. "We knew we were going to win, every time." Despite the superficial ease with which he lived, Merry began to feel the heat. He knew that he could easily become addicted to gambling if he let himself go, if he stopped looking at gambling as work. All around him, he saw what gambling wrought on the people who let it control them. The cocky young card player began to wonder, When would it be his turn? Then, one afternoon, Merry's next-door neighbour shot his wife and put the gun to his own head. Gambling had claimed another statistic. Merry took this as a sign. He left Las Vegas and a couple of years later had a new career. He became a comedian who dabbled in magic.

Twenty years later, on May 20, 1996, at the age of forty-three, Merry was doing a different kind of counting. He was counting the hours. That morning, David, a Yuk Yuk's comedian, had driven the five-hour trip to Toronto from Sudbury, where he'd done a show. Once in Toronto, he'd played with his three children for a few hours and then hopped back in his car and taken a four-hour drive to Owen Sound. After the show there, he'd drive the four hours back to Toronto. That would make a total of around thirteen hours on the road and four hours of show for Merry. While it was a taxing schedule, it was nothing compared to the pressure of Vegas. Merry wouldn't even break a sweat; he was as cool as they came. Merry didn't "handle" pressure, he lived for it.

In Owen Sound Merry had been joined by Johnny Gardhouse,

another Yuk Yuk's stand-up from that city, who'd spent the previous night at his parents' house. Gardhouse was just back from vacationing in Bermuda, where he'd scuba-dived and slept with a girl named Alice. Tonight he'd be playing his home-town crowd, but he seemed more enthusiastic about how much he was going to drink and smoke after the show. "I'm still a young pup," the twenty-six-year-old said. "I can still get wasted."

The last of the triumvirate on the bill, Larry Horowitz, had driven up from Toronto that morning. Horowitz had over twenty years' experience as a stand-up and countless road gigs under his belt, all for Yuk Yuk's. Some referred to him as "the Dean" because he had seen and done so much. Others, when he was not around, referred to him as "the Hack" because he had seen and done so much. Of all the Yuk Yuk's regulars, Larry was the most consistent crowd pleaser. He wasn't edgy or highly experimental, but he was the closest to a sure thing that Yuk Yuk's had. Eight or eighty, crippled or crazy, they'd laugh at forty-three-year-old Larry Horowitz. Larry, a former swimmer, now topped two hundred pounds after years of eating fast food on the road. He had a broad laugh and a sharp memory. Larry could recall anything, from gigs he'd done fifteen years ago to what kind of shoes he'd been wearing on his first amateur night.

That day, Owen Sound High School was celebrating its 140th anniversary. In honour of this auspicious occasion, virtually every shop and restaurant in the small central Ontario town was closed. As if this wasn't reason enough for celebration, those with no connection to Owen Sound's high school were busy preparing for the Victoria Day long weekend. After a winter of excruciating cold, warm weather had arrived, and for Canadians everywhere Monday was a holiday. Heaped upon this bonanza would come another delectable treat. Three comedians were coming to town to perform at the high school anniversary celebration at the Roxy Theatre. Big-time comedy was coming to Owen Sound, and the town would show up in force.

The three comedians did not share the small town's excitement at the prospect. To them, it was all money. To Merry, Gardhouse, and Horowitz, it was just another piece of road work.

Road work is an unavoidable rite of passage. Once a comedian has graduated from amateur night, clawed his or her way into an opening spot, and then become a middle, he or she is ready for the road. Yuk Yuk's booking agency, Funny Business, begins to send middles on one-night gigs and regional tours. One-nighters can be presented in venues ranging from small theatres and bars to shopping centres and bowling alleys. These shows are held for one of two reasons: there's a celebration (like a high school anniversary), or the owner wants to draw a crowd and thinks comedy will get thirsty customers through the doors. These establishments are notoriously poorly equipped. Frequently there's no microphone, mic stand, stage lights, or even a stage. Funny Business tries to protect the comedians from poor conditions but there's only so much it can do. Quite simply, road work is bottled insanity. Comedians who survive a year or two on the road earn themselves the title of "road warrior."

The biggest challenge facing a road warrior is mileage. Canada's size has always challenged Canadians and determined much of our cultural life, so it is not surprising that the country's mammoth and sparsely populated geography has played a key role in the development of our stand-up comedy. America offers comics a wealth of densely populated urban centres. During the comedy boom of the late eighties, the Boston area had six full-time comedy clubs, ten suburban full-time clubs, almost twenty college and university sites, and over one hundred one-night venues. An American comic working the Boston circuit could earn a healthy living, up to $50,000 (US), and never have to drive more than an hour to a gig. Canada, by contrast, is spread as thin as tissue paper. Canadian stand-ups must travel farther to find an audience. Toronto in 1996 had two full-time clubs and one club in Mississauga. There are one-nighters in the city, but not enough to sustain all the comics who live and work there. Stand-ups who want to live by their craft must tour. Touring means driving to one-night gigs. Driving means eight to ten hours a day, every day. It means braving snow, hail, torrential rain, wind, moose, wolves, mechanical problems, and boredom.

Road warriors are similar to the *coureurs de bois*. They are comedic *voyageurs* who cart jokes across Canada. It's a brutal lifestyle that claims many casualties, but it must be mastered. Those who don't become road warriors become ex-comics.

In the pre-Yuk Yuk's days, road gigs existed, but they were haphazard and disorganized. The comics were vulnerable to a variety of abuses. Nova Scotia-bred Wayne Flemming started in comedy during the mid-seventies. Today he's forty-eight and a respected headliner. He also has the distinction of being Jim Carrey's mentor and closest friend. Flemming is as bald as an eagle and has the demeanour of Jack Nicholson on a good day. He is amiable and devilish. For example, Wayne once appeared at Johnny Gardhouse's hotel room door, stark naked. He had wedged his penis between his crossed legs, to make himself "look like a girl." Flemming then asked Gardhouse for a cup of tea.

Such wildness has its roots in Flemming's early road days. He was in his late twenties and had given up a career as a draftsman to hook up as front man with a musical duo called Lisle. The trio played bars and hotels throughout northern Ontario. He sang and performed comedy bits. Lisle would play tunes and musical interludes. According to Wayne, there is a word in the English language that sums up the audiences they played for: *vicious*. During his time on the road he required more than ten stitches for cuts, all, coincidentally, sustained in Owen Sound.

"I saw the bottle fly by me and I felt it brush," he recalls of one occasion. "Then I thought to myself, It must be hot; you're really sweating. I licked the sweat and realized it was blood. They threw the guy out and later they told me they had banned him for life. A year later they begged me to come back and offered me double the money. So I did it reluctantly. Again I was hit with a bottle and took another four stitches."

But it wasn't the bottles that were the most dangerous, Flemming says. "Believe it or not, it was the pennies. These audiences had a joke which they generally played on strippers who would come into town. They'd heat quarters with their lighters and then throw them to the stripper, who thought they were tips. The strippers would stoop to pick up the coins and burn their fingers on the hot metal. These guys thought that was the funniest thing in the world. When it came to us comedians, they knew that we weren't going to pick them up because we didn't get tips, but they still wanted to hurt us, so they'd heat pennies and flick them at you. If you took one in the eye it would blind you. It was their way of booing. It was a fucking horror show."

Flemming did thirteen or fourteen shows a week with Lisle, for which he would get $250. The threesome stayed in scummy motels or above the gig they were playing. There's a saying that road warriors have, "If the place you're playing has the word *Theatre* in it, that's a good sign; if the place you're staying has the word *Arms* in it, you're in trouble." Hallways were uniformly crooked and slanted, making the drunks feel like they were walking straight. Flemming says conditions were often so repugnant that he would be afraid to shower. "There'd be hair already on the soap." Wayne picked up a method of testing for infestation. When you first arrived you turned on every light in the room. Then you warmed up a bar of soap with water until it became mushy. You pulled up the covers of your bed and made a small sort-of tent on one side of the mattress, large enough for the soap. Then you placed the soap in the tent, flicked the lights off, and left. Two hours later, "every bug in the fucking room would head for that damn mushy bar of soap. You would see the scariest things. That was the bug test. If you got a room like that you wouldn't stay, but nine times out of ten you had no choice. It was 'Get your own room.' How are you going to get your own room if you're doing thirteen shows a week and making two fifty?"

Along with the audience and insects, road comics had to worry about the people who paid them. It wasn't unheard of for the bar that booked the comic to pay him and then pay someone else to mug the comedian and get the bar's money back. Shortly after leaving one such gig, Flemming was accosted by two thugs and had a gun put to his head. He immediately soiled his pants. Flemming handed over his wallet and the thieves fled. Flemming was forced to try and hail a cab with feces coating the inside of his briefs. Matters were made worse by the fact that Flemming was wearing an all-white disco suit.

Comedians quickly learn that they can trust no one when they're travelling. They learn this the hard way. Kenny Robinson is a Yuk Yuk's headliner. He is a massive black man and an imposing figure. He hails from Winnipeg via Chicago. He's a tough individual. After one road gig in Saskatchewan, Robinson was invited to attend a party that was being held at a local pawn shop. When Robinson arrived he didn't find much of a party, just a few dubious-looking Prairie boys drinking hard liquor. The shop had signed dollar bills strewn across its walls. Robinson noticed another odd decorating choice. There were numerous pictures of Adolph Hitler hanging up. Robinson realized he'd stumbled into a nest of white supremacists.

He also realized he had been invited not for a drink but as the evening's entertainment. Still he couldn't keep his mouth closed. One of his hosts, whose name was Mongo, threatened to shoot him. Robinson did not flinch and Mongo backed down. He even asked the comedian to sign a dollar bill. The stand-up was happy to oblige. Robinson wrote, "Jesse Owens fucked Eva Braun up the ass, signed Kenny Robinson." Then he left.

Pragmatic road paranoia includes being wary of potential lovers. Says Wayne Flemming, "You never know what you're dealing with. You may be stepping on some guy's grass. A woman can lie to you and tell you she's not married. I was in the midst of something with this woman and I hear a door slam downstairs, and I say, 'Who the fuck is that?' And she says, 'My husband.' I say, 'I thought you said you weren't married.' She says, 'Well, I figured you wouldn't come home with me if you knew, and he's not supposed to be home until next Thursday.' I say, 'But he's home *now*.' So out the second-storey window I go, with my clothes in my hands, barefoot. I run ten minutes across a field of freshly cut corn. The stalks cut my feet. They're shredded. Then I walk seven miles to the hotel with my bloody feet wrapped in my T-shirt. After that, if I'm going to be in the company of a lady, she comes to my room. And I don't fucking care what it looks like."

These stories worry comedians. They remind them that every time they go on the road, they're rolling the dice. They remind comedians, who generally crave control, that there is a limit to their capacity to navigate their surroundings. At least you can see audience trouble coming. Gardhouse was once assaulted at a gig on Vancouver Island. He took a punch in the face from a very nasty woman. He'd used the word *fuck,* and an inebriated lady had taken exception. "She said I was disgusting and that I should leave. I told her, 'Hey, if you don't like the show you can get the *fuck* out.' Then she charged the stage and began to wrestle for the microphone. I grabbed it and tried to keep it. Then she wound up and punched me, knocking me to the floor. The bouncers removed her. The audience didn't even bat an eye. I said, 'What? Do you people see this every night? Anyway, here's your headliner.'"

Virtually every comic has been attacked at one time or another. Timmins-born Derek Edwards had an angry biker charge him with a knife, yelling, "Don't ever say that about my dick again!" Tim Conlon and Harry Doupe played a Victoria bar on Superbowl Sunday. The crowd, which was all male, had been drinking for five hours when the comics went onstage. There were no male staff or bouncers present. Insults and food were thrown as the crowd grew restless. Suddenly, the bar doors flew open and a man riding a Harley Davidson started driving around the bar. He stopped directly in front of the stage, about forty feet back, popped a wheelie and charged Conlon. The road warrior threw his microphone at the rider and leapt out of the way as the biker flew off his bike. The comedians had had enough. They crawled to an adjoining bar and hid under a table. Fifteen minutes later a waitress came out and asked, "When are you going to start the next show?" Doupe told her, "You don't understand. We have a rule — when a guy on a motorcycle charges the stage there is no second show. And why the hell don't you guys have any men working? It's Superbowl Sunday, for Christ's sake."

"We do," she tells him. "The manager is working."

"Well where is he?" the angry comic asked. "I want to see him."

"He was the one riding the bike."

In 1980, Yuk Yuk's launched its first tour. Breslin's empire consisted of only one club at the time. Tours, he believed, would open up new markets and help finance the Toronto club, which required plenty of liquid cash. The first three tours were utter confusion. Breslin's crew included Horowitz, Mike MacDonald, and Lou Dinos, a young kid whose sole purpose for going on the road was to get laid. One legendary road story has Dinos calling up a fellow stand-up in post-coital bliss to tell him, "Jim, I just got laid." Fifteen minutes later he called back: "Jim, I just got robbed."

Travel arrangements were improvised. The comics took everything from eighteen-hour train rides to endless car trips, and stayed wherever they could find shelter. They played for crowds that had never seen stand-up before, in venues ranging from Harvey's hamburger joints to colleges to biker bars. They ate little, and when they had nothing to eat would have competitions to see which stand-up could make the others' stomachs ache most by describing food. Pay was abysmal, anywhere from zero to around three hundred dollars a week. But since no one really expected to make stand-up a career, they ignored it. Tours lasted three weeks and the troupe did two shows a day. They made up for a lack of money and food by partying. There was plenty of marijuana and booze. For entertainment the comedians smoked a few joints and went to the movies. On the way out of one theatre Horowitz noticed that Steve Shuster was wearing reflective ski goggles. Explained Shuster, "I'm wearing them so no one will know I'm stoned."

The tours made big news, and the gang of comics got countless reviews. Critics and small-town reporters wanted a look at this new phenomenon. The notices were generally positive, and the early tours set up a circuit that exists to this day. They created an overnight demand that would eventually allow Breslin to open his cross-country chain. They also enlightened Breslin and company to the dangers of road travel. There were many concerns: the weather, road conditions, thieves, and as ever, the audience. When a one-nighter in Dunnsville, Saskatchewan, sold no tickets, an angry bar owner forced the comedians to do the show anyway, for him. During the performance the disgruntled publican sat in the audience heckling the comedians. Occasionally he would yell, "Where's that Jew, Breslin!" Dinos was so traumatized by the experience that he sat in the back seat of the car on the way out of town chanting, "Fuck off, Dunnsville."

The comics also brushed with death. On a later trip, Shuster almost drove their car off a twenty-foot cliff. The comedians had to creep out of the automobile on one side, so as not to tip the car over.

It is amazing that more comedians don't die on the road. They log as many hours as truckers in vehicles that are often far inferior. Stand-up Mike Gottli hit a moose in Northern Ontario and fell into a coma.

Now, hitting a moose has a comic ring to it, but it is in fact an extremely dangerous accident. Moose weigh as much as small cars and tend to kick their legs as they fly over the hood of a car. They can actually rip the top of a car right off. Gottli spent a year in a coma and gradually began to regain his ability to function. His memory is gone. Gottli has sent letters to his friends that read, "I'm told I know you."

It can, believe it or not, be worse. A few road warriors have perished. Monty Cohen, a young comedian, was killed roller-blading in Grand Prairie, Alberta. He'd gone out after his gig to get some exercise and clear his head. He was struck by a pick-up truck and died instantly. "It was a horrible place for him to die," said a friend and fellow comic, Craig Campbell. "He hated those shows. He hated baseball-cap-and-beer crowds."

But perhaps more dangerous than the physical threat that the road presents are the psychological perils. The road is lonely, boring, and usually unrewarding. There is no place for creativity. It's just, do your routine and get out. This bleak and aimless lifestyle can take its toll.

In March 1987, Doupe, then twenty-six, and his friend, fellow stand-up Colin Campbell, were in Montreal, three-quarters of the way through a North American tour. Thus far it had been a bizarre and taxing trip. Doupe had been chronicling it in short notes that recorded sundry road adventures. One entry read:

> Unbelievable collection. Guy chugs antifreeze to impress girl . . . Speeding ticket, allegedly doing 80 in 55 mph zone. What a cop scam. Pay $20 fine to cop directly.

The jaunt, which the British Columbia pair dubbed the "Lobster to Salmon Tour," had begun in Vancouver and thus far taken them through the United States and to the Maritimes. If all went as planned, they would tour across Canada and finish in late May back on the West Coast. Doupe and Campbell would do seventy shows in seventy-four days. They would travel 16,640 kilometres by car and another 5,900 kilometres by train, bus, and plane. The tour would pay each comedian about seven thousand dollars.

Doupe's March 30 entry was more than the usual daily rehash of road life:

> Open at The Comedy Nest, Steve Brinder says, "You're great but keep away from the bars." Says club owner Ernie, "Want a drink?" After a lot of pressure from Ernie, Colin falls off the wagon on 29th. Train to Ottawa, Colin drinks whole way.

The next two months of Doupe's diary are littered with similar observations:

> Soon as we get into town, Colin takes off . . .
> Ottawa. Colin is hammered. Howie sees Thursday show. Says, "You can say you saw him when he was alive"
> Colin seems all right . . .
> Colin nowhere to be found . . .
> Branigan's. Richmond Hill. Worst show I've seen Colin do. He hassles with a guy, makes friends, pukes on bar, pukes on car, pukes and moves all over the Brownstone. Keep him moving so he doesn't choke. I brace myself for his imminent death.

Death: it's odd how that word is constantly linked to comedy, how often it comes up in conversation. Death, depression, addiction are as much a part of the business as the punchlines. Mention comedy at a cocktail party and you're bound to find the conversation steering towards the legendary anguish beneath the laughs. The comedians themselves deny that they're any more troubled than the average citizen. "We just make our living turning troubles into comedy," is their refrain.

Comedy is an all-or-nothing proposition that offers those who do it well the rush that comes from turning a room full of strangers into a room full of admirers. Those who don't do it well experience unparalleled humiliation. The worst quit, the agony of failing at comedy having become unbearable. Their pain ends. Those who are merely average suffer the most. They exist in a comedic limbo. Occasionally they kill, but the next night they may run up against dead air. In their minds they are close to bursting through, just a couple of breaks away from the top. There haven't been studies done, but it's a good guess that contrary to what the comedians believe, there is a disproportionately high number of depressed, hurting people working in comedy.

The comedy business is full of tales about those who couldn't leave the game but no longer had the strength to play it. Mickey Rush, for example, was a middle comic for Yuk Yuk's in the early nineties. At best, he was average. Unfortunately for him, however, all he wanted in life was to be a stand-up. All he wanted was to be a headliner. He never made it. At age twenty-five, after a break-up with his girlfriend, Rush jumped to his death from his ninth-storey balcony. He did not leave a note.

Brett Weir was a good writer. He was not a good stand-up. Weir was well liked by his peers and had a reputation as a gentle, friendly guy. As a performer, he didn't have the goods. Weir spent ten years working as an opening act. His career went nowhere. In 1995, Weir also committed suicide.

Comedians deal with the Mickeys and Bretts of the world in the only way they know how. Privately it may trouble them but publicly they use it to get laughs. Gallows humour. Boyd Banks dealt with Rush's death by singing the pop song, "Oh, Mickey." After Ron Vaudry had learned that the roller-blading Monte Cohen had been killed by a hit and run driver he quipped, "When is a headliner going to die so I can take their material?" Breslin suggested that he issue a "Yuk Yuk's dead comedians Franklin Mint commemorative plate series."

Comedians like Mickey Rush and Brett Weir are both sad cases. They entered comedy looking for salvation and instead found despair. Their contemporaries could always find solace in the fact that "they weren't any good." When it comes to Colin Campbell, however, there is no such refuge. Colin Campbell was not only good, he was great. In the early eighties he had been the most promising comedian on the west coast. Canadian comedy icon Don Harron had called Campbell "one of the brightest comics to ever come from this country." In his time, Campbell performed on every Canadian comedy show and most of the

American ones. He was the winner of countless comedy competitions. He was one of the best.

"All the comics would gather by the side of the club when he was doing his set," says Doupe, "just to see what he was going to do. He was amazing. He was the way all comics are supposed to be, except we've all grown too lazy."

Colin Campbell was born in Calgary on January 28, 1958, the only son of Vera DeBalinhard and Alex Campbell. Colin's father died when he was three. The only memory he had of his dad was a picture of Alex Campbell standing before a car, holding a bottle of beer. Like Mark Breslin, Colin had been a late baby, his mother forty-three when he was born. She credited him for keeping her young at heart. Vera Campbell eventually remarried. Colin Campbell never embraced the new man in her life. He never called him Dad, just Howard. Campbell did not have a cushy upbringing. His family had moved to the down-trodden neighbourhood of West Vancouver when he was one year old. Growing up, Campbell was privy to, in the words of Doupe, "a lot of weirdness. Guys would come to the school yard and give the kids a quarter each to spit on them — that is, the guys would pay the kids twenty-five cents each for *them* to spit on the *guys*." Such episodes left a mark on Campbell, filling him with a seething cynicism.

Campbell was a natural jock and was named athlete of the year at his high school. Basketball was his favoured pastime, and his skill at the game won Campbell an athletic scholarship to the University of British Columbia. Around the same time, Campbell was diagnosed with a serious form of degenerative arthritis of the spine. He failed the physical for his scholarship and lost it. Campbell did not have the financial means to attend university without it, so after graduation he took a variety of jobs including bike courier, waiter, and airport security guard and, says Doupe, "spent a lot of time drinking."

In 1979, when he was twenty-one, Campbell tried his luck on amateur night at Punchlines, the first stand-up club to open on the west coast. Rich Elwood started it in 1979 and stayed in business until 1995. Punchlines was in direct competition with Yuk Yuk's during the early eighties, but Elwood was not expansion-oriented like Breslin and did not challenge Yuk Yuk's domination of the national scene. Every comic to come from west of Winnipeg got his or her start at Punchlines. It was a club held in great affection by the stand-up community.

Amateur nights were in their infancy when Campbell did his first. Crowds weren't yet jaded by stand-up, and the young comic got three or four laughs. Still, Colin felt bad about his performance until a few audience members told him, "You were pretty funny." Campbell came back two weeks later for another shot, and after that he was hooked. He went on to make twenty-five dollars a show. This apprenticeship was followed by years of road work. Harry Doupe met Campbell in 1982. Harry was trying his first amateur night and was impressed by the veteran's skill. They began to do tours of the West Coast. The two struck up a friendship that would last the rest of Campbell's life, but the relationship was conducted on Colin's terms.

When he was twenty-four, Campbell's mother died on Christmas Day. Doupe was unaware of her death until Colin did a bit on it in his act. "There wasn't a lot of give to him," says Doupe. "I didn't even know if he liked me until 1985."

Campbell had already been stuck with the nickname that would survive him: "The Chief." He'd earned the label for two reasons: he was the pre-eminent comic on the West Coast, and in the comedians' typically politically incorrect terminology, "he drank like an Indian."

No matter how much alcohol Colin consumed, he scrupulously rose every morning and wrote jokes. He had closets of notebooks crammed with grade A material. In the early stages of his career these books were neatly printed. By the end he wrote in a muddled shorthand that only close friends could decipher. Some notes were merely columns of words, as many as one hundred and fifty per page, each one signifying a joke. Campbell composed sheets of spontaneous banter for any calamity that could occur in a comedy club. For example, the code "broken glass, joke fails, WH" indicated what to do if during a show a glass breaks, killing the joke, and then there is an insult from a woman heckler.

Campbell's skill was legendary. He is responsible for many of what are now classic lines of stand-up. Campbell, for example, is the comedian who wrote the opening line, "Hi, my name is Colin Campbell and

I'm an alcoholic. Oops, sorry, wrong meeting." His jokes were lean and punchy. There was no excess fat or superfluous patter. They were 100 per cent laughs. Onstage he had a distant, almost disinterested presence. He had a tight-lipped delivery and used static rhythms to clip his jokes. Campbell gave the impression that comedy came so effortlessly to him that he was almost watching his own act:

> I'm originally from Vancouver but I consider Toronto my second home, 'cause my dad comes and beats me here, too. I had a real strict dad. He used to say, "I raised that boy and I never hit him once in anger." Which is true — he enjoyed every minute of it. My mother's weapon of choice was the kitchen spoon. It really didn't hurt much. I cleaned up my act, though, when she got a food processor. I'm actually trying to quit drinking myself. Another fifty-one-and-a-half weeks and it'll be a year. I never make it home. That's my problem. You ever have that happen? You wake up in a neighbour's satellite dish and you've got nothing on but a pair of flippers and a chef's hat.

"Even when he was bad with the drinking," says Doupe, "he'd get up in the morning and go over to his note pad and work things out. I saw him onstage in Ottawa once and he was so drunk he could barely stand, and he still did nine new bits. I couldn't believe he could remember anything, let alone work new material." Says Joel Axler, who ran Yuk Yuk's' Vancouver club during Campbell's era. "You could put a bullet in Colin's head and he could still ace his set."

It wasn't until 1987 that Campbell's drinking began to noticeably destroy his life. By any normal standards he would have long been considered an alcoholic. By comedy's standards, however, he was just normal. Drinking is as much a part of comedy as running is a part of the Olympics. Booze is ever present. If you don't drink, you're considered a freak.

Put it this way. Imagine that the first thing you heard when you showed up for work at nine in the morning was, "Do you want a drink?"

When you looked up from your desk you saw a fully stocked bar. Then, when you finished your assignment, you were offered another drink. Then your co-workers came over and brought you more drinks, to celebrate your successful work. Now imagine that you're on the road and don't know anybody and are staying in a rotten hotel room. You have no reason to go home, no home to go home to. If they're not drunks when they go into the business, many comedians become drunks after a few years.

When drinking, Colin was prone to violence and blacked out almost automatically. When he was sober, he was quiet and shy. By 1987, Campbell was missing gigs and getting beaten up. In Vancouver, the police beat him one time after he had been disorderly in public. "Luckily," recalls Doupe, "we knew the police pretty well because they used to hang out at the club. They took him out and roughed him up a bit. Banged up his ribs. He had to have a reminder that he had done something bad, but they didn't want to take him in and charge him." Campbell blew countless opportunities for success. Don Harron wanted to hire him as a writer. All Campbell had to do was show up for the interview. He got drunk instead. Once when Campbell was opening for country singer Reba McIntyre, all he had to do was ace one more show and he'd get signed to a six-week tour. He got drunk instead. "He had a fear of success," says Doupe. "I don't know if he felt unworthy or just scared. There was almost no opportunity he didn't screw up."

Campbell made attempts to quit drinking. He and Doupe once made a thousand dollar bet to see who could go on the wagon the longest. Both fell off on the same day but in different cities. Campbell sank to his lowest after his lapse in Montreal in 1987. He was drinking from the moment he woke to the minute he passed out. He became more and more violent. In Toronto, Campbell tried to throw Doupe off a twentieth-storey balcony. Then he threw him through a glass coffee table. In Edmonton, at dawn after a night out, Campbell smashed Doupe in the face with his elbow. That was it. "At that point it was, 'Okay, fine, let's go outside,'" says Harry. "He was way drunk. We had a big fight. It lasted five minutes. He'd run at me and I'd hit him a few times and he'd fall down. I took some photographs of him. I knew he wouldn't remember. I wanted to show him what he was like, otherwise he'd shrug it off. The next morning he got up and said, 'Who did this to me?' I said, 'I did.' He said, 'Well, I guess I must have had it coming.'" That day he checked into rehab. After a stint in detox, he seemed hopeful. Campbell had decided to marry his girlfriend, Deb, and settle down. But when he got back to Vancouver, Deb told him she didn't want to see him. He went back on the bottle. He would binge and sleep under highway overpasses. When Campbell was determined to sleep outdoors, Doupe would occasionally lend him a bright orange blanket, and then go out looking for it. Doupe isn't sure himself why he stuck with Campbell. The best reason he can conjure is, "He was my friend."

Colin Campbell made many attempts at sobriety. Joel Axler recalls one occasion vividly. "I remember I played tennis with him and he looked great. Of course, he kicked my ass. Afterwards, we sat on a bench and it was this beautiful West Coast day, and I said to him, 'This is so great. You look great. You're healthy. You're working out and swimming. I can start booking you again. Things can work out.'

"Right then a little bird — a chickadee bird or something, the kind that picks at ice cream cones that get dropped on the pavement — landed at the foot of the bench by Colin's feet. Colin looks at me and he says, 'Joel, I hate life.' Then he makes a big hork and he spits right in the bird's face, right between its eyes. And he turns to me and says, 'You know what I mean? I hate life. This is as good as it gets and I hate it.'"

Campbell eventually became unbookable. He and Doupe lost contact. Harry says he was resigned to the fact that Campbell was not going to live much longer. Then Campbell married Beverly Brendan. She had met Colin at Punchlines back in 1979 and had been "impressed from the start." Campbell had taxied her home across the Granville Street Bridge on his ten-speed bicycle one night after her car had been towed. Doupe's first thought when he heard that Campbell had wed was that he had gotten married so that he'd have a family to bury him.

By the early fall of 1991, Colin and Beverly had settled in Qualicum Beach on Vancouver Island. Doupe says Campbell was still drinking and had been arrested a few times for stealing liquor. He faced two charges for theft and a charge for failing to appear in court. A jail term seemed inevitable. On the ferry ride back from a hearing at Vancouver Provincial Court, he got a bottle and told his wife he could not stand going to prison. Campbell's arthritis was also worsening, and he began taking more and more medication to fight the pain. On September 21, he had a mental collapse, Doupe says. Campbell had taken too many painkillers and was having paranoid delusions. He thought the army had surrounded his house and were coming to seize him. Beverly tried to stay up and comfort him but finally fell asleep from exhaustion. When she woke up, he was gone.

"There was no organized search to speak of," says Beverly Campbell. "We were strangers in a small town, since we had just moved there a few weeks earlier, so it was kind of difficult to rally support. The local RCMP seemed to believe that he'd hitched a ride with a trucker and was long gone. The day that Colin went missing, I asked the local radio stations to make hourly announcements that there was a man missing, disoriented due to medication, and for people to look in their backyards and around their neighbourhoods. I put up 'missing' posters with Colin's picture on them in gas stations along the Island Highway. I went back to Vancouver and called hospitals, police stations, old friends of Colin's, and detox centres in hopes that someone knew his whereabouts. For months, I couldn't drive the Island Highway without checking the sides of the road for a piece of his clothing or something. Mostly, I just waited in Qualicum at the place from which he'd gone missing."

Campbell remained "missing" for more than three months. Then, on January 1, 1992, a discovery was made. "A local coroner says it will take about a week to identify a body found near Qualicum beach," read a small article in the Nanaimo *Daily Free Press*. "The remains of the body were discovered Wednesday in some bush near the Island Highway. Parksville RCMP believe the person died three to five months ago."

It was Colin Campbell, or what was left of him. He had been decomposing for over three months and had been picked pretty clean by rodents and small animals. So far as the coroner could tell, he had wandered off, perhaps looking for the highway. Doupe says Campbell either had a heart attack or simply laid down to sleep and died of hypothermia. There was no foul play suspected. Few were shocked to hear he'd passed away. "I was not surprised when I got the call," says Axler. A number of memorials were held, one at the University of Victoria and one at Punchlines. Comedians performed in Campbell's honour and money was raised and given to charities such as Big Brothers.

According to Anne May Sirois, rodents were not the only creatures picking over Campbell's bones. Not long after his death there was a "feeding frenzy on Colin's material. Everybody started stealing it," she says. To this day, many claim that there are one-nighter comics on the West Coast living off Campbell's work.

His style lived after him. Campbell established observational humour in Canada. "He was better than Leno," Axler claims. "He was that good."

Harry Doupe says, "He had the most tragic life of anyone I've ever known. But I think the demons that made him drink are the same ones that made him funny." Beverly Campbell doesn't agree. "Performing was one way that Colin dealt with his problems, but I don't think it's accurate to say that demons were what made him successful. Colin had more than his share of burdens, but he was also gifted. I wouldn't call his life a total tragedy."

So why do comedians submit themselves to the hardship? You will never get a comedian to answer that question. Stand-ups don't know why they're in the business. They'll tell you it beats work, or that they wanted to be Johnny Carson as a kid. Or that it's fun to make people laugh, or they'll tell you they don't know. Most will say the big attraction is the buzz they get from drawing laughs from a crowd. David Merry says it is as good or better than breaking the house in Vegas.

"You can never underestimate the rush from getting on a roll," maintains Larry Horowitz. "When you get on a roll, the high is better than a lot of other things, like drugs and alcohol, that people forsake everything for. It's indescribable."

Stand-ups want laughs, but they are also searching for something deeper, something they didn't get growing up. Laughter is a tangible sign of approval. It is affection you can measure with a sound system. To some comics it represents vindication. It is proof that those who wronged them in the past — ex-lovers, parents, employers, friends — were wrong.

"When I was a kid I hated being laughed at,' Canadian stand-up Chris Finn told me in the spring of 1996. He later went to Los Angeles and became a writer for the television show *MAD TV*. "If something embarrassing happened to me and people laughed at me, I went nuts. I figured if I could control it, I could beat it. It's a control thing. To this day if somebody laughs at me at a time when I don't want them to, it drives me nuts. I need the control. That's why really, really tough guys don't make good comics. They can fight with their fists. I don't know any comics who are real thugs. They get back with their jokes. Justice. Kicking some sand back in faces. There are very few comics who were captain of the football team and dated the head cheerleader."

To others, like Colin Campbell, the rush represents redemption. During their brief time onstage their self-loathing is eased. They can kid themselves into thinking that they are worthwhile people. The laughter is proof that they are loved. After all, two hundred strangers can't be wrong, and they have no reason to lie, no motive for faking the laughter. The minute it stops, however, the comics are back down to zero and feeling worse.

Stand-up is one of the loneliest professions in the world. There's a cliché about public speaking: If you want to relax, just imagine that all the people you're talking to are naked. Stand-up is the opposite. Imagine that you are naked standing before a room of strangers and all the people you're talking to are using binoculars. Stand-up comedians expose themselves to an audience like no other performer does, with the exception of strippers. The stand-up is the writer, the director, and the performer. If you fail, don't blame anyone but yourself. And if you suffer, take a look in the mirror. Stand-ups are all volunteers. No one, as so many veterans will tell you, makes you become a comedian. No one is forcing you up there. You're up there because you need the laughs more than you fear the silence and the hecklers. Mark Breslin says stand-ups are the crack addicts of the show business world. An actor will wait until the play is over to get applause; a singer will wait until the end of a song. A stand-up needs laughs with the same frequency as an addict needs hits off a crack pipe: every twenty seconds.

The road multiplies the obstacles between the comic and his high.

To enjoy its ups and downs you must have a gunslinger mentality. You blow into town, check into your room, shower, eat, and do your set. If all goes well, you kill and everybody loves you. People are buying you drinks and everybody wants to be your friend. There is also a rush that comes from doing something that terrifies most civilians. The road warrior takes on the elements. He braves the climate and handles the unpredictable. Road work is a comic's initiation into the brotherhood. You pass that test and you earn respect among your peers. A comic without road experience is like a soldier who had never seen combat. When a comedian has done enough road gigs, the club engagements look easy. He can no longer be intimidated. He has voluntarily placed himself in strange and volatile situations and fought his way out of them. It's an extremely macho mind-set.

The road did not kill Colin Campbell. He had problems that would have plagued him no matter where he was. But would his demons have burned so hot if, instead of life as a road warrior, he had chosen a career as a security guard? Campbell knew he had the talent to rise from road-gig hell, but he lacked the strength. When you're on the road you have no nine-to-five. You carry your talent and you carry the psychological needs that drive you to use it, twenty-four hours a day. Comedy isn't a job, it's a way of life. You can't put it on and take it off like a piece of clothing. For Campbell, the road became an unendurable nightmare that he could only end with a bottle. As Harry Russell said, nobody leaves comedy. A stand-up is a stand-up, even in death.

When they found him, Campbell's body was so badly decomposed that the coroner thought the only way to get a positive identification was through dental records. This was unnecessary. Anyone who knew Colin Campbell would have had little difficulty identifying him. The troubled comedian, who had once told a reporter, "You'd be surprised at what you can get people to laugh at," was wearing a Yuk Yuk's sweatshirt when he died.

SEVEN

∎

Just For Laughs

If they don't die, or quit, they march on. Mediocre stand-ups reach their plateau and stagnate there. The gifted keep rising up the ranks. Eventually, even the best hit a roadblock. It's at this point that comedians realize they have gone as far as they can go in Canada. They have no bigger future, except the slight possibility of work at the CBC. The comedian faces a life of road gigs and the occasional headline club work.

The scarcity of comedy-career opportunities was not much of a problem back in 1975. Stand-up comedy was considered a hobby, not a profession. Being a comedian was so undesirable that those who aspired to it risked losing parental approbation, societal acceptance, and, of course, any hope of a middle-class existence. Comedy wasn't something you chose to do if you had any sense. Like alcoholism or sexual perversion, it was something you were compelled to do. This had been true throughout North America until the mid-seventies. In Canada, this mind-set held for another decade. Some might argue it still holds true today.

"Steve Martin and I were talking not too long ago," Lorne Michaels told me in June of 1996, "and we were reflecting on the money that's come. It's funny, because if you told us back then [the seventies] that we'd never make more than fifty thousand dollars a year doing what we were doing, we would have been happy to keep doing it. The money that came later was unfathomable. Today a junior writer on my staff makes a minimum one hundred grand a year."

Americans have always believed in the possibility of striking it rich, and it was therefore only a matter of time before the guerrilla comics, like those who pioneered *Saturday Night Live* (*SNL*), realized they could make the same kind of money that Sid Caesar had. Up north, it took a while to understand that American riches were available to Canadians, too. There had been the Dumbells, Alan Young, and Wayne and Shuster, among others, followed by Rich Little, David Steinberg, Dan Aykroyd and the whole *SCTV* gang, then Mike Myers, whose popularity on *SNL* and in the *Wayne's World* pictures hit new heights for a Canadian kid in the American comedy sweepstakes — until Jim Carrey came along and eclipsed all who had gone before him. Carrey became not only the biggest comedian in America, he became the highest paid and arguably the biggest star in America. He got right up there with Elvis.

At the time of Carrey's ascension in 1994, I was writing for *eye WEEKLY* and immediately noticed the impact of Carrey's fame. Stand-up became a gold rush. It became the Canadian version of the black American take on super-success through basketball (as chronicled in the documentary *Hoop Dreams*). There was a flood of young, mostly male, stand-ups swarming the stage. Unlike their predecessors, they were all armed with the knowledge that it could be done, the "it" being monumental success in America. These comics had grown up in the seventies and eighties watching *SNL* and *SCTV*. To them, comedy was a ticket to fame. It was a pass into a world of riches, cars, unfamiliar Californian sunshine, unlimited access to super models, and public adoration. Screw hockey. In 1995, Jim Carrey got twenty million Yankee dollars for making one picture, *Cable Guy*. It took at least a couple of years for Wayne Gretzky to make that playing hockey. Who could afford to wait? Comedy was the fast track for enterprising Canadian boys and girls with attitude and talent. All you needed was the right set of breaks and good management.

The old-school comedians were ill-equipped for the business end of comedy. To Gary David and the Starvin' Marvin's burlesque comics, comedy money meant $250 a week for eighteen shows. The gang at Yuk Yuk's in 1976 thought taking money for comedy was just a dream. The new breed obsessed over fiscal rewards. Neophyte comedians often carried business plans. These young hustlers spent more time discussing immigration law and the advantages of American super-agencies over Canadian managers than they did on jokes and comedy.

Hopeful Canuck kids weren't the only segment of the market to dream of cashing in. The American industry began to realize that there was a glut of talent up north, and all a sharp producer or development executive needed to do was pull the right fish out of the water. This epiphany predated Carrey's success. Hollywood has had a long history of Canadian cherry picking. Since the days of the silent movie, Canadians have found a place in Los Angeles. Hollywood, however, has always waited for Canadians to come to it. A Canadian had to leave Toronto, St. John's, or Moose Jaw. The big change, by the early nineties, was that Hollywood was making the trip north to scout talent. They were not making it often. In fact, they made it only once a year. That trip was to Montreal, for the Just For Laughs Festival, known in French as Juste Pour Rire.

The Just For Laughs Festival had grown alongside the Canadian stand-up game. It was born in 1985, out of the ashes of a failed French rock-and-roll festival. Its promoter, Gilbert Rozon, had raised some government money to throw together a summer music fest. It was a categorical flop. One observer told the organizers, "You have the worst festival in the world." The only aspect that worked was the comedy portion of the festivities. So, they kicked out the music and kept the comedy.

The engine that drove this new comedy convergence was Andy Nulman, a short, tenacious Montrealer who had spent time working as a journalist and as Howie Mandel's road manager in the early eighties. Working with Mandel had taught Nulman the importance of business in the comedy world. "Howie was the consummate businessman," Nulman recalls. "He would go onstage, kill, and then as soon as he got

offstage he would say, 'How many T-shirts did we sell?'" Nulman was
the right sort of man to get a festival on its feet. A master diplomat,
Nulman can work a room with the same aplomb as a seasoned politician. He is fluently bilingual and at ease working in the French community. He's a workaholic who can juggle a dozen problems at once.
Perhaps most importantly, Nulman understands Montreal. He knows
what the city wants and has learned over the years how to deliver it.

In 1986, he organized Just For Laughs and was paid a total of nine
thousand dollars. It was a small affair. Nulman's motto was, "Let's listen to everyone but not *everyone*." Over the next two years it began to
grow. Nulman brought up relatively unknown American comics such as
Jerry Seinfeld and Jay Leno. He also showcased Canadians like Norm
MacDonald, future star of *SNL*. In 1987, the American industry awak-
ened to Montreal's possibilities. The *Hollywood Reporter* published a
special issue profiling the festival and painting it as a hotbed of comedy talent. They portrayed it as the equivalent of one-stop shopping for
agents and development executives. American television picked up the
story. Bud Friedman, owner of the Improv comedy chain, came up.
Robert Morton, producer of *Late Night with David Letterman,* came up
along with Stu Smiley, president of HBO. The Canadian federal government helped out by providing a grant that paid the expenses of
American producers who flew up to the festival. It is particularly ironic
that one of the few times the Canadian government has funded comedy,
it was to help bring Americans up to Canada — especially since the
express purpose of these Americans was to take the best back down south
with them. The following year, Americans came in droves, and they've
been coming up ever since.

Of course, the Americans aren't drawn solely by the idea of Canadian
talent. The Just For Laughs Festival features plenty of American comedy
— a majority, in fact. It also showcases acts from Australia, Britain, and
the rest of the world. Hollywood comes to Montreal for two reasons —
one mercenary and one political. On the mercenary side are the patented
Hollywood motivators fear and greed. The executives are afraid to miss
out on a talent and greedy to cash in on the next big thing. Says Nulman,
"If you miss it, you get shit and then get fired."

Politically, it's a chance for the industry to take its own temperature. Agents, development people, producers, talent, and the media all mass together to talk shop. So, in a way, the festival serves the same purpose for the American comedy business as a convention does for a political party. It rejuvenates the foot-soldiers and fills the generals with grand ideas. The balloons and confetti are provided in the form of the city of Montreal. As one American executive puts it, "I get thirty cents on the dollar, the beer is good, and the women are unbelievable."

The notion that Montreal is a hotbed of female beauty is prevalent among the Americans. I often find them slack-jawed as they sip coffee in a café or walk down the street. "What is it with this city?" one American stand-up once asked me as we strolled down Ste. Catherines Street. "Every fucking woman you see is drop dead gorgeous. I can't take it." This fixation is accompanied by the stereotypical belief that all French women are sexually adventurous. Given that this group hails from Los Angeles, a city known for its beautiful people and libidinous character, I've always found this lust for Montreal women a telling comment on the appeal of Just For Laughs.

In July of 1996, I was gearing up for my fourth Just For Laughs Festival. I'd seen it before in every way imaginable. My first year, I'd driven up with a carload of comedians and slept on a hotel floor. It proved a tumultuous journey. The comics, who were all scheduled to appear on a taping of the American television show *Comedy on the Road,* drank excessively. Tempers rose and the evening ended in conflict. Mark Farrell, a young guy from Halifax, began to goad his friend Chris Finn. Farrell had been part of the comics' rebellion of 1990 and had left Yuk Yuk's to join the independent circuit. When sober, he claimed to have little animosity left for the chain. When drunk, his bitterness spewed forth.

"That's okay," Farrell, slurred in his inebriation, "if you want to suck Breslin's cock, go ahead. Just admit you suck his shaft down to the balls for the money. I'll be happy with that. Admit it: say, 'I suck Breslin's cock!'" The two comics came to the brink of a fistfight. Then tempers cooled suddenly and the two men retired for the evening still the best of friends. I, however, was badly shaken by this vicious display.

To calm my agitated state, Finn emerged from the bathroom, in his underwear, and extended his hand. Between his thumb and forefinger he held a pill (which turned out to be a vitamin) the size of a cashew nut. "Take this," he suggested. "You'll feel better." I declined the offer.

By the time I attended my fourth festival in 1996, I had the routine down. Maybe because I had some experience under my belt, it proved to be the most enlightening festival I'd attended. I saw things about the comedy business and the people who drive it (the Americans) that I had never seen before.

All the hurly-burly was fixed firmly in one spot — the Delta Hotel. The talent was housed there. The media tables and hospitality tables were there. All festival seminars were held there, and most importantly, the Delta bar was there. I hit the Delta at around seven in the evening. Its foyer is bright, with plenty of yellows and golds. There is a grandiose atmosphere; the decor is regal. The hotel was already buzzing. I made my way up to the media table and picked up my badge. Badges are key at the festival. They are colour coded, laminated cards — red for media, green for talent, and a shiny metallic colour for super-talent. Festival goers wear these badges like dog tags. They hang obtrusively around their necks, allowing others to instantly identify them and their status. Just For Laughs industry types make no effort to play down this comedy class system. It is perfectly acceptable to pick up a person's badge, read it, and decide not to talk to him or her. My badge, obtained in the course of doing research for this book, was a source of bewilderment for many. It read, "Andrew Clark, Doubleday Canada." Conversations often went like this:

"What's Doubleday, a production house?"

"No, it's a publisher, like Doubleday in the States."

"What are you doing?"

"I'm writing a book on Canadian comedy."

"Why? Can't you write a book on American comedy?"

Of course, the responses I got from Americans were worse.

Armed with my badge, which gave me access to all festival club shows, I headed to the Delta bar to gauge the temperature. There was a smattering of players inside doing some preliminary networking. It was

Wednesday and not quite peak time for the festival. The locusts wouldn't descend until Thursday and Friday. By then, a seat in the Delta bar would be as hard to come by as a guest spot on the *Tonight Show*. Having surveyed the battlefield, I opted to take an early shuttle over to Club Soda to catch an 8 P.M. Canadian show entitled "Comedy Night in Canada."

Club Soda is a music venue that goes comedy during the festival. It is a perfect room for stand-up — square and not too deep — so the comic energy bounces off the walls and back into the crowd. During the festival it is consistently sold out. "Comedy Night in Canada" was no exception. The club was flush with native Montrealers, many of whom had come to see Mike MacDonald, who was hosting the show. MacDonald, a favourite at the festival, holds the record for consecutive festival appearances. He had been in every one.

The American industry insiders are not hard to spot. In fact, they're about as difficult to spy in a Montreal crowd as Little Richard would be at a Klu Klux Klan meeting. There is no mistaking them for talent. For starters, the industry people are in much better shape. They have tans, while most comics emit a fluorescent hue. The most pronounced clue that you're gazing at an agent or development executive is the "look." They dress casually, but you can tell that somewhere in some magazine is a picture of the original ensemble.

So you get your middle-aged man with a baseball cap, ironic T-shirt ("France"), highlights in the hair, brown eyes, once-handsome face, semi-stubble, conservative running shoes, six-thousand-dollar watch, drinking a light beer. You get your twenty-eight-year-old development executive with her *Friends* haircut, thin lips, skin that gets a lot of attention, close-fitting summer dress that coincidentally holds tight to her small bosom while going loose over her slightly (despite the roller-blading) wider hips, with black boots and black socks, eyeing the crowd like it was an Olestra buffet. You get the executive type in a suit but no tie, with his closely trimmed grey beard and blue eyes, who has been to the Far East, has an M.A. in English, and once planned to become an art critic but now sees TV comedy as the modern equivalent of Aristophanes. You will notice his blue eyes again later in the evening intensely focused on a much younger woman with whom he is trying to deal in private while she wants to deal in public. And you get your young agent in the olive-drab suit, goatee, tan, martini in hand, destined to be a success, or die trying.

All of them, at the Just For Laughs Festival of 1996, were smoking cigars. Tobacco and red meat were the latest craze to hit Hollywood, and they brought it north. They were excited about cigars, talked about cigars as if they'd smoked them all their lives, and spent lots of money on them. I mention the cigar mania because it illustrates the herd mentality of the American industry. Comedy agents and executives are people who believe that life can be separated into two categories: good things and bad things. The media and the town (Hollywood) determine which is which. They were excited by cigars, and I overheard many heated discussions about how these rolled tobacco leaves had changed people's lives. Newspapers, television, and magazines said cigars were good. Arnold Schwarzenegger and Sylvester Stallone smoked cigars. So cigars were hip in 1996. Hollywood people love to get worked up and enthusiastic. If they indulge in something it must be *the big thing*. They convince themselves they have found the answer to life. And yet, these powerful players are plagued by self-doubt. Inside every head there is a tiny voice whispering, "You're wrong." Hollywood, American stand-up Andy Kindler later observed, is the only place where people get a second opinion for everything, where everything is up for negotiation. It's crazy, he said. "You didn't see Einstein saying, 'I've come up with the formula $E = MC^2$ but we can change that, if you think we should.'"

Hollywood applies the same premise to comedy talent. Once the players decide, by osmosis, what's hot, they pursue it madly. At the festival this manifests itself in the quest for the two or three promising properties who emerge in the club shows and late-night showcases. A couple of lucky comics get "heat," and they become unstoppable.

At the "Comedy Night in Canada" show, Mike MacDonald played up the industry presence. "Here's some new meat," he told the crowd, "for the Americans to take home. Let's send some more beef south!" He would bring on comedians with introductions like, "I see our next performer as a kind of wacky-next-door-neighbour type." Later, MacDonald diverted into some set material. He mused on death preferences. "You want the shark to bite your head off, not start at your feet and work his way up. If I have to die, I want it to be quick and painless."

I'm sure many of the comedians were feeling the same way about the show that Wednesday night. If they had to die, at least let it be quick. Ironically, "Comedy Night in Canada" had not even finished before the festival claimed its first casualty. Three-quarters of the way through, Steve Levine told me that an American named Brian Regan had made an historic bomb at the St. Denis Theatre, a cross-town venue where a gala show was running concurrently. Gala shows at Just For Laughs are large-scale, star-studded TV tapings. They are the marquee gigs of the festival. Only the best acts get on.

"I've never seen anybody bomb worse," Levine said, with a glow of sheer delight on his face. "He came out and he didn't get what he wanted. So he told the audience, 'Let's try this again,' and he came out again. He did that four times. Each time he was worse. He walked off to silence. He may have set his career back four years." Regan's bomb was so severe that it became the talk of the festival. He was a good comic — a favourite of many industry types — who had never died like that before, not even close. His failure was the ultimate choke: he had gone onstage a virtual sure thing and departed a failure. Comedians and agents alike relished it. Revelled in it. They bathed in it and nourished themselves on it. It was so catastrophic that the Montreal *Gazette* did an entire eight hundred word feature on it two days later.

This meant that at least no one at "Comedy Night in Canada" would be shamed. The casualty list already had its first name. Not that there was too much to worry about. The talent that Wednesday night was solid. On the bill were Derek Edwards, a top comic from Timmins; Russell Peters, an East Indian comic from Toronto; Corky and the Juice Pigs, a sketch troupe that had its own series in Britain but had been ignored by the CBC; and Mike Wilmot, who did blue humour. Wilmot's signature bit was his riff on male Truth or Dare. "The conversation always ends up with, 'What would you do for a million dollars? Would you suck a cock for a million dollars?' Everyone says no. For a million dollars? Are you kidding? For a million dollars I'd not only suck a cock, I'd wear a T-shirt with a picture of me doing it. Per dick? Line 'em up. I'd play them like a trained seal . . . Only show me the money first. I don't want to fall for that one again."

When the room emptied at the end of the night, there was no clear winner. A young comedian from Toronto named Lynn Shawcroft had turned a few heads. Shawcroft was twenty-eight and had a slacker look, cute but not gorgeous, and a perfect sense of timing. Her jokes were delivered with a laconic swing that made them seem unrehearsed. Shawcroft had a tendency towards self-deprecation. Her most notable bit was a riff on a fantasy sitcom starring herself. "I call it 'Boozy.' I play a bar fly by day, and by night. And in it I go to the bar and drink until I black out, and when I black out I travel back in time. Like, I could go to the Civil War and be bandaging troops and just hankering for a whisky sour. At the end of every episode I vow never to drink again." Shawcroft was fresh and new and marketable. She created a spark. The development executives from ABC had heard about Shawcroft prior to the festival and had come with an eye out for her. Shawcroft's manager, Louise Parent, was also on hand to stoke the fires. She got hard at work shaking hands and talking Shawcroft up. I began to realize that most of what mattered in the festival, as far as career building was concerned, happened offstage. Managers and comics spun tales that network executives were supposed to eat up.

"It's like winning the lottery," Nulman would later tell me. "You know your chances are slim to none, but you're still willing to try. It's climate-controlled comedy. The Club Soda audiences are the best in the world. A good comedian can turbo to the next level. It's a high-speed proposition if they play their cards right. At the same time, the development people have to come back with something. They're here spending money and time. A lot of stand-ups come out of it with dipshit development deals. You tell a Canadian you're going to get seventy-five grand in American dollars to sign and they think they've struck it rich. Not much is going to happen except that the development executive gets to keep his office. It is truly perverse."

This rags-to-riches mentality fuels the Canadians at Just For Laughs. It doesn't happen often, but when it does the sound is heard around the comedy community. These meteoric rises quickly gain a place in the mythology of the festival. Back in August of 1995, a Toronto-bred university student named Michael George was as hot as you got.

Mike George is handsome, boyish, and very personable. His story is of the "Once upon a time . . ." variety. One day Mike George decided he wanted to have a go at stand-up, so he went down to The Comedy Nest in Montreal and did an amateur night. He did okay and he kept going back. He found he loved stand-up and wanted to make it his career. Then George decided to try for a place in the 1995 Just For Laughs Festival's "Montreal Show," a Club Soda presentation that feature's the city's best comics. The "Montreal Show" is often one of the festival's hottest gigs, partly because the talent is comfortable and on its home turf. George methodically set about crafting a solid five minutes of material. He worked it and worked it and worked it. Finally, one day, after much pain and suffering, *it* worked. George had his golden five minutes, and his five got him a spot. That, so far as George was concerned, was enough. He had accomplished his goal. So on opening night, George, a fresh-faced kid with eight months' experience and absolutely nothing to lose, went out and took his shot.

George is the sort of comedian who drives other comedians insane. Mention his name to Ron Vaudry and you'll get, "Is he still shit?" Some veterans hate George because he landed in a matter of minutes what they still haven't obtained after decades of trying.

The industry was floored. George super-killed. That night his manager, Willie Mercer, got a call from ABC executives. They told him, "We're flying out, but we must meet Mike George. Is he free for a meeting at two?" Two o'clock in the morning, that is. Then NBC called, then FOX, then CBS, then HBO, Disney, Paramount, then a fistful of others. Without even trying, George had created heat. Everywhere he went throughout the rest of the festival, George was met with grins and handshakes. His head spun. Offers were made, but Mercer decided to let things get even hotter before signing anything.

A month after his killing set at Club Soda, George and Mercer flew to Los Angeles to do meetings and create a career. It was D-Day. From the moment his feet touched the ground, Mike George was hit with waves of adulation. Everybody loved him. He did seven meetings a day. As Mike tells it, "I'd do one at 9, at 9:45, 10, 11, noon, I'd have one at lunch, then meet a lawyer and at night we'd go to meetings over dinner and then parties. It got to the point where, honest to God, I'd walk in and forget why I was there. People would say, 'I've never seen you, but I hear you do great in meetings.'"

Mike George had, in his own words, become "flavour of the month." Mercer kept a close rein on his hot commodity. For instance, Willie decided not to have George perform any sets at comedy clubs while in Los Angeles. "If you have enough heat for your client, you can get the deal," he says. "Going onstage isn't going to help you. It can only hurt you. Even if you have a great set, hey, they were already willing to make the deal."

George eventually decided to sign a holding deal with NBC and move to Los Angeles. The deal meant that he agreed to work exclusively on NBC shows. If NBC didn't use him, he could do no other television, although he could still do feature film work.

There are many different kinds of deals. There are development deals, in which a network or studio agrees to build a show around the talent, and there are step deals. Holding deals usually have step deals inside them. These deals agree to give money in stages — for example, $15,000 for a script and $10,000 for presentation (in which the show is pitched to executives). George's deal was worth $80,000 (U.S.) Along with his deal he had four managers, six agents at the UTA agency, two lawyers, and an accountant.

"They give me a cheque for twenty grand and they say, 'Go buy a car and rent an apartment and furnish it,'" Mike recalls. "In college I was a bum. I was the guy you had to run down to get me to pay the phone bill. It was so fast I felt like I was being thrown into a fire. It was so hard to accept what had happened. I mean, Disney? NBC? How far away are those deals? Venus!"

George's rocket ride is in the back of every comedian's mind at Just For Laughs. This goes for American as well as Canadian acts. The difference is that for the Americans, the festival is one of many shots. If things don't pan out, they go back to Los Angeles or Atlanta and wait for another chance, which will come in another few months. If things don't pan out for the Canadians, it will be a minimum of three years before they get another festival shot, if they get one at all. If they still want to go south, they'll have to do it illegally or amass enough money to live in Los Angeles until they can get an agent. For the Canadians, the Just For Laughs Festival is their one chance to shine.

The second day at the 1996 festival began at the Delta at three in the afternoon with a tribute to Bill Hicks. Hicks, who died in 1994 of pancreatic cancer, was without question the most important comedian to come out of America in the eighties, and no one in America has ever heard of him. Americans don't know who he was because Hicks said things that made America uncomfortable. His material was political, religious and, like the title of his 1992 album, relentless. Hicks used comedy to expose the hypocrisy of American society and make unpalatable truths digestible. His take on the Gulf War was, "Let's call a massacre a massacre." He suggested that Americans avenge the Iraqi assassination attempt on then president George Bush by assassinating Bush themselves. "That way," Hicks explained, "there would be no loss of innocent life."

The tribute was chaired by John Lahr, an author who was a regular contributor to *The New Yorker*. He had written an article defending Hicks after David Letterman's people had cut him from Letterman's show for doing a joke about Christ. Hicks had pondered the reason Christians wear crucifixes. ("Nice sentiment, but do you think when Jesus comes back, he's really going to want to look at crosses? Ow! Maybe that's why he hasn't shown up yet.") Lahr said that Hicks had failed to reach Americans because the American axiom is optimism. Hicks had been successful in Britain. Lahr maintained that he was embraced there because Hicks traded on irony, and the British axiom is irony. It was a somewhat simplistic premise but it sounded right.

It got me thinking about the Canadian axiom. I remembered the Dumbells, Canadian comedians who had used comedy to cope with the ugliness of World War I, and they made me wonder if the Canadian axiom is fatalism. There is an inevitability about our place in the world that leaves us powerless on some fronts.

They say geography is destiny. No matter what we do, we will always have to deal with the consequences of living in the shadow of a colossus. We will always struggle for survival in a vast and largely uninhabitable land. And we have been left to sort out the volatile legacy of eighteenth-century Franco-British colonialism on a continent that Europe abandoned centuries ago. What can we do but laugh? Laughter helps us fend off the cold, fight off the Americans, and excuse the increasing irrelevancy of the two solitudes. We know that there are some things you just have to accept and that it's much easier to do so with a grin.

I gazed out around the Thursday afternoon Just For Laughs audience. The Bill Hicks tribute had drawn a full house. The crowd sat stone-faced, serious. They loved Hicks, many of them stood up and told us after Lahr's presentation was finished, but you couldn't work with Bill. He wouldn't do the same jokes twice. He wouldn't bend. The big issue, if you went by their observations, was what a shame it was that Hicks never had a sitcom or made lots of money. Bill Hicks hadn't capitalized on his talent. Sure, he'd written some incredible material, but he hadn't cashed in. That was sad. That was a downright tragedy.

Finally, a man rose up at the back and told us, "I knew Bill Hicks, and I think what many people are missing was the fact that Bill wanted success, he would have liked to have been rich, but he wasn't willing to compromise to get there. That's all. He measured himself on a different scale." This was Andy Kindler.

Kindler was a renegade from Los Angeles. He'd grown up in Queen's, New York, and drifted into comedy after failing as a musician. He was a short, forty-year-old bespectacled guy, who you would never notice in a crowd. He appeared meek but his comedy was volatile. Kindler was a renegade because he routinely attacked the industry. The previous year he had given an afternoon session called "The Hack's Seminar." It was a thrashing of the low standards Hollywood kept and the shoddy, often racist work the comedians put forth. It was a hit. An hour or two after the Hicks tribute, Kindler presented his "State of the Industry" address. The entire industry turned up. It was standing room only. They were there to hear Kindler unleash a diatribe, and he did not disappoint. Kindler lashed out at Hollywood for using the term *urban* to describe African American shows. "That is the most racist statement going. That's like me having a show and calling it 'Jewy.'"

Kindler named names. He called HBO evil. He offered "ONE MILLION, I repeat, ONE MILLION dollars to anyone who can provide me with footage of Whoopie Goldberg actually being funny." He fantasized about locking Robin Williams in a room without any props. Kindler said that Jay Leno, host of the *Tonight Show,* had "won the *Guinness Book of World Records* title for going the longest amount of time without having an authentic moment."

I was struck by two points. The industry, just as it had dismissed Hicks, appeared to dismiss Kindler. They loved him and they loved his sharp attacks, but they all agreed that the American public would never get it. There was no money there. I was also hit by how utterly un-Canadian Kindler's comedy was. Here was a person standing, holding his ground, and publicly attacking the powerful, and he was doing it as himself. He wasn't appearing as a character or a comedic creation. He did not need to adopt the mask of a rural hayseed in order to call attention to wrongs. Here was Andy Kindler, as Andy Kindler, railing against the establishment. Not only that, he was attacking the very people who would, a week later and for the rest of his life, decide his future. A satiric mask can be just as funny, but there is something exhilarating about watching a comedian cast fear aside and speak his or her mind directly. The optimistic notion that a single voice can be heard is appealing. Then, as quickly as the session began, it was over. We'd had conscience for a few hours. Now it was back to consumption.

Later Thursday evening, most of the development people went to The Comedy Nest, Montreal's full-time comedy club, to see the "New Faces" shows. These gigs were favoured by industry types because they promised virgin goods. The comedians were chosen by the festival's Canadian talent co-ordinator Willie Mercer and Just For Laughs English festival producer Bruce Hills. These two travelled the globe going to comedy clubs and by the end of the spring had a list of unknown comedians for the "New Faces" shows. Virgin did not mean young. Many of the new faces were in their thirties. The standout of the evening was again Lynn Shawcroft. The heat kept intensifying. She was beginning to look like this year's Mike George.

Friday offered more shows and galas, but these gigs were becoming less and less consequential. The industry was beginning to thin the herd. The time for grazing had passed. All agents and development executives who were in a buying mindset had their short lists, and now, like high-tech missiles seeking the heat, their sights were set. The last public opportunity for schmoozing would be the Comedy Central Breakfast.

The breakfast is a staple of the festival. It starts at midnight on Friday and goes well into Saturday. The network puts on an enormous buffet of free food and booze in a vast ballroom at the Delta. The industry descends and indulges. The buffet, laid out on a huge circle of tables, offered every sort of cuisine. There were Chinese noodles and stir fry, egg rolls and fortune cookies, fajitas, croissants, scrambled eggs, fruit, cold cuts, pastries, bagels, smoked salmon on rye with capers, chocolate truffles, and custards. Opposite this cornucopia of food were two batteries of bars that provided strong drinks. Those in attendance devoured the food as they circled the room, metaphorically feeding off each other.

A pair of younger types, a man and a woman, approached me. They were both white, blond, clean-cut and trendy. The man shook my hand eagerly and said, "Hi, how are you?"

I replied, "Fine."

"Are you still with Warners?"

"No, I —"

"You're still in Los Angeles, though."

"No."

"Well, where do we know you from? Did we meet in New York?"

"No, we've never met. I'm Canadian. I'm not in the business. I'm a writer. I'm here researching a book."

"On comedy?"

"Yes. Canadian comedy."

"Oh."

"What do you two do?"

The woman piped up, "We're development executives at Twentieth Century Fox."

"So you're here scouting talent?"

"Yes."

"That must be very interesting. Do you see anything you like?"

With this, they shot each other a glance then flashed a pair of blushed grins. "Oh," the woman said sweetly, "we just say, 'We like the script but it needs work.' That's all we do. If we do it before everyone else, then we're doing our job."

"Really," I said. "Do you —"

The woman beamed at me. I thought she was going to kiss me. Then she said, "Well, see ya." I never got their names.

The party went on. More and more people arrived. The din of the politicking was a mixture of loud laughs and sibilant whispers. Unlike at the afternoon seminars there were plenty of hangers-on present. There was eye candy — female and male — to divert comics and suits alike. The lower-rank Canadians talked among themselves. They stood, bemused, just happy to be getting free food and drink. I ran into Jay Sankey, a stand-up from Toronto who was doing the "New Faces" show. He looked lost. He waved to me and called over the noise, "What would Fellini make of all this?" The party went until dawn, at least that was what I was told. I left at 3:30 A.M. Before I absconded, I met Louise Parent. Was it true, I asked her, that Lynn Shawcroft was getting a lot of advances from the industry? She grinned. "We're doing meetings all night," she replied. "I'll tell you tomorrow."

As I left the hotel, I recalled a conversation I'd had that afternoon with Andy Nulman. I was to meet him in the Delta's lobby. As I waited, Montreal stand-up Barry Julian sat behind a grand piano, which was located in one of the hotel's hallways. He began to play *The Battle Hymn of the Republic*. It was the song American Civil War General William Tecumseh Sherman's troops had sung as they made their infamous march from Atlanta to the sea, during which they raped, looted, and pillaged the South. Julian, who, besides being a comedian is a jazz drummer, placidly indulged his musical talents. I asked him, "Are you trying to make a point with this song?"

He just smiled and told me, "I can't believe anybody recognized it."

Nulman appeared a few minutes later. He gave me his impression of the proceedings. "Every day is unique. Every day is a year and every year something happens." The festival's success has spawned a host of imitators. There is now an Aspen comedy festival, and one in New York City.

"I hate all competition," he admitted. "If it exists, I'm happy it's people like the ones who run Aspen. But people told me, 'Hollywood won't come to Montreal, now that they can go to Aspen.' Okay, I don't care. The industry is a very small slice of the pie. Don't come. Boycott. The Just For Laughs Festival is a public event. We exist because Montrealers go to our shows, not because a TV network or Time Warner throws money left and right. And besides, if you don't go, your competition will and you'll miss out. So far there's been no drop in interest or attendance at the Canadian event. The talent Hollywood finds here is just too strong a draw."

I also thought about something Jay Sankey said that afternoon. Sankey, who at age thirty-three had been performing for seven years in Canada, was sombre. He claimed not to care about the Americans. "I'm not too thrilled about being here on earth, so I do fantasy that's comedy. The money is the last thing involved in what I'm doing. It's the first thing they're thinking." He figured that because of his style he was pretty much out of the running. Sankey paused a moment and lowered his gaze to the table. He swirled his drink and then turned to me and said, "You know, tomorrow they'll pull up the stakes, the tent will be gone, and we'll all be back at the bar gigs."

All except for Shawcroft. Shortly after the festival she signed a development deal with ABC, who told her to go take acting lessons and gave her $75,000 (U.S.). She got half up front, and by the time the government had taken its share and her manager and agent had each taken their 10 per cent, she would have very little left over. But in the spring of 1997, Shawcroft flew to Los Angeles to take part in a bizarre migration as mystifying as anything salmon do. Shawcroft headed south for "pilot season."

EIGHT

■

The Season of the Snowback

A Canadian newcomer to Los Angeles must overcome the belief that his or her visit to California is going to end in a flurry of machine gun bullets. That is the first hurdle. For years we have been brain-washed by television reports of chronic, senseless violence. The L.A. riots did nothing to dispel the notion that Los Angeles is one step removed from hell. As Roseanne put it, "If Los Angeles doesn't fall into the ocean, God owes Sodom and Gomorrah one hell of an apology." Circumstances are not improved by the fact that Los Angeles *is* a dangerous place, though not the iniquitous zoo conjured up in Canadian fantasy. It is a city that demands that those who wish to survive there use their heads. Ironically, keeping your head in L.A. is just about the hardest thing you can do.

First, you must make it from the airport. In March of 1996, I found myself driving through Inglewood, a tawdry Los Angeles slum, trying to find the 405, the megalopolis's biggest highway. After a five-hour flight from Toronto, I'd rented my car from Alamo, and now I was worrying that maybe "Alamo" wasn't the best choice for a Los Angeles visit. It was around nine in the evening and I had an hour's drive to the Sunset Strip where my hotel, the Hyatt, was located. The Hyatt sat right next to the legendary comedy club, The Comedy Store. During the seventies and eighties The Comedy Store had showcased such future stars as Richard Pryor and Garry Shandling. The Hyatt, where many visiting comedians stayed, had become known as "the Riot" because of the wild parties that occurred there. It had the added distinction of being the only hotel in Los Angeles from which a comedian had jumped to his death. Steve Lubetkin was a disgruntled stand-up who leapt off the roof of the Hyatt in an attempt to hit The Comedy Store, to protest what he felt was unfair treatment. The Comedy Store's management wasn't giving the comedian enough sets. As a public statement, it was a pretty spectacular move. As a career builder, it seemed counterproductive.

I was in Los Angeles for pilot season, a four-month stretch between January and early April, when Hollywood studios and networks create pilot episodes. Pilots are test episodes, examples of how a show would appear were it to in fact become a television series. Pilots have writers, sets, actors, directors, producers — everything real shows have. Like any other season, pilot season has its own distinctive character. In autumn geese fly south, and shortly before pilot season literally hundreds, maybe thousands, of Canadian stand-ups and sketch comics hop on planes and depart for L.A. It's an annual gold rush with producers, agents, and talent alike scrambling for that nugget. Even a small find can translate into a small fortune, such as one hundred thousand American dollars. The goal, for a comedian, is to find work on, or sell an idea for, a television series pilot. My aim that March was to observe Canadian comics in migration as they sought shelter in the warmth and money of America.

Hollywood exerts as much effort in getting a show on the air as keeping it there, maybe more. Pilot creation is a complex science. The process is often far more interesting than the product that results. To start, the stakes are high. The average cost of a pilot varies from five hundred thousand dollars to over a million. Once all the pilots are finished production, television executives view them and decide which ones deserve to "go to series." Going to series means that the show has been picked up by the network and guaranteed a minimum number of episodes, usually thirteen.

Between two and three hundred pilots are produced each year, and of those about twenty are deemed worthy of picking up. Those that get picked up can make the people who write and star in them rich. The wealth is not instant. The real money doesn't flow until the sitcom goes into syndication. Even the most successful sitcom loses money — on average it's losing a million dollars an episode. That means that during its height of popularity, a sitcom could be suffering a substantial loss. When it goes into reruns it becomes worth tens, even hundreds, of millions of dollars.

The success of television shows inspired by stand-up comedy, like *Seinfeld* and *Roseanne,* has made pilot season an important period for comedians. This has not always been the case. Although television has often used stand-ups for variety programs, they weren't always the prime choice for situation comedies. *The Dick Van Dyke Show* and *Sergeant Bilko* were the exceptions. The big sitcoms of the seventies and early eighties generally featured actors, not comics. This changed in the mid-eighties with Bill Cosby's success in situation comedy, but not because the "suits" decided to tap into the comedy market. Until that point many producers were quite happy to let their writers sit at the back of comedy clubs and pilfer material from the stand-ups, changing it enough so that they couldn't be caught. "They used to twist it, turn it, and burn it," says one source. The leap to stand-up as a sitcom vehicle was caused primarily by the bust of the live stand-up circuit. During the height of the boom, which ran from the late seventies until around 1986, a top comic could easily earn $7,000 (U.S.) a week. Life was good. There was no motivation, or precedent, for staying in Los Angeles.

Howard Lapides is an American manager who represents Canadian comics Mike MacDonald and Pat Bullard. Lapides is intimately familiar with both the American and the Canadian comedy business. He ran a Yuk Yuk's in Buffalo during the early eighties and watched the development of Canadian stand-ups who went on to earn a place in Los Angeles. Lapides is a large man with a large appetite, for both comedy and deal making. He is devoid of pretense. "When the boom burst, all these comedians came off amateur nights. Instead of using better comics the clubs figured they could use these amateurs and book them cheaper regionally," he says. "The quality went down. Clubs started to close like crazy. It even affected the better crowd. Most stand-ups got into sitcoms because the money in live stand-up dried up."

At the same time, producers began to realize that by building shows around stand-ups, they could cut out many steps, like thinking of a concept. The comic was the concept. Executives could pick the stand-up they felt would click with viewers and get writers, who were often other stand-ups, to write for that comic's voice. You find a top comedian like Jerry Seinfeld, for instance, and you make him the show. *Seinfeld* becomes an extrapolation of Jerry Seinfeld's stage act. The success is built in, because if you can get what Jerry Seinfeld does onstage onto television, you know it is going to work. If you surround him with top actors and get writers who can write episodes that resonate his act, you've got a hit. Now, this is a terrific oversimplification of the process, but that logic is what spawned the trend towards building shows around comics. It's simple.

There was and remains only one problem: who is the next Jerry Seinfeld? Every comedian who goes to Los Angeles for pilot season has the answer to that question: "Me." Some come to Los Angeles with their immigration papers in order and obtain a green card. Getting the right to work in America requires lawyers, money, and newspaper clippings that state the comedian possesses a "unique talent" not found in the United States. Canadian green-card holders generally have an American manager, like Lapides, or an American agency, like William Morris, behind them. There is, of course, an easier way to get one: convince a major movie studio or television network it needs you. Then you get your green card pronto. That, of course, is the catch-22. You can't get the card without the work, and you can't get the work without the card. It can take years to win these prizes. Many Canadian comics never do. The law, however, does not have to stand in the path of an ambitious comedian.

Two days after arriving in Hollywood, I found myself sitting on the roof of the Hyatt with "Steve" (not his real name), a stand-up who had taken the alternate route down to California. Steve was one of America's millions of illegal immigrants. But he was not your stereotypical illegal, who scratches a paltry living picking oranges in the San Fernando Valley. Steve was a Montreal-born Canadian who made good money doing stand-up. It's been over thirty years since Frank Peppiatt went south to America, but Steve and those like him are still referred to as "snowbacks."

Steve had an edge over the average snowback. For starters, he was signed with a respected agency. He could audition as much as he liked, that was legal. He only got into difficulty if he took money for work. Having an agency behind you is essential for any comedian who wants a chance in Hollywood. Agencies like United Talent Agency (UTA), William Morris, and Creative Artists Agency (CAA) wield tremendous power over who gets what part. Probably the most important advantage they bring their clients is early access to "breakdowns." Breakdowns are lists that specify what roles are up for grabs. They are the studios' wish lists. Agencies get the breakdowns early, before they are even posted. This means their clients are up for roles that the rest of Hollywood doesn't even know exist. In fact, by the time most breakdowns are released publicly, many of the roles are already cast. Not having an agency behind you is like constantly arriving at dinner parties to discover that you've missed the main course.

Steve was bitter about the charade he was forced to play. He was angry that a Canadian comedian who wanted to work in America had to go under the table, while the Canadian government allowed Americans to work in Canada at a whim. Thanks to the Free Trade Agreement, an American comedian can pay a nominal seventy-five dollar fee and work anywhere he likes. This disparity drove Steve crazy. "It's nuts. Not only can I not work down here, but they can come up and take work away from me." Americans have a different take. They say Canadians come down to Los Angeles and take jobs away from Americans. Even bitter Steve, after a couple of months in Los Angeles, quickly found work as an opening act on road gigs for American headliners (for which he is paid in cash). He had a tan, sunglasses, a decent apartment, and a $150-a-week rental car.

The most frightening part of his illegal journey had been getting through customs. Steve was careful and played all the standard tricks —

he mailed his résumés and photos across the border, got a tourist-style ticket — and then spent a tense half-hour waiting for his turn to walk across the customs line at a Canadian airport. The entire time he worried that he would hear the words "Somebody call immigration."

Steve was philosophical about his chances of survival. He was going on a steady round of auditions, and, if he were ever to land a part, hoped to get the studio to do his immigration paper work. Steve's strategy was to get the role first, then break out the "I'm not really sort-of supposed to work here legally" speech. So far, he'd been up for a few big roles, and for half of one glorious day thought he'd landed a starring role in a feature film. It had been so close that his agent vowed he had never seen closer, but Steve had lost out in the last minute. He was also, he said, getting worried about being caught. Like a soldier who was nearing his discharge, Steve was afraid of "catching one" just before he shipped home. He felt that his luck was running out. Still Steve swore that any trip back home to Canada would be temporary. He was not going to give up on Hollywood. He'd spend the summer in Toronto or Montreal and then be back in Los Angeles for another tour of duty. And why not? Steve liked L.A. Sure, life was tense, he said, but it beat the hell out of Canada. "Nobody forces you to be a comic," he said. "Canada isn't a very big country. You have to leave if you want a life. I'm tired of hearing comics who whine about not being taken care of. Some would do better here, and others would die. That's the way it should be." When I asked him if there were any differences between the Yanks and the Canucks, he said, "Yeah, we're not fucking rude."

The stakes might be high and the rewards so large they're almost inconceivable, but for most Canadian comedians it is not greed but desperation that drives them to Los Angeles for pilot season. In the spring of 1996 there was an enormous Canuck migration. An entire generation of comedians had come of age and cut their teeth in cities like Toronto, Montreal, and Vancouver, and then embarked on a mass exodus. The Canadian comedy community had lost all confidence in its own television industry. The CBC was rightly viewed as a closed shop. Canada's public broadcaster had produced no new comedy series since 1993. They had done a few one-hour specials and nothing more. To make matters worse, if you weren't a political comedian, the CBC had no place for you. Yes, the CBC had produced the apolitical sketch troupe, the Kids in the Hall, but many comics believed that the only reason the CBC had kept the Kids on the air was that the troupe's American backers, Broadway Video and Comedy Central, had forced them. Comedians saw the CBC as a clique for political punsters. The CBC's executives only understood comedy as it related to the news. If the show did not use the headlines to turn out laughs, there was no "distinctive Canadian" ingredient they could use to justify funding it. The network's top comedy shows were two topical revue shows: *The Royal Canadian Air Farce* and *This Hour Has 22 Minutes*. Shortly after pilot season in 1996 ended, the CBC unveiled plans for a new series, *The Newsroom*. It is a situation comedy, shot in a documentary style that is totally derivative of the American hit *The Larry Sanders Show*. It is a decent series, but the only thing Canadian about it is its Canadian showbiz references and occasional mild digs at the CBC. Which of course suits the CBC just fine. The comedians' disenchantment was captured by Dan Redican, who had been a member of the Frantics, a sketch comedy troupe that had run on both CBC Radio and Television. Redican had spent years trying to work in Canada and, he believed, had been abused and lied to by the CBC. At a benefit concert, shortly before flying to Los Angeles to work in American television, Redican had sung a song lambasting the network. It ended with the words "Fuck off, you bastards." His audience, which consisted mostly of comedians, burst into applause. Private broadcasters like the Baton Broadcasting Corporation were worse. They did so little they were not even worth resenting. Comparing the comedy output of Canada's private broadcasters to the CBC was like comparing the morgue to the intensive care ward. The vital signs in either location were not encouraging.

As the CBC continued to do less and less, what little reason there had been to stay in Canada completely disappeared. There were so many Canadians in L.A. for the 1996 pilot season that it was proclaimed a "second wave," the first wave being the early-eighties migration of the *SCTV* cast. There were Canadian parties, chance Canadian meetings, Canadians everywhere. Paul Greenberg, a member of the sketch troupe the Vacant Lot, said he met more Canadians in Los Angeles than he did in Toronto. The one sentiment all the Canucks shared was a feeling that they had been run out of their own country. The Canadian comics I spoke with sounded like immigrants who had left a dead and corrupt Third World state.

Mike Elliot had done stand-up for eight years in Canada and then moved to Los Angeles in 1990. He works doing stand-up and supplements his income by writing film reviews for the Hollywood *Reporter*. He is a short man, with short dark hair and a fast clip to his voice. Elliot told me, "There's this idea that as Canadians we're putting on our happy little shows back home. All of a sudden an American guy says, 'Come do your shows here,' and the Canadian says, 'Oh, okay, I'll leave home and see what it's like.' No, that's not it. Everyone from Lorne Michaels on down came to the States because they couldn't get the time of day in Canada and they are bitter. We are very angry and very bitter."

Steve confirmed the sentiment. "You have to come down here. It's unavoidable. What was I supposed to do? Sit around on my ass and wait for the fucking CBC to give me something?" The CBC was the whipping boy for every Canadian I met in Los Angeles. The CBC was, in fact, a four-letter word to most Canadians in Los Angeles. It was the bad relationship in all their pasts.

The Vacant Lot, whose members were, along with Greenberg, Rob Gfroerer, Nick McKinney, and Vito Viscomi, had been dubbed by many as the next big thing in Canadian sketch comedy. They had sharp writing skills, great collective timing, and an original take. In 1993, the CBC had signed them to a six-episode deal in conjunction with *SNL* creator Lorne Michaels' production company Broadway Video, and with Comedy Central in the States. The CBC ran the shows and then left the Vacant Lot dangling, just as it had done with others, from Peppiatt and Aylesworth to Wayne and Shuster. What irked Greenberg and Gfroerer was not the fact that the CBC had dropped them, but the way it had been done. "I would say it was prison bad," Paul Greenberg said, "that's how bad it was. They seriously left us hanging for six months. We lost all our momentum."

Pat Bullard is a Toronto-bred comedian who worked his way

through the Yuk Yuk's chain. He was a headliner and one of the original first string of stand-ups who came out of the early eighties. Bullard had done his time trying to get things happening at the CBC. It was a wash. A few shows, like *Downtown Saturday Night,* came and went. In 1988, after eight years as a stand-up in Canada (and one failed marriage), Bullard decided to go to America. He was ahead from the start, since he had the papers that allowed him to work legally. Still, this did not make the decision any easier. "That was the biggest move. I remember the months leading up to July, when I was due to leave. I recall praying to God for some reason, for some phone call, for somebody at the CBC to give me something, for someone to say, 'Don't go.' It's scary."

Bullard's angst didn't last long. "I was here two weeks and I was totally acclimatized. In two weeks, I had meetings with NBC, CBS, ABC, and all the industry players. They didn't want to take a chance of not knowing who I was. Canada? The CBC? I can't even get a fucking meeting. The CBC is not going to give me a fucking meeting because they've already got their guys. It's frightening to think how much untapped talent there is in Toronto that is not going to get used because those guys aren't motivated to find it."

After eight years slugging it out in Los Angeles, during which time he wrote for *Roseanne* and *Grace Under Fire,* Bullard had recently been awarded his own afternoon talk show. It was produced by Multimedia Inc., the syndicate that produces such shows as *The Jerry Springer Show*. Bullard's show would fill Donahue's time slot.

What's interesting is that, although Canadians who've left can relate to what those who remain suffer, they generally have little sympathy. Says Bullard, "No one is going to ride in on a charger and make you a star. If I hear one more time, 'If I was in New York or L.A. . . .' Then get your ass to New York! What good is it to sit up there and say, 'If only I was somewhere else.' You're in Canada and you're not making a living, then go to *New York* and don't make a living. What's the fucking difference?"

According to Jim Carrey, "Everybody who's not from L.A. has an inferiority complex. I got down here and I realized, Hey, shit, I'm just as good as these guys are. There's incredibly talented people down here, but I've got my own thing. I'm different. When you get down here you realize that there's a hell of a lot of incredibly talented comics in Toronto. I mean, an amazing amount of talent."

Californian Canadians kept telling me the thing they liked most about L.A. was the respect they got. I found this particularly puzzling since Hollywood is famous for being one of the most dehumanizing industries around. But time and again I kept hearing the same sort of thing. "You feel much more appreciated here," says Greenberg. "In Canada, they make you feel like they're doing you a favour by just seeing you."

Hollywood's respect is not without self-interest, of course. In fact, it is extremely pragmatic. The town's number-one sport is finding the next big thing, as is illustrated at the Just For Laughs Festival. Nobody knows who or what the next big thing is, but they all know they want it. They just don't know if you're it. You might be the next Jim Carrey. If they slight you now, you might knife them later. Most importantly, they might miss out on making money off you. At any rate, life is easier when everyone gets along, at least on the surface. That is why producers and casting agents say, as Greenberg puts it, "Thank you, that was great," after each audition.

Lapides offers a golden example of Hollywood's unpredictability. In 1985 he was running Yuk Yuk's in Buffalo. "There was a girl there who'd done a one-woman show and was a USC theatre grad. I let her do a set, and she had the goods but needed work. She was always hanging around the club and she was broke. So I let her run the box office. I said, 'You're here anyway, you may as well make some money.' That girl was Stephanie Miller." Miller later became a huge radio personality and briefly had her own late night TV talk show.

"Now, before her TV show is going to production, I get a call from a guy called Jim McCauly. He was the guy who, for the seventies, eighties, and nineties, told Johnny who to put on *The Tonight Show. He was the guy.* He was the gatekeeper. McCauly and I have been friends for years and since *The Tonight Show* finished, he's been bouncing around from one thing to another. He's been real sick and he's looking for work. He said to me, 'I understand you've got Stephanie Miller. I understand you're looking for a booker. Jeez, would you mind giving her a call and see what you can do for me?' I said absolutely, I hung up the phone and I started to dial Stephanie. And I had to hang up the phone. I had this flash: if, in 1985, somebody came up to me and tapped me on the shoulder and said, 'Ten years from now you're going to be calling your box office girl to get Jim McCauly a job as a booker on her show,' nobody would have believed it. Nobody. He didn't get the job. He was really concerned, and one of his big concerns was, 'Did Stephanie Miller know me? Did I ever turn her down?'

"Canadians think they get respect because they get treated like everyone else. In a way they're right. It may be self-interest disguised as respect, but they're getting treated equally." This code of conduct is a good example of what makes Hollywood click. There are plenty of nasty things that can be said about the system, but no one could ever accuse Hollywood of failing to produce product. The town pumps out reams of garbage, but it also produces the best comedy in the world. Critics often disparage Hollywood by holding up British comedy as the epitome of excellence. They cite the best Britain produces, like Rowan Atkinson's *Blackadder* series, conveniently forgetting all the tripe, such as the odious comedy of the hack stand up Bernard Manning. They also forget to mention that in Britain, television producers only have to create six episodes to get a series to air. In Hollywood, producers are looking at a minimum of twenty-six. Take the best six episodes of *Seinfeld, Roseanne* or *The Larry Sanders Show,* and they will not only equal anything the Brits produce, they will nine out of ten times surpass them. To meet these pressures Hollywood works hard.

Whatever their accomplishments in Canada, expatriates start at square one in Los Angeles. Most decide to play down their Canadian identity. A veteran stand-up told Elliot, "Don't tell them you're Canadian or they'll spend the first five minutes of your act staring at you like you're a freak in the zoo. They'll stare at you until they identify some characteristic that they think is Canadian." Elliot went so far as to construct a list of Canadianisms to delete from his vocabulary and replace with American versions. *Rubber bands, sorry,* and *about noon* became *elastics, sawry,* and *around noon.* He dropped the terms *running shoes, bloody caesar, rye, broadloom, washroom, chocolate bar, serviettes, brown bread,* and *homo milk,* and stopped referring to vinegar as a condiment.

Being unknown can have its benefits. Having no record means Hollywood has not stuck a label on you. You're new goods, but unlike American unknowns, who are generally new to the business, Canadians, as former road warriors, generally come to Los Angeles with more experience than any comic will ever need. This makes them potent threats — unknowns with experience. They are seasoned veterans with no Hollywood scars. It's like starting high school with a university education under your belt. This combination has the potential to generate heat.

Creating and maintaining heat is the key to survival. Mike George moved south a few months after his coup at the 1995 Just For Laughs Festival. He arrived in L.A. and got his apartment. He then dropped himself into the social scene, but Hollywood did not turn out to be the Babylon he'd been expecting. "This is the cleanest town I've ever seen. I mean, I totally drink, I'm Canadian. The parties here are no different than university parties. The only difference is that here there's all the free booze you want, but which nobody drinks, and all the free food you want, and it's in somebody's very nice house and there's all these twenty-five-year-olds talking about buying houses. I mean, everybody drinks Evian and gets to bed by nine."

After six months in Los Angeles things had gone well for George, but not well enough. He'd had seven auditions at NBC and come close to getting a role in a Tom Hanks movie. But after a good try it looked like NBC and Mike George did not have a love connection. We met for a beer at the House of Blues, a night club owned by Dan Aykroyd. George was up-beat, but I could tell he was smarting a bit from the ride he'd taken. It was March and he hadn't scored yet. Pilot season would end in May. George's holding deal would expire in June. After the heat and hype, the twenty-two-year-old kid would most likely return to Canada and begin touring northern Ontario. "That's the downside for the client and the manager," says Howard Lapides. "A year later it may not work. And let's face it, look at how many do work. If it doesn't work, you've got a client looking at you from the other side of the desk, saying, 'What now?'"

Lapides says it is a manager's responsibility to guide his client through the heat. To act as a sort of sun block to all the sycophancy. "If you were my client and there was going to be a lot of heat on you, I would explain to you who was going to say what . . . Then you'd say to me, 'Oh no, that's not going to happen.' Then all of a sudden they'd start saying it, and it would play itself out. But you'd know in advance who was coming, what they're coming with, and how they're going to come in. What you have to do is be true to yourself and your inner voice, the one that got you into the business in the first place. Make sure the things that happen around you are true to that inner voice . . . with obvious flexibility."

"Development deals are like putting a deposit on something you like at a store," claims Mike Elliot. "The networks don't want anybody to get you. They're basically saying, 'We're not sure you got it, but we're not sure that you don't got it, and we don't want other people to get it. So, with the holding deal we can keep you here, and if a year goes by and nothing turns out, you can go to someone else.'"

"When it happens, it's bizarre," George admitted. "Everyone wants a piece of you. But you're only flavour-of-the-month once. Now they all know me. So no matter how great I do, they know me. The big thing everyone wants to do out here is find the next *somebody*. Even though I haven't done anything, I've been found. To find me now isn't a discovery. Now I'm part of the game. At first, you get excited about every fucking little thing, like my deal with NBC. They tell you, *You're going to be a star. You're going to be huge.* There is a time and a place when I'll be a star, but you have to look at things from a business standpoint. Reality is different from what you see.

"Hollywood is a business. This is not a fucking dreamland where there's a wizard with a little wand, saying, 'You're a star! Run and frolic!' I'm a realist. I know it's a matter of, you've got this far, now what do you do to maintain it? You can't take anything personally here, because as much as it is personal — you know, 'I'm your buddy, I'll be on your side' — they're just in it for the money. *As they should be.* What? They're in it for the love? It's the money, and there's nothing wrong with that. What do you want them to do? Come over and make you dinner?" With these words George stopped himself and appeared to take stock of his situation. "I don't mean to sound like an asshole. I mean, did I ever get lucky. But man," he muttered, "this is my life's dream. It came true too quickly."

Not all Just For Laughs flavours-of-the-month ended up with a handful of promises. John Rogers, an American who claimed to be Canadian through the fifteen years he lived in Montreal, had also scored at the 1995 festival. Rogers had gone farther than George; he'd had a CBS pilot built around him. It had scored well with test audiences, but the network had passed on the final product. That meant he could forget doing any of his own series for at least three years. Rogers finally landed on his feet after the 1996 pilot season with a job writing for Bill Cosby's new sitcom.

Following my meeting with Mike George, I returned to the Hyatt and relaxed on the roof by the pool. Across the street was a giant billboard for Gucci sunglasses. The enormous spectacles were a cherry red with gold trim, set on a white background. The glasses seemed to be eyeing the street and following pedestrians as they moved down Sunset Boulevard. They reminded me of Dr. T. J. Eckleburg in *The Great Gatsby*. They were all-seeing, all-knowing, but completely cold and analytical. In L.A. if a "suit" could see all, he or she would become a star of the industry, a superagent like Michael Ovitz. They had to see everybody, no matter how big or small, if for no other reason than they could then summarily dismiss you. Los Angeles was as open to Canadians as it was to anyone, provided that they could make someone money. If not, they were out. That was the big difference between working in L.A. and working in Toronto. Comedians were treated with scorn or envy in Toronto. They were resented. The stars in Canada were not the comedians, they were the bureaucrats at the CBC and the producers who toiled for them. In America, talent ruled — although the Hollywood definition of *talent* was an ability to make Hollywood money. Bill Hicks had been the best there was and he had registered almost nothing inside the industry. Canadians, I thought, had no real trouble fitting in in Los Angeles. They had the talent, they spoke the same language, sounded more or less like Americans, had the same cultural references, ate the same food. It was an easy fit. As I stared across the street at the Gucci glasses, I found myself thinking of Mark Rowswell.

Mark is a blond, six-foot, blue-eyed man from Ottawa who wears glasses and has an intelligent, perceptive gaze. He has a knack for absorbing information and is highly adaptable. He had stumbled into a brief career in comedy in a country where it was not quite as easy to fit in. In fact, it was damn near impossible. Mark Rowswell had not gone west to Hollywood; he had gone east, to Beijing. In China he'd become a comic superstar.

Rowswell became a comic sensation on New Year's Eve in 1988. At the time, he was a twenty-three-year-old student of Chinese literature at Beijing University and had been enlisted to take part in a multicultural New Year's variety show. The performance was being held at a large theatre on campus, and the university's administrators wanted some of the school's foreign students to play roles in small comedy sketches. These sketches were performed in the *xiang sheng* (pronounced see-ang sheng) style, which translates roughly as "crosstalk." Crosstalk is a 150-year-old comic dialogue characterized by plenty of word play and punning. It has no real Western equivalent. The closest we come is Abbott and Costello's "Who's on First" comedy routine.

Rowswell, who had studied Mandarin at the University of Toronto before winning a scholarship to Beijing, was fluent in the language and was an ideal candidate for the performance. He was chosen to play the role of a workaholic named Dashan (meaning Big Mountain) who stays late at the factory every night and always misses dinner. His wife becomes fed up with him and locks him out. While he has been praised for being a "model worker," with awards in family planning and rat extermination, he can never get home on time. The bit was a generic piece of crosstalk. Rowswell's mastery of Mandarin won over his audience of five hundred students. His uncanny ability to mimic Chinese slang especially garnered an enthusiastic response.

The following day, as he made his way to class, Rowswell found himself swarmed by admirers. Cries of "Hey, Dashan" greeted him at every turn. Rowswell dismissed the attention, thinking it was only a bit of university fun. A friend clued Rowswell in a few days later.

Unbeknownst to the kid from Ottawa, Chinese Television had broadcast the show live to the entire country: 550 million Chinese had seen the program. Rowswell was an instant celebrity and was hit with a torrent of offers. Promoters wanted Dashan in sixty cities from Shanghai to Chengdu. Filled with youthful exuberance, Mark embarked on a comedy career. He performed for small gatherings and for stadium audiences of twenty thousand. Rowswell would pair up with local crosstalk performers in whatever city he was playing in. He earned around one thousand American dollars for every gig. Fan mail began to arrive. Mark Rowswell became so famous that admirers had only to write "Dashan, Canadian, Beijing" on an envelope and mail would reach him.

While performing in the northern port of Qing Dao, Rowswell joked with reporters that he was up there looking for a wife. The next week a woman showed up at his university residence armed with pictures of her daughter. More proposals arrived. "I'd get letters from girls who would make it very clear that they were young and female and would like to be friends. I'd get letters from parents that said, 'My daughter is a really good person, and why don't you be friends with her?' The euphemism is always 'friends.'"

In 1989, Rowswell took a step up. He met Jiang Kun, China's foremost *xiang sheng* practitioner. Jiang Kun liked Mark and saw in him the ability to become a master. He also saw the potential for a broadening of East–West relations. Rowswell, as Dashan, made crosstalk accessible to foreigners and the Chinese more accepting of the West. Jiang Kun had been following the young Canadian's career ever since his first TV appearance. The elder comedian was so certain of Rowswell's success that he told me, "Mark is going to become an emissary of crosstalk whether he knows it or not, because that is what he is destined to do."

Despite Kun's prediction, the Canadian continued his career in comedy but opted to keep his involvement on a semi-professional level. Rowswell never really wanted to be a comedian; he just loved comedy. He graduated from Beijing University in 1992 and went to work in the communications branch of the Canadian embassy in Beijing. Mark married a young woman named Gan Lin in 1993 and continued to perform as Dashan, hosting television shows and appearing at cultural benefits.

His life as a star in the biggest market in the world shifted gears in 1995, however, when he and his wife moved to Toronto where Rowswell now owns and runs a Sino-Canadian marketing company.

Rowswell's Dashan appealed to the Chinese because he symbolized what they believed was the Canadian approach to East–West relations. The American approach was imperialist, just as the British had been in the nineteenth century. Americans, in the Chinese mind, were money-mad capitalists intent on forcing China to westernize. Dashan was the opposite. Dashan loved China and spoke Chinese better than most of the natives. He embraced Chinese culture and immersed himself in all facets of China's history and literature. He had a simple, honest face that the Chinese could trust. That was a very important element. The Chinese chose to see Rowswell as a logical extension of Norman Bethune, the Canadian doctor who sacrificed his life for the Chinese people. Like Bethune, Rowswell embraced China. He was a friendly example to the Chinese that the West and the East could find middle ground.

Without realizing it, Mark Rowswell carried a Canadian comedic tradition to a whole new frontier. For decades, Canadian talent had achieved enormous success bridging the tiny cultural gap between British and American entertainment. Like some official good-humour emissary, we would continue our diplomatic forays into the U.S. Rowswell proved, however, that our talents weren't limited to one continent. His contribution to the business of comedy suggests something larger than the clichéd quiet-observer-from-north-of-the-border theory of why we as a country produce, per capita, such an overwhelming amount of talent. Perhaps being constantly reminded first by Britain and then by our neighbour to the south that we are not number one allows us to understand and appreciate the spectrum of diversity the globe offers. Being number one can create a dangerous myopia: it's not always easy to remember that you are not the world. If nothing else, Mark Rowswell proves that our talents are not based solely on, nor limited to, our proximity to American culture and our insights into its sitcoms. When one nation produces the biggest comedy stars in both America and China, you've got to begin to wonder whether maybe it's something in the water.

Mark Breslin, *centre,* the most controversial man in Canadian comedy. He has had critics, such as Steve Levine, *lower right,* and Boyd Banks, *upper right,* as well as fans, Ron Vaudry, *upper left,* Brian Ainsworth, and Anne May Sirois, *lower left,* "My whole life I've been falling apart, and the pieces burst into flames as they're hitting the ground. I see the comedian and comedy as a way of extinguishing those flames," says Breslin.

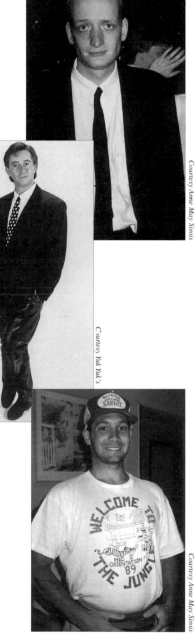

Just For Laughs Festival impresario, Andy Nulman, being "strangled" by Jerry Lewis. The comedy icon was angry that he had been filmed earlier that evening at a gala show. According to Nulman, Lewis was trying to harm him. Here, Nulman tries to hide his pain under an industry-friendly smile.

A master diplomat, Andy Nulman can work a room with the same aplomb as a seasoned politician. "Every day is a year," he says of the industry schmoozing that goes on at Just For Laughs, "and every year something happens."

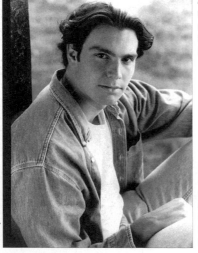

Mike George was hot at the 1995 Just For Laughs Festival. Networks were battling to get access to him. He was wooed to Los Angeles and signed by NBC to an $80,000 development deal. Six months later the deal ran out, and George was back in the comedy herd.

A seasoned road warrior, Wayne Flemming. Here, Flemming does his Jack Nicholson.

Lawrence Morgenstern, *left,* and Lou Dinos share a smoke break, and the bohemian advantages of the stand-up lifestyle.

From left to right: Mike MacDonald, Jim Carrey, Brian Ainsworth, Mark Breslin, Howard Glassman, Tim Conlon, and Larry Horowitz. Yuk Yuk's alumnae returned to toast the club and its founder.

Sandra Shamas. To her fans, she is a ferocious, funny, estrogen superhero.

Hart Pomerantz, *left,* and Lorne Michaels. The duo, known as Hart and Lorne, broke up in 1973. Michaels headed south to the States and created *Saturday Night Live.*

The Kids in the Hall. *From left to right:* Kevin McDonald, Scott Thompson, Mark McKinney, Dave Foley, and Bruce McCulloch. They emerged in the mid-eighties from Toronto's alternative comedy scene with a surreal, non-political style. The troupe went on to cult popularity in both Canada and the United States.

Courtesy the CBC

Courtesy Hart Pomerantz

Courtesy the CBC

Jim Carrey began his career at age fourteen. Carrey chose comedy to win acceptance. "I didn't have a friend in the world until about Grade Three," Carrey says. "I started to realize, hey, I can act goofy and people actually respond." He spent the early stages of his career as an impressionist.

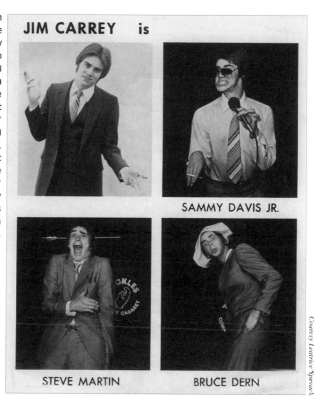

JIM CARREY is

SAMMY DAVIS JR.

STEVE MARTIN

BRUCE DERN

Scarborough, Ontario-raised Mike Myers had watched the first episode of Saturday Night Live at age eleven. In the eighties, after working at Second City in Toronto, Myers became a member of the SNL cast. One of his characters, Wayne Campbell, became the quirky hero of the blockbuster movie *Wayne's World*.

The Toronto Second City 1974 cast: Eugene Levy, Dan Aykroyd, Gilda Radner, Rosemary Radcliffe, and John Candy. Says Levy, "There were nights when we were brilliant and nights when we weren't. It was tremendous for establishing material."

"Bob and Doug were an insult to the CBC," says SCTV cast member Dave Thomas. "We said, 'What do you want us to do? Put up a big map of Canada . . . sit there in toques and parkas, and fry back bacon?' The CBC said, 'Yeah, that would be great.' Our producer said, 'If you could put a Mountie in there, that would be good.'"

The Toronto Second City alumnae return for a reunion. *From left to right:* Martin Short, John Candy, Rick Moranis, Dave Thomas, and Eugene Levy.

The cast of *This Hour Has 22 Minutes*: Mary Walsh, Rick Mercer, Cathy Jones, and Greg Thomey. The show mined the news to dig up laughs. "In my family, watching the news was a spectator sport," says Mercer. "You were free to make snide remarks."

The Newfoundland sensation CODCO: Mary Walsh, Andy Jones, Tommy Sexton, Greg Malone, and Cathy Jones. "CODCO was less a troupe than it was a lifestyle," remembers Mary Walsh. "CODCO appealed to the marginalized. We were Newfoundlanders in Canada and Canadians in North America.

Greg Malone (as Barbara Frum), and Tommy Sexton, from their 1987 special The S & M Comic Book. *The Jugular*, their satire of the CBC newscast, *The Journal,* became a staple of the CODCO television series.

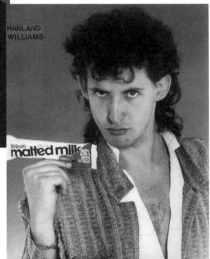

HARLAND
WILLIAMS

In 1996, Harland Williams was on the verge of meteoric success. He began his career in the mid-eighties doing surreal gags, such as his bit with bald puppet Luke Emia. In 1991, Williams had reluctantly cut his hair and cracked the Hollywood system.

NINE

■

The Best Stand-up, Live

Mike MacDonald and I met the day after I'd talked to Paul and Rob from the Vacant Lot. It was 10:30 A.M., very early in the morning by the standards of those who work in comedy. MacDonald had suggested he come to my hotel, so we met in the lobby. That morning, before going down to meet MacDonald, I went up to the roof for a swim and became distracted by the thought of Steve Lubetkin's legendary leap. So it was that suicide was on my mind even before I met Mike MacDonald that morning.

The weather was vintage Los Angeles, dry heat and smog. This climate made MacDonald's entrance jarring. Out of the blinding sunshine he emerged through the lobby's revolving door, with eyes wide and focus narrow. His hair was shaved almost to the skull in an unflattering style that made his head appear misshapen. His shoulders and chest were hunched.

I waved hello. I'd interviewed MacDonald a couple of times before, and he gave me the biggest grin he could muster, which amounted to a grimace. Together we walked into the Hyatt's restaurant and settled at a table. MacDonald ordered white toast with two bowls of butter. Then he let me into the contents of his head. As he spoke, my thoughts wandered back to the roof of the Hyatt, because being privy to Mike MacDonald's thoughts was like staring into a basket of snakes.

Once upon a time, one could assume that everyone knew who Mike MacDonald was. He had been the undisputed king of stand-up in Canada throughout the eighties. Yet that doesn't say enough about MacDonald's prominence. Mike MacDonald isn't a talented guy who has gone from "Oh *him!*" fame to "Oh . . . him" notoriety. He is a pivotal character in the history of Canadian stand-up.

MacDonald began comedy surreptitiously, at the end of the seventies. He had just graduated from Brookfield High School in Ottawa and was heavily involved in the music scene. At first he would make comedy tapes with his friends, which were so offensive that people "would have had to wait in line to kill us" if they'd ever been broadcast, he says. A friend asked MacDonald, who was known for his work in school plays, if he'd do some comedy at a new folk bar that was opening. MacDonald was to perform a set before each band. Sure, he figured, why not? So Mike MacDonald, innocent that he was, sat down and wrote two forty-five minute sets, showed up opening night, and whipped them off. He killed.

It's hard to explain what an incredible feat that was. I'm sure most people who watch stand-up think that the comedians perform new jokes every night. This is understandable, since stand-ups try to give the impression that gems flow from their lips like rain from the clouds. In truth, it takes most stand-ups four to ten years to work up forty-five minutes of killer material. Working forty-five minutes of top-grade material can be compared to writing a novel. It requires the same talent, sweat, and tenacity. And just as most writers never finish their novels, most stand-ups never work up forty-five minutes of material. This makes MacDonald's start — in which he worked not one, but *two* full feature sets — one of the wonders of the stand-up world.

MacDonald's precocious debut was no fluke. It transpired that the club attracted mostly regulars. Mike was playing to the same hundred people, so he figured he'd better write a new forty-five minutes every week. It got to the point where, exhausted, he created a geek character who would do his entire act, but badly. "I would come out in a stupid tie and shirt and glasses, and say things after the punchline like, 'Mike makes a face here.' It still got laughs."

MacDonald's accomplishment did not remain a secret for long. Mark Breslin, who was then busy laying the foundations for his Yuk Yuk's chain, caught Mike's act and began to give the kid bus fare to Toronto. MacDonald was an angry comic, just the sort Breslin adores. He railed and mimed extreme acts of violence. One comic who saw him then observed that if all the people MacDonald pretended to kill or maim could be placed onstage, the boards would be soaked with blood. In MacDonald, Breslin saw the stand-up equivalent of the Sex Pistols. Soon MacDonald had moved to the big city and set up house with a few other comedians from the Yuk Yuk's stable.

It was 1979, and the first blush of Canada's golden age of comedy was just peeking over the horizon. MacDonald was centre stage. Around him a hard-core gang of stand-ups formed. The crew consisted of Ron Vaudry, Lawrence Morgenstern, Simon Rakoff, and Howard Nemetz. They all worshipped Richard Pryor and his autobiographical yet pointed approach to stand-up. Their lives revolved around two pursuits — comedy and mind expansion, not necessarily in that order. MacDonald and company did not sit around sipping herbal tea while reading Proust. Mind expansion and comedy meant drugs and alcohol. LSD was the hallucinogen of choice, primarily because it was cheap and offered a long buzz. MacDonald hosted countless acid parties at which comics would drop a few tabs of LSD and riff jokes. Tape recorders were always present to capture killer bits for posterity. All told, MacDonald guesses they taped at least one hundred hours of acid trips. He became known for chiding other comics. If they threw out a good bit he'd tell them, "Use it in two weeks or it's mine."

"I wish you could go back in time and drop acid at one of those parties," Joel Axler, who attended many of these shindigs once told me. "It was magical. Mike would go off on hour-long bits; everyone was spritzing [improvising]. They were incredible."

This environment was conducive to comedy. MacDonald and his gang could drop acid, party all night, watch Sunday morning religious programs with the sound off, and then show up for their sets. Their drug use was no secret. It wasn't uncommon for a manager to see an entire show featuring tripping comedians. "Oh well," MacDonald recalls one saying, "I guess you're all on acid again." Those nights (which bled into days) were wild, to say the least. Regulation paraphernalia included clown costumes, straight-jackets, and paranoia.

As MacDonald's stand-up success continued to build, other comics became envious of his success and tried to cripple his act. "Steve Brinder [a Yuk Yuk's headliner in the early eighties] would try to block my material," Mike says. "They knew I did bits on Honda, so they'd mention Honda. They didn't even have a joke. The thing is that it backfired. It made me write new material." MacDonald became known for his explosive shows. "He was truly dangerous," says Ralph Benmergui, who was a minor figure in the stand-up firmament at the time. "The audience didn't know if he was going to beat the shit out of them or what."

MacDonald traces his anger back to his upbringing. MacDonald is the eldest of three boys. His father was in the air force and MacDonald was raised as an army brat. The family eventually settled in Ottawa. It wasn't an easy childhood. "Back then it was normal discipline; now they call it child abuse," he says. "I was always getting whacked for not taking things seriously. I always thought things were boring, so I'd cut up to make them interesting. Now they call that attention disorder. I remember one home movie. I'm sitting there drawing and it's Christmas. It's obviously Christmas because there's Christmas cards on the mantelpiece. As soon as the camera lights go on it's *bam,* I go right to the camera, and I walk over to the Christmas cards and knock them all over. Then the camera gets turned off. Then it comes back on and I'm colouring, and I've got an unhappy look on my face. Guess what happened when the camera got turned off."

Comedy, just as it had for the Dumbells, meant survival. It was MacDonald's life preserver. The adulation he felt onstage soothed the wounds he harboured inside. Stand-up was a way of disarming his inner demons, which MacDonald says raged so fierce he had only two choices: comedy or physical violence.

Despite his aggressive exterior, MacDonald was not the sort to make a career of bar-room brawls and street fights. There is a gentle side to his character that would not allow that. As a teenager, for example, MacDonald had worked as a volunteer at a school for retarded children. He spent hours working closely with the kids, "just trying to understand them." MacDonald chose comedy, he says, because "it's a lot easier on your fists."

When he was at the microphone he felt free to unleash his dark side. He often took his angry character offstage with him. MacDonald was known for trying to shock people, particularly strangers. Says Benmergui, "He would say the most offensive things. He'd go for your heart. I saw him make people cry. I would tell them, 'It's a test. If you can get past this, you'll be all right.' Mike's attitude was, 'If you take me at face value, fuck you.'"

"He was egomaniacal, immature and funny," says Axler. "Like Robert De Niro in *Taxi Driver*."

By 1983, MacDonald had made substantial inroads into the American scene, regularly touring the southern states. He had done the stand-up showcase programs like *Evening at the Improv* and was Canada's number-one headliner. Breslin continued to be his biggest booster. The comedy mogul made no secret that MacDonald was the chosen one. MacDonald got the choice gigs. On the downside, MacDonald's carefree experiment with mind expansion had turned into a ten-year research project. He was now addicted to heroin and cocaine.

Cocaine was easy to get on the road, especially down South, and MacDonald made a point of getting it as much as possible. He continued to be productive, obsessively trying to prevent his affair with the "king and queen" from harming his career. Despite his drug habit he made sure to take a nap before every show, to ensure a good set. Afterwards, however, it was party time. MacDonald remembers being on the road in Atlanta and scoring a gram of cocaine from the bartender. He did the entire gram in one shot — half a gram up each nostril. Then, while sipping a drink, he began to see FBI agents coming out of the drink coolers. His condition was obvious to those around him. MacDonald says waitresses would often insist on driving him to the airport after his gigs were done. They felt MacDonald was so far gone they'd never see him again. "So many people thought I was going to die," he says. "They thought they were going to open up the paper and read about me on page fifty-three."

His drug use began to peak at the same time as he was writing and starring in his first feature film, *Mr. Nice Guy.* MacDonald was collaborating with Mark Breslin and Axler on the script. He was not the most reliable partner. At one meeting, Axler recalls, a producer asked the strung-out stand-up what he'd written. "I've got a great joke for you," Axler says MacDonald replied. He then laughed and pulled up his shirt-sleeve to reveal an arm strewn with needle marks and bruised veins. MacDonald soon began to miss meetings altogether. On one particular night Breslin and Axler went to his apartment in Kensington Market to find him. MacDonald would not answer the door. While Breslin continued to ring the bell, Axler climbed the fire escape and went to MacDonald's living room window. He found MacDonald, crouched on a chair, holding a brick. He was staring at a white shirt that was hanging on the back of the front door. "I couldn't make the meeting because I was watching the shirt's arms flailing," MacDonald confessed. "I thought I had to kill it with the brick or it would kill me."

The scene so disturbed Axler that he quit comedy and moved to Colorado. "Mike was my hero, and the guy had reduced himself to that. He was trying to prove the existence of God by seeing the devil. The comedy business was so ugly I couldn't stand it. I thought, I'm finished with this shit. I just fucked off and got a degree in communications." But like any good addict, Axler could not stay away from his drug, comedy. He returned to the business three years later, his disgust overcome by his passion, as well as his need for cash. He accepted a job running Yuk Yuk's' Vancouver club, where he was to meet Colin Campbell and glimpse the dark face of comedy again.

Despite the drugs, MacDonald's work kept improving. At one show, during a Christmas holiday run, MacDonald delivered a two-hour concert that fellow comedian Al Rae remembers as one of the best stand-up shows he has ever seen. MacDonald built the crowd into a roaring frenzy, then said his final words: "If it wasn't for you people . . ." He formed his hand into the shape of a pistol, placed it against his temple, and mimed pulling the trigger: *boom.* MacDonald strode offstage. The audience sat in stunned silence.

Eventually, the substance abuse crushed him. MacDonald found himself on his knees asking God to help him quit. "And that was it," he recalls with pride. "No withdrawal, no nothing." Nothing except that MacDonald became a born-again Christian, although he says he is "on the far left of the born-again movement."

After he cleaned up, the CBC gave Mike a sitcom, *Mosquito Lake.* The show was the brainchild of CBC programming boss Ivan Fecan. Fecan later departed for Baton Broadcasting's less glamourous shores, but while at the CBC he had had some hits like *The Kids in the Hall* and *The Royal Canadian Air Farce.* He'd also had some close misses, like *Material World* and *In Opposition.* But *Mosquito Lake,* which ran from 1989–90, was deemed so bad that to this day it lives in infamy in the Canadian comedy community. The Toronto *Star* summed it up as "prime time pestilence." When Ralph Benmergui was given his late-night talk show and subsequently vilified in the press, MacDonald breathed a sigh of relief. "At least," he said at the time, "maybe now they'll forget about *Mosquito Lake.*"

Mosquito Lake proved to some that at the same time as MacDonald found God, he lost his edge. Many of his peers feel the absence of malice cost him his ability to be funny. "He became Father Knows Best," says Vaudry. "He lost it." In the *Globe and Mail,* John Haslett Cuff reviewed MacDonald's one-hour CBC Television special *My House, My Rules* this way: "Mike — there's a lot to be angry about. But quit trying so hard to be loved, go back to being nasty. You're a lot funnier and more likable when you do."

MacDonald dismisses those who pine for the days of his troubled past. "People say, 'I liked Mike better when he was angry, or in the dark days,' because they want to refer back to when they still had hopes and desires. That dark and angry thing got tired real quick." Says Axler, "Mike's edge is what killed Mike's edge. His lifestyle and drug abuse were so horrendous, they could have killed him, but they killed his edge instead."

After the *Mosquito Lake* fiasco, MacDonald left Canada and made the trip to Los Angeles, the city where all successful Canadian comedians eventually find themselves. He has since done a few CBC Television specials and little else. He was deeply into video games for a while and would play for hours a day. He continued to pitch studios and showcase for roles, but nothing stuck. Each year a former upstart overtook him. First Jim Carrey ("Jim's not so hard to take; he earned his place"), then *SNL* star Norm MacDonald ("He's a little hard to take; he is a guy who trips over silver platters"). One by one he watched them pass by. Every new success for another comedian festered under MacDonald's skin like a tick.

"In L.A.," he explained, "I drive by my dreams every two seconds. Look at that billboard, there's the movie I should have been in. Look at that beautiful woman, that's the woman I should have been married to. Look at that car, that's the car I should be driving. Every two seconds — overload."

Rumour in Toronto had it that the day an act named Carrot Top — a red-haired comic who used props as punchlines — bagged a million-dollar contract, MacDonald had a mental breakdown. The reality was less drastic but far from rosy. MacDonald's money was beginning to run out, and he was becoming more and more reclusive. Ultimately, he was gaining a reputation as a sort of Colonel Kurtz of Canadian comedy, and when I met him that day at the Hyatt, he seemed like he'd reached the river's end.

While preparing for the interview, I'd thought it would be necessary to do a lot of prodding and massaging to get him to discuss the drugs and depression, and what had gone wrong in Hollywood. I knew he was combative, and I figured he would not want to get too personal. I could not have been more mistaken. MacDonald poured out his guts, as if he wanted his version of events on the record for posterity. He was frighteningly eager to talk. His response to my opening question, "So how have you been?" was, "You mean other than trying to kill myself?"

Then MacDonald unleashed his story. It wasn't packed with laughs. It was loaded with obsession, envy, and depression. In other words, it had all the right ingredients for humour, but they just weren't put together in a particularly amusing way.

For starters, MacDonald said he was more financially unstable than he had been in eighteen years. He was six months away from having to sell his house and move back to Toronto, "a city I don't mind, but most of the people there I don't like." Money was the least of his problems, however. Los Angeles had got to him. It is a city where everyone says yes all the time. You smile all the time and you are excited all the time. You are nice all the time. These are not exactly MacDonald's strong suits. In Los Angeles, when industry people would tell him, "I love what you do and I want to do something with you," MacDonald would say, "Give me a dollar." When the stunned executive asked what MacDonald meant, he'd reply, "If I had a buck ever time somebody said they wanted to do something, I'd be rich." This was not Hollywood's style.

In Mike Elliot's view, that was the problem. "He was hot for a while. They were expecting big things from him, but he would not play the game. He treated a lot of people like shit. I remember one of his Ottawa homecoming gigs three years ago. We were both on the bill. The deal was, I do twenty minutes and then he comes out and does two hours. Every night I would do less and less time because I was doing too well, according to him, and he didn't want me to get too many laughs. The whole weekend I was there he never said hello to me, he never said a word. Never said boo to me, nothing. Came on and did his thing and had a question period about his career for the last fifteen minutes of his act. I was thinking, 'This guy is an asshole.' MacDonald was just an asshole, and he was like that with a lot of people. He had it, and it didn't take. I honestly think a lot of it has to be attitude. I took his name off my résumé. No one has heard of him anymore."

MacDonald was well aware how L.A. perceived him. He recalls, in particular, a 1995 industry party. MacDonald came in, saw a few friends and then met a few not-so-amiable folks. "They gave me *that look,* and that look said one thing and one thing only: YOU DO NOT HAVE ANY HEAT, and then they turned their heads. After two or three of those I thought, I really do not need this. I said hi to all my friends and I was out of there. There is no getting these people. [My] resentment and [the] revenge factor building up with the natural anger and the manic-depression, you can see where that was going."

Where it was going was towards suicide. Six months before our interview, he'd gone to the edge. "[The business] was too unfair. It didn't make sense. Here I was and I had these projects that were turned down by networks, and then the networks would come out with the *same thing* . . . They're telling me something's not going to work, when they have something exactly like it. That would throw me for a loop . . . I always thought that talent would be enough, but boy, it's not even close."

MacDonald went so far as to shop for a gun. "I was ready to just blow my brains out. I was on the way to do it. I came home. I was going to write the note, change my clothes, and go. Change — I don't know why you have to change. I had to have clean underwear.

"My wife and I had had a series of fights. She had taken the dogs and cats and she'd split. She took off knowing that I was in this state and she phoned Howard [Lapides]. Howard phoned me and he had a doctor on the other line. They talked me into going to another doctor and that doctor talked me into going to the hospital and the hospital talked me into going to the psych ward. I spent a week in the psych ward, which I loved. Oh man, I was home. It was perfect. There were all these nuts. All of a sudden I was Jack Nicholson in *One Flew Over the Cuckoo's Nest*. I had everyone's number. It was amazing. One guy, all I had to do was walk by and buzz my lips — gone! He'd crack up. That was his button. Just tape it down and put a roll of quarters on it.

"A person like me would get more benefit from going to the psych ward for two weeks than the Bahamas. I hate the sun, I hate the beach. But there in the psych ward I relaxed. I thought, Thank God I got here. I finally got here. *I feel great.*"

Yes, MacDonald felt great. He had been diagnosed as manic-depressive and had started on medication. But he was not well. Since his crash he had been writing a lot. Sometimes he was writing sixteen hours a day. He was also working with a series of different writing partners (in Los Angeles no one seems to work solo). But MacDonald wasn't scribbling furiously for himself. "I'm writing so my wife can make money off it later. 'Cause I'm going to die, and I'm not going to get my shot, and here's something that maybe my wife can support herself with sooner or later."

Sooner or later. These have become the words that have epitomized MacDonald's career. He has been perennially on the edge of something big. "I've done a lot of the shows where it's, 'Here are some up-and-coming guys!'" he told the Toronto *Star* in 1992. "Uh, excuse me, but can I move on to the current category now?"

By 1996, MacDonald's life preserver had turned into a stone. Comedy had been a way of destroying the pain that plagued him. When it became a Hollywood game of who's got more work, more money, more fame, comedy got twisted and became a self-inflicted wound. MacDonald was not alone in this club. Colin Campbell had destroyed himself, and so had many others. It was MacDonald's talent that elevated him above the pack. MacDonald was haunted by the car he should have been driving, the woman he should have married, and he failed to see his real victories. MacDonald led the first movement in Canadian stand-up. He epitomized it. He was its Jim Morrison. MacDonald's stand-up attacked everything that Canadian comedy had previously been, such as *Don Messer's Jubilee* and *The King of Kensington*. MacDonald was aggressive, angry, urban, and increasingly insightful. His timing and delivery were relentless. He hammered jokes the way Bobby Orr hit pucks. MacDonald was unpredictable, taking his audience for a breakneck ride every time he went onstage. Of all the miserable things I heard MacDonald say that morning, one in particular sticks in my mind because it illustrates the depth of his despair: "I get young kids coming up to me in the clubs, saying, 'You're the reason I started.' I tell them, 'Don't blame me.' If I'm their influence, God help them."

When we said goodbye at the Hyatt, I wanted to tell him, "Don't do it." But all I could get out was, "Take care of yourself."

TEN

■

The Girl Who Scared Boys

Sandra Shamas had it all back on April 30, 1995: the perfect husband, the perfect career, the perfect home (a farmhouse on a hundred acres of Ontario land). The comedian, who had made herself a millionaire through her autobiographical one-woman shows, was poised for the perfect future. She was wrapping up a final show in Ottawa and then it would be on to her sabbatical, a year of rest and domestic bliss.

But on May 1, her husband, Frank (the "perfect male" fans will remember from her *My Boyfriend's Back and There's Gonna Be Laundry* trilogy), telephoned her from Montreal where he was working. He told her he wasn't coming home. It wasn't just a matter of Frank missing a plane. Frank wasn't coming home, period. Frank had let his fingers do the walking and left his wife by phone. Three days later, Sandra got a letter from the American producer of her San Francisco show. She had performed *My Boyfriend's Back* at San Francisco's Alcazar theatre the previous November. Shamas had been held up at the border due to work permit conflicts and had had to cancel performances. When she'd finally cleared immigration and performed the show, it did not do well. The letter said that the American producer was suing Shamas for $50,000 (U.S.), claiming that the shows she'd missed had cost him money.

In less than a week, Shamas watched her life implode before her eyes. It was a tale not so new as it was lamentable.

All this I found out when I met Sandra in November 1995 at a bistro in Toronto's Little Italy for the first of a series of interviews. She was in rough shape. She opened up and confided the anguish her separation had wrought. She may have felt freer to talk because she knew I was going through my own matrimonial upheaval at the time. Of course, I wasn't taking notes. It was always the case with Sandra that I didn't take any notes. Primarily our conversations were personal. I had known her for a couple of years and had quickly realized that Sandra froze the minute she saw a pen hit paper. Her mouth would keep moving and facts would come out, but what you were getting was tripe. If you wanted to find out what Sandra Shamas was really thinking, you had to look her right in the eye, the way she looked her audiences in the eye, and dare her to tell the truth.

I didn't get much out of our first interview except that — big surprise — the break-up had left Sandra an emotional cripple. Home and marriage were the stars Sandra set her course by. During the course of her ten years with Frank, she never did a national tour, because she thought it would hurt her relationship with Frank, who was a puppeteer. Instead, she would play a city, return home to Frank, and then a few months later she'd fly out and do another out-of-town gig. Frank, on the other hand (according to Sandra), would take work out of the city for months on end. So when the bottom fell out for Sandra, there was nothing there to break her fall. She exiled herself to her dream farm in the autumn of 1995 with her two kittens, Buster and Minnie, and began to live a hermit's life. She wouldn't let people come and visit her.

Unfortunately for Sandra, the news of her dilemma was received with relish, or at least mute satisfaction, by some in the Toronto comedy community. Deservedly or not, she had gained a reputation as a spoiled diva. She had climbed to the top of the comedy scene by never compromising her artistic vision. This strategy proved utterly successful. Sandra could get away with stunts that would get other performers executed. When powerful TV producers phoned other comics asking for complimentary tickets, they got roses to go with them. When a powerful TV producer called Sandra to ask, "What do I do if I want to see your show?" she told him "Call the box office."

The anti-Shamas sentiment can be summed up by comedian and one-time Shamas friend, Dan Redican. "She was going off the deep end of being a star. She was dispensing pearls from the heavens. She wasn't talking to you, she was blessing you. I guessed her next show was going to be about having kids or getting divorced." For her part, Sandra says Redican hasn't done anything funny since his first wife left him.

A big part of the bad blood came from envy. Each Sandra Shamas production was more of a hit than its predecessor. Her competition kept waiting for her to screw up but she never did. *My Boyfriend's Back and There's Gonna Be Laundry* was a hit in 1987, *My Boyfriend's Back and There's Gonna Be Laundry II: The Cycle Continues* topped it in 1989, and *Wedding Bell Hell,* which opened in 1993 and broke box office records at the one-thousand-seat Elgin Winter Garden, was the biggest hit of all. Of course, if you had any doubt about her achievements, all you had to do was ask Sandra. Modesty was not one of her attributes. When it came to talking it up, she was the Muhammad Ali of Canadian comedy. Nor did Sandra have any problem telling people who she felt had slighted her where to go. Once, after I had written a piece on her for the *Financial Post,* she telephoned to chastise me for printing her husband's last name. She felt the use of Frank's surname was an invasion of privacy, despite the fact that she earned her living exposing her personal life, and Frank in particular, to paying audiences. After that we didn't talk for a couple of years. As much as I admired her work, I decided to put a moratorium on Sandra Shamas scribbling until fate dictated that it was time to write the inevitable "What's Wrong with Sandra Shamas?" piece.

When I got the book deal, I was back in the position of needing Sandra. I had to interview her. There was no getting around it. Sandra was, and is, a gigantic star among Canada's female population. She has a lot of male fans, but their fervour pales in comparison to the esteem in which women hold her. For a lot of women, seeing one of Sandra's shows is a rite of passage. Probably seven out of ten times that I'd tell a woman I was writing a book on Canadian comedy, she'd ask me, "Do you get to meet Sandra Shamas?" All my divorce lawyer wanted to know, after we'd finished our first meeting, was, "What is Sandra Shamas like?" To her fans, she is a ferocious, funny, estrogen superhero.

She's not the first. There have always been independent Canadian women making headway in comedy, even those born at the turn of the century. Beatrice Lillie was born in Toronto in 1898. As a child, she was expelled from her church's choir for making a "ridiculous" face. Her humour paid off. Lillie became one of the finest comic actors of the early twentieth century. She first performed in 1924 and went on to a glowing theatrical career that spanned the twenties to the sixties. Lillie dominated Broadway and appeared in a string of Hollywood feature films. Noel Coward said of her, "Beattie has been for years and still is the funniest woman of our civilization." Like Shamas, Lillie was a forceful comedian. She didn't play the ingenue, and her favourite targets were social hypocrisy and, in true Canadian fashion, authority figures, most of whom were male. Critic Kenneth Tynan once wrote, "Almost without exception, American [women] comedians get their laughs by pretending to be pop-eyed man hunting spinsters. Miss Lillie is as far removed from these as a butterfly is from a guided missile." In 1972, she published an autobiography entitled *Every "Other" Inch a Lady*.

Lucille Kallen, who grew up in Toronto around the same time, became a successful television writer. Kallen was a trained pianist and honed her skill working on Toronto satiric revues such as *Let's Be Offensive*. In the mid-forties she drummed up one hundred dollars and rented a run-down movie theatre. There she helped launch the Belmont Little Theatre, which performed avant-garde theatricals. Like many talented comics, Kallen was rejected by the CBC. They felt she was unfit for a thirty-dollar-a-week job as a continuity writer. Max Liebman, the creator of Sid Caesar's *Your Show of Shows,* saw more potential. He hired her as a writer. Kallen went on to script much of Caesar's material and to write for comedian Imogene Coca as well.

These women comics shared Sandra's chutzpah. They were funny and they were ambitious. They weren't afraid to grab the spotlight. Generally, women in comedy have characteristics that society considers male. They are independent, assertive, occasionally profane, and don't shy away from confrontation. In any case, it was certainly true of Sandra, who said her "male" side was so strong that she "frightened boys."

So when I called Sandra after not speaking with her for over two years, I was hoping it wouldn't be her "male" side I encountered. I recounted my life in twenty seconds or less — baby, book, divorce. She went through hers — farm, divorce, kittens — and we arranged to meet at the fashionable Bar Italia. Misery loves company, and it also loves caffeine. At our first meeting we just commiserated. I drank coffee. She drank cappuccino. Afterwards I accompanied her as she shopped for leggings at Holt Renfrew, where she gave the sales clerk hell for putting people's names on mailing lists. Sandra gave me a lift home and took a look into my apartment, which held a bed, a chair, and a desk. After surveying my squalour, she gave me a big fat look of pity and suggested we get together again. I proposed a trip up to her farm. Sandra was taken aback. She said she was very careful about who she let up there. So I left things at that.

A few days later she called and invited me up. Sandra said she had really enjoyed meeting me. "It's good to be around healthy people," she told me. "But it's also important to . . . be . . . to . . . be . . . ."

"Around people like me?"

"Yes."

We agreed I would visit the following Friday, December 1. I'd make an early start and catch a GO bus up to her central Ontario farm, which she had appropriately named Wit's End. It was an hour and a half ride. I decided to roll tape on the life and times of Sandra Shamas.

Sandra Shamas was born in 1957, in Sudbury, Ontario. Her parents were Lebanese and were partnered as a result of an arranged marriage. She had one younger sister and one older brother. Sandra was very close to her brother. To hear Sandra talk, her parents hated each other. Sandra's fans will recall many scenes of domestic warfare from her trilogy, such as her father locking himself in his car and turning up the radio to block out his wife's screams. This parental feuding left deep scars on Sandra's psyche. My guess is that they made her long for an ideal of domestic bliss (since she saw none) but left her without the tools to achieve it. In this respect she was like most people on the planet. Sandra muddled through childhood, didn't have much use for school, left home at an early age (sixteen), and found herself in Toronto in the late seventies.

Between 1980 and 1983 Sandra worked at various forms of wage slavery — bartender, cleaning lady, waitress. In 1983, she joined the Second City National Touring Company. The company travels the province of Ontario and a few other spots around the country, presenting its *Best of Second City* show. In 1984, Sandra, along with the entire touring company, was let go. After her dismissal Sandra called up her director, Jeff Ellis, and asked him what her next step should be. She needed some direction and encouragement. He kicked her in the face. According to Sandra, Ellis told her, "Let's face it, Sandra. You're not a pretty girl, but I *have* seen you with make-up on and you *can* be attractive."

These words dug themselves into Sandra's soul and never left. They told her everything she needed to know about the comedy business. If she was going to succeed in the milieus that existed — the stand-up clubs and sketch venues — she would have to get on her knees and admit to being "not a pretty girl." She'd either have to put on the make-up and play the ingenue (which she knew she wasn't) or eschew it completely and pass herself off as ugly (which she knew she wasn't). Like many women, she'd have to choose between being smart and being beautiful. That was the choice for women comics: you could be the ugly hag with the brain or the bikini-clad bimbo. Instead she decided to blow off the rules. She refused to be divided. Sandra vowed not to play anywhere she was being dictated to. The establishment tried to make her say "uncle" and she said "fuck off."

Not many people have her kind of strength. That's one reason that only 10 per cent of working stand-up comedians are women. The comedy business is a man's game. The hours, the road work, the stigma of being a woman in comedy (the number-one heckle a female comic hears is "Take your clothes off") make it rough going. For some women, the pay-off is not worth the lifestyle. Still, there are those who try. The extra obstacles they face often turn those with enough raw talent into killer comedians. In America, you have the likes of Paula Poundstone, Ellen

DeGeneres, and Rita Rudner. Canada has yet to produce one. One reason for this gap is the amount of road work Canadians traditionally must
do to earn a living. In America, the greater number of urban centres cut
down driving and make it a little more bearable. DeGeneres, for example, started out working the New Orleans café comedy scene.

By the nineties, a lot had changed. Canadian women stand-ups had
adopted a strategy for coping with the system. They cut road work out
of the picture. In cities like Vancouver, where comedians such as Sherrie
O'Brien were based, and in Toronto, where a host of young stand-ups
were working, women were concentrating on club gigs and shows in
non-comedy venues such as coffee houses and rock-and-roll bars.
Instead of earning their living on the road, they took part-time jobs, and
focused on working as many in-town gigs as they could. The results
were almost immediate. By 1996, some of Toronto's best young stand-
ups were women. Comics such as Ophira Eisenberg, who did dry, acerbic
one-liners, were burning up stages around town and also producing their
own shows in small venues.

Sandra took a different route. In 1984, instead of letting someone
else pull her strings, Sandra decided to literally pull a few of her own.
She became a puppeteer after landing a job on the international children's
television series *Fraggle Rock,* which was filmed in Toronto. (When she
performed improv at a Jim Henson Christmas party, Henson was so
impressed by her performance that he gave her a six-week contract,
despite the fact she had no puppetry experience.) Sandra went from
making $100 a week as a cleaning lady to $530 a week as an artist. She
thought she'd won the lottery. The six-week try-out became two years
of employment. The Henson experience was a revelation for Sandra. "It
was the first time in my life when I was surrounded by people who were
all working at the top of their intelligence. They encouraged me to work
on a higher level."

But Sandra didn't last in muppet land. She felt the Canadians in the
company were being mistreated by the Americans, and she walked off
the set one day, never to return. Not, however, before she met the man
who would become her husband and the centre of her work, Frank.

Just before she turned thirty, Sandra saw Lily Tomlin's one-woman show in New York City. More than any other influence, Sandra credits that show for changing her life. It drove home the power of solo performance. "I saw a woman onstage with two chairs and a riser and I thought, I can do that." She opened her first show, *My Boyfriend's Back and There's Gonna Be Laundry,* at the 1987 Edmonton Fringe Festival. It was an instant hit. Sandra's popularity grew exponentially. She moved the show to Toronto, where it scored again at the Factory Theatre. From that point on she had nothing but success.

The key to that success, along with her performance, was Sandra's insistence on having complete control of her productions. She was the producer and she made all the decisions. Comedy was Sandra's first love; her second was business. Sandra wanted to make money, and she had a solid plan to achieve that end. She kept things simple. Sandra rented the theatre so that it would be her space. She controlled advertising, marketing, and technical aspects, and had only one assistant, her stage manager Scott. She has also ruled out television and film. After her appearance in Gail Singer's film *Wisecracks* (a documentary on female comedians) she refused to appear again on TV. Sandra believed that every time possible ticket buyers saw her on television, they lost interest in seeing her in person. If you wanted to see Sandra Shamas, you had to buy a ticket to a Sandra Shamas show. If you bought a ticket to her show, you had to pay the producer, and the producer was Sandra Shamas. The formula worked. More than 42,500 people saw her *Wedding Bell Hell.* She eventually became a millionaire.

Sandra's entrepreneurship flies counter to the idea that Canadians are funny because they are more modest and deferential than Americans. Comedy is at every level a free-market proposition, and the free market rewards those who raise capital and invest it wisely. These people are generally not modest or deferential. Sandra raised capital and wisely invested it in herself. The more successful she became, the more capital she acquired; the more capital she acquired, the more comedy she produced. Money meant artistic freedom. Sandra never had to explain or justify her work. Her attitude was: if people pay, then I don't have to explain anything.

One result of Sandra's entrepreneurship is that she's developed an animosity towards the so-called artistic theatrical community. Once her shows became proven money makers, many regional theatres (which were supported by government funding) would ask to book her. It was an obvious cash grab. These theatres needed to make some revenue from ticket sales to fill the gap where funding stopped, and their artistic directors knew she would sell out. But when she quoted her going rate, they would say, "We don't pay anybody that" and offer a dismal sum. To that Sandra would reply, "My price just went up five grand. And every time you argue with me, it's going to go up another five grand. I sell out. You're going to make money off my run. This is what I'm worth, and you're going to pay it or I'm not working."

Shamas felt that since she was a profit maker, they didn't consider her an artist. She's never been nominated for a Dora Award (Toronto's theatre awards). "They want the whore," she has said, "which is what I am to them because I'm commercially successful. They want the whore, but they don't want to pay her."

Sandra was the most successful "whore" going until her ill-fated trip to California in 1994 to introduce America to her trilogy. She recalls the trip as a "crock of shit." San Francisco audiences did not respond to Sandra's material. Her heart wasn't in it. In retrospect she realizes that the trip south was the act of a performer who didn't know what to do for an encore. She was burnt out but didn't know it, or couldn't admit it. "I wasn't listening to myself. I was tired but I didn't know what to do. I scrambled and did a gig. I thought I'd start a career in America."

Instead she got her ass handed to her on a platter. Shortly after San Francisco Sandra realized she needed a break, a sabbatical, some time to cultivate her marriage and maybe have a kid. She decided that after her last gig, in Ottawa in late April 1995, she'd take a leave of absence. So she and Frank bought the farm and got ready for bliss. Dream homes and cottages should come with warnings. "Caution: purchase of your dream home may trigger the collapse of your marriage." Almost immediately after her last show, her life crumbled, but no one knew. Her fans read in the May 11 Toronto *Star* that she was telling people at parties that the theatre was losing her to domestic bliss; she was never going to perform again. They didn't know that the bliss had already ended, and that

Sandra Shamas was that very day up at Wit's End trying to sift through the rubble of her marriage. She was there alone, living for that brief moment between falling asleep and waking when she could actually believe that Frank hadn't left, that everything was as it used to be, or at least how she thought it had once been.

I ran this little biography through my mind as the GO bus entered Georgetown, Sandra's new "hometown." The timing of my trip was a bit odd. I was recovering from my break-up (I had a copy of the separation agreement in my briefcase), and she was trying to bounce back from hers. I wondered how we'd keep to the subject of comedy. To me, Sandra had always been an urban celebrity. I thought that extracting her from the concrete of the city would be like taking a flower out of the sunlight. It would be hard to find a place less like Sandra than Georgetown. Maybe that's why she liked it. Downtown was four blocks long. It had the standard one set of traffic lights, a Chinese restaurant, a pizza place, and a fancy restaurant (the Cellar). Georgetown had one apartment building, and a page of the local paper was devoted to covering its machinations. The weather that day was unseasonable. We'd had snow, but it had been followed by a warm snap. So, in essence, we were getting what felt like an early spring melt instead of an early winter cold.

"It feels nice," Sandra would say later. "But it fools you, because you know by night it's going to freeze solid and kill somebody."

I'd arranged to meet Sandra at the corner of Mill and Main streets. I popped some gum and kept a lookout for her black pick-up truck. In Toronto it was very easy to spot Sandra; her pick-up stood out. Here in Georgetown, I gave up looking. Everybody drove one. In about fifteen minutes she showed up. I hopped in and Sandra asked if I would mind going to the Salvation Army Store. I figured she was going to drop some clothes off, but she wanted to shop. Unfortunately, that day there wasn't anything that caught her interest. All the while we made small talk. Sandra made a few references to "how good it was" that I had come up. How was I? How was she? Yes, it's up and down. You feel good one moment and devastated the next. That was the gist of our conversation.

Wit's End was about half an hour from Georgetown. It was a quaint farmhouse set on a huge spread of land. Sandra's property stretched out of sight. There was an orchard, large tracks of field, ridges of brush, a small lake, and countless trails. It was all dusted with a layer of snow. By the time we arrived, the weather had turned bitterly cold. So we stayed in and spent the afternoon eating risotto and drinking wine. I took out my tape recorder and set it aside, as I always did. It was a ritual similar to leaving your gun with the sheriff before entering Dodge City. It eased Sandra's mind. After a bottle, we both had a nicotine fit, and an emergency trip to the country store was arranged to score a few packs of cigarettes. Conversation touched on topics ranging from Frank Sinatra, of whom Sandra was a big fan, to comedy and relationships. Hours went by. Ash trays filled. Small talk was exhausted. We decided to walk Sandra's property before night fell.

This journey took over an hour. We crossed hills of brush and found her lake, which she had not yet named. It was small but deep. At one end a damn blocked a small creek. Underneath it water splashed into a reflecting pool. Here, Sandra told me, she and her friends skinny-dipped during the summer. Not far away was the orchard. Apple trees speckled that landscape in twisted, shrunken shapes. The care with which they had been planted many years before still showed, although much of the original orchard was gone. While the scenery was beautiful, it wasn't an easy walk. We were trudging through deep snow and the temperature continued to drop. As we left the orchard, the sun was beginning to dip under the horizon. Sandra joked about wills and hypothermia. As we walked and froze, all we spoke of was summer. How much better everything was going to be then. All those apple trees were going to bear fruit. The fields were going to be green. Sandra was going to have a huge party and invite all her friends. Then, as we passed through a fence, I heard swift rustling behind us. I turned to Sandra and she jumped three feet towards me. A herd of deer blew past us. They didn't make a loud rumble, in fact we could barely hear their hooves brush the snow. They flew by and melted into a clump of trees far away. One straggler, a doe, stayed back and studied us. We looked back. In an instant she too disappeared.

Maybe it was shock therapy, but the sight of all those deer gliding by stirred something in Sandra. She grew serious and began to tell me how much this farm meant to her. I began to realize, however, that it wasn't really hers yet. There was too much of her old life here, and it was being kept alive underneath the snow. When spring came Sandra could work the land, dig it up, farm it, and make it her own. That was months away. It became apparent that for Sandra, walking the snowy land was like strolling through her old dreams. She felt like a ghost. More emotions began to seep out as we drew closer to the farmhouse. They were the kinds of emotions that are born of separation. They began with thoughts like, "You try so . . ." and, "I thought that . . ." and, "Sometimes . . ." I listened and walked. Then I stopped to turn and realized that Sandra was twenty feet back, knee-deep in snow, crying.

Back at the farmhouse it was decided that it was too late for me to return to Toronto. The fact that neither of us was in any shape to drive was also a determining factor. So, we had another bottle of wine. Then I began to get to the bottom of what Sandra's comedy was all about. Sandra's first revelation was, "Nobody in comedy is young."

Comedy required weary insight, she said, reconciliation to the sad state of things. It meant growing up in a messed-up environment. For women, it meant fighting the roles that were pushed on you. Women in other professions encountered the same roadblocks, but comedians tackled them publicly. Comedy, to her, was all about confronting your life. Sandra did not do political material, mocking the day's headlines, because she didn't know enough about them. The only topic she felt she was entirely expert on was her own life, not because she was dull but because she believed comedy demanded total understanding, the sort that only came from autobiography. That was what had eventually worn her down. The joy Sandra got from performing was immeasurable. She said being onstage she had a sensation of "smooth, solid, smooth." I think she meant it was a state in which she was 100 per cent at ease and 100 per cent in control. This sublime state was anchored in fury. What made her funny? That was straightforward. "My anger is what makes me funny. The tension holds it all together."

If you asked a roomful of female comedians what single trait they shared, they'd tell you it was a need for the laughter. That need springs from a compulsion for approval, just as it does with male comedians. The difference is that women don't generally get approval for publicly displaying their anger. Society will tolerate an angry and dissatisfied male, but an angry and dissatisfied woman is considered a very dangerous force. We'll accept an angry man because in traditional Western society, men are the doers. Women are the mothers and muses. They and their children are the reason that the providers (men) provide. If the muse takes the stage and begins to expose her discontent, all hell could break loose.

That is what many women comedians are craving when they perform: the freedom to voice their discontent. They exhibit their discontent but sugar-coat it with comedy and the laughter they receive represents unconditional approval. The woman has revealed her darker emotions, her sexuality, her anger, and the audience responds by saying, in essence, We accept those elements of your personality, and we still love you. That is the core of the phenomenon. From this relationship many different styles of comedy are born. Some women, like Mary Walsh of the sketch troupe CODCO, turn their comedy outwards and comment directly on society. Others, like Sandra, turn it inward: they air their own dirty laundry.

Sandra did this almost literally. Her shows hinged on a mutual understanding between herself and her audience. Her material was often a catalogue of rules and institutions that are foisted on women. In *Wedding Bell Hell,* for example, she chronicled the rituals of marriage. She lampooned the traditions that are used to homogenize women: the bridal shower, the wedding ring. By doing so she acted as a surrogate for her crowd. She voiced the discontent, and the audience enjoyed a vicarious catharsis. Her shows also contained a big slice of warmth and compassion. They were not judgmental in tone. Sandra did not assign blame. She merely laid out a chain of events and took her audience on a ride through them. There were two constants. Sandra was the locomotive; the track was always anger.

Perhaps she has reached the point where she doesn't want to be angry anymore, at least not professionally. Each of her shows dealt with anger — against her mother, father, the powers that be. Wit's End was supposed to have been a refuge for Frank and her. Instead, it was now the place where she pondered her failed relationship. Sandra was bruised, she was reeling. She was pretty much knocked out cold. When I asked her in a roundabout way if there was another show in her somewhere, she said no. She was planning nothing and didn't even want to think about performing. But I could sense there had to be one in there somewhere. Sandra may have been tired, but there was no way she could leave comedy. "It's like being hungry all the time," she had said of the impulse that drove her. There was, of course, a catch. "It's like being hungry all the time and being born without a mouth."

Five months later we met again, this time back in Toronto, to catch up. Spring had arrived, although it was still miserably cold. The time had worn well on Sandra. She was coaching girls' soccer up in Georgetown. She had taken figure skating lessons and had spent the winter "learning how to be a girl." She had a farmer's tan from spending April tearing up her farm, with the help of her farmhand, Ray. She had cleared acres of bush, dead trees, brambles, and rocks. The big news was her return to the stage. Not in a show, just speaking engagements. But the show that wasn't there when I had talked with her last, the one she wasn't working on or thinking about and wasn't going to do, had surfaced. She was writing every morning. We could expect it in a year.

"You should come up to the farm this summer," she said. "You won't recognize it."

ELEVEN

.

The Ambassador for the Counter-culture

When summer arrived, however, I was as far away from Sandra's pastoral retreat as you could get. I was in Manhattan, in the heart of NBC's offices in the Rockefeller Center, sitting in Lorne Michaels' office. For more than twenty years, Michaels had been one of the most influential people in American television. His office fit his stature. Out its window, there is a beautiful view of the plaza's fountain, which in the winter feeds a skating rink. Lorne's decor is a combination of kitsch and cool. The furniture is of extremely high quality. I gazed at his desk and chairs and thought to myself, I'll be sitting on at least two months' rent. There is a fish tank and, of course, a television set. The aroma of popcorn is perceptible in the air. Popcorn is everywhere. Michaels keeps it handy for all meetings and writing sessions. In fact, there is a popcorn maker on the *Saturday Night Live* stage floor to cater to his addiction.

Outside, on the way in to the *SNL* offices, you encounter a series of photographs from old *SNL* casts. There's a receptionist who grills you as to your purpose. Michaels' office is situated along an L-shaped corridor. It fronts on a common area containing a battery of assistants.

There is a lounge with a coffee table and stacks of trendy magazines and a few television sets. Various assistants trot through the halls carrying coffee, scripts, or both.

You sense that you are on hallowed ground, walking a comedic battlefield. Every kid with comedic aspirations, and who grew up after 1975, has dreamt of performing on *SNL*. When he was in grade school, Mike Myers wrote an essay on Lorne Michaels. He hoped that it would lead to a spot on *SNL*. When Jim Carrey appeared to host the show in May 1996, he told Wayne Flemming that it was the moment he had been working towards his entire life. Comedians do not crave a spot on *SNL* because it is the hottest show on the air — *SNL* goes up and down in popularity. They want it because once you've appeared on *SNL* you've touched the thing that inspired you to do comedy in the first place. You've walked through the television screen into your teenage comedian-wannabe fantasy.

The wizard who makes these lollipop dreams come true is Lorne Michaels. I'd say the most telling statement his office makes is not anything that he has in it. It's the location. Michaels' office lies on the seventeenth floor, midway between the suits upstairs and the street. This reflects the secret of Lorne Michaels' success — his ability to bridge the gap between the streets (the comedians) and the powers that be. At *SNL* they called him "the ambassador for the counter-culture."

As a kid growing up in Toronto during the mid-fifties, he was nowhere close to that title, nor was he close to being Lorne Michaels. He was Lorne Lipowitz, and in one of the most serendipitous twists of Canadian comedy, he was seated most nights at Frank Shuster's dinner table. It was not the quest for a mentor that led him to that table, although Shuster would later assume that role, as well as the role of surrogate father. It was Michaels' heart that had driven him there. Lorne was in love with Shuster's daughter, Rosalind. She and Michaels had gone to the same summer camps, the same junior high school, and they lived in the same Toronto neighbourhood, Forest Hill. They had been an item from the moment each hit puberty. Lorne was five years older than Rosie. "He'd seen me and some friends out in the neighbourhood jumping on boards," Rosie Shuster says. "You know, young girls having fun.

He got curious about that energy and showed up at my doorstep. Then he never left."

Michaels had been born and raised in Toronto. His grandparents ran a movie theatre. His father was a furrier, who died when Lorne was fourteen. His childhood was not unusual in any way. He played sports, hockey in the winter and baseball in the summer. "Toronto was still a very, very safe environment," he recalls. "I can remember sitting on the curb and waiting for a car to pull down the street. That would be exciting. The men left in the morning and went to work, the kids went to school. There was order and safety, and parents weren't terribly concerned. You played after school and as long as you were home for dinner, nobody worried. You didn't have to travel with a beeper."

Lorne Michaels wasn't a show-biz kid. He had no aspirations towards the stage. But jokes came naturally. There was a currency, both in the neighbourhood and within his family, as well as in Rosie's, in being funny. You scored points for being witty. Michaels vividly recalls his first encounter with the power of comedy.

"I made a joke in the second grade, which was a cruel joke, I think. The teacher said — about a girl who was slightly overweight, what we called then a fat girl — that if this girl didn't stop talking, she was going to put her in one of the lockers at the back of the class. I said she wouldn't fit. I think I was trying to be funny, rather than trying to be cruel. I think I was trying to relieve tension, and I was showing off for the teacher. As a result of the joke, I was given the strap. They had a leather strap and you had to hold your hand out. It was just corporal punishment. They hit you till you cried, because the point was to humiliate you and send you back to class so everyone could see you."

Like many of the baby-boom generation, Lorne was drawn to radio's successor. While radio was linked forever to the wartime generation, television was locked firmly in the fifties. It seemed to belong to the young. Says Michaels, "Early in the fifties, television came into our home. I remember radio a little bit. What I remember most is that my mother *watched* radio. Once television came, she leafed through magazines. She didn't pay as much attention to television as she did to radio. But I couldn't get enough of it.

"You'd wonder why they'd put certain shows on after school. There was a show out of Buffalo called *The Kate Smith Show*. I remember thinking, 'This isn't for kids.' There were so few choices. That's an experience that is exclusive to my generation, the idea that you had to live through shows to get to the show you wanted. I have a four-year-old son who just assumes that there is always something on. They — television's producers — never explained anything. The CBC would air an Indian's head graphic throughout the night when they weren't broadcasting. My brother and I used to get up every day to see if the Indian head was on yet."

Michaels struggled through high school, dating Rosie Shuster all the while, and went to the University of Toronto for a bachelor of arts degree. Like Frank Shuster, Lorne directed the student revue *University College Follies* and won positive reviews. Comedy, however, remained only a diversion in Michaels' mind. He did not consider it a career. He and Frank spent many hours discussing its nuances, and although Michaels wasn't serious about comedy as a career, he was serious about it as an art. "He had these strange ideas for this show he wanted to do," recalls Frank. "He was very passionate and clear about it. I had no idea what he was talking about."

After graduation, Michaels did not want to commit to a future. He was restless. To buy time, Lorne and Rosie travelled to England in 1966. London was then the Mecca for youth culture. The music scene was at its peak, and unlike the London of today, it was a very affordable city. Michaels earned fifteen pounds a week, and lived "quite well and had an incredibly intoxicating time."

In 1967, Lorne and Rosie returned to Canada. Michaels had been out of university for three years and was no closer to finding a calling than he'd been on graduation. He was beginning to run out of "excuses not to go to law school." On a whim, Lorne applied to the CBC. They turned him down, but an old friend from U of T named Earl Pomerantz suggested Michaels meet his brother, Hart Pomerantz. The younger Pomerantz was a natural-born performer, who had already been through law school. Pomerantz was looking for a scriptwriting partner. Michaels decided to take up his offer. The team of Hart and Lorne was born.

The duo first spent time working on CBC Radio with a show called *Five Nights a Week at This Time*. They wrote and performed satiric sketches on Canadian themes and developed a crisp writing style. These efforts were followed by a trip to New York (orchestrated by Pomerantz), during which the pair wrote for various stand-up comedians, such as Joan Rivers, Dick Cavett, and Woody Allen. Allen, Michaels recalls, would often have the writers over to his apartment to work. He was very gracious and friendly, but used little of what they produced. In June of 1968, the pair were hired to punch up the West Coast NBC television series *The Beautiful Phyllis Diller Show*. The program, which starred the burlesque comedian famous for her self-deprecating humour, ran thirteen episodes and was unceremoniously cancelled. Shortly afterwards, Hart and Lorne were picked up as junior writers for the hit CBS comedy series *Laugh-In*. The program, which starred the comedy duo Dick Martin and Dan Rowan, epitomized the free-love attitude of sixties counter-culture comedy. The jokes were standard issue, but the show used new technology that produced quick edits, to create a hip new style. It featured a multicultural cast, fast sketches, and bubbly air-heads played by Goldie Hawn.

By Canadian standards, Hart and Lorne had made the grade. They had succeeded, albeit modestly, in the United States. The CBC asked what it would take for Hart and Lorne to come back. Michaels told them creative control. "The CBC was so much more likely to give you control than money," he says. "We would write and produce and star. It seemed perfect. You've got to remember, after Expo '67 nationalism was at a peak, and people of my generation believed that we would be the first generation of Canadian artists to be able to stay in Canada." In 1970, *The Hart and Lorne Terrific Hour* was launched. Michaels and Pomerantz would do four specials a year, each airing on a Sunday. The show was a hit with Canada's baby boomers. The first *Hart and Lorne* show was titled "That's Canada for You." It might as well have been called "That's the CBC for You." For example, the show's signature sketch was a bit in which Michaels interviewed Pomerantz dressed in a beaver's costume. The show ran successfully until 1973, after which Hart and Lorne split up.

During its run, the team discovered they had different interests. Pomerantz wanted to concentrate solely on performing and writing. Michaels began to find himself more comfortable in the role of producer. With each show the pleasure he got from performing diminished. "I noticed that just before a take, my eyes would be checking lighting and looking all around the studio," says Michaels. "There'd be a look of enormous concern on my face. The slate would come and then I'd be smiling. I thought that was not a good sign. I was a worrier, and that's better suited to being a producer than a performer."

As *The Hart and Lorne Terrific Hour* was finishing its third season in 1973, Michaels had been promised the opportunity to develop a pilot using two comedians from Ottawa named Dan Aykroyd and Valri Bromfield. Had it ever seen the light of day, it might have resembled in many ways Michaels' most famous achievement, *Saturday Night Live*. In fact, had it ever gone to air, there might never have been a *Saturday Night Live*. But the CBC reneged on the promise to produce the pilot, and Michaels began to find himself falling victim to the negativism of Canadian TV comedy.

He was fielding offers from America but wanted to remain in Canada. "I didn't want to go. I wanted the assurance from the CBC that the pilot would go," Lorne remembers. "But instead, the head of CBC variety said to me, 'If you're that good, why are you here?' It was clarifying for me. Sidney Newman [the head of CBC programming at the time] recited something that James Joyce had written, about Ireland being an old sow that eats its young. There was a certain kind of self-loathing that Canadians who stayed had for each other. The attitude was, Hollywood was bad, and yet anybody who was any good went there. I began to think that it didn't really matter if Van Gogh was a Dutch artist or a French artist. What really mattered was his work. He went where the light was. The light for me was more and more in California."

Michaels had other issues to grapple with. His marriage was ending. He and Rosie had then been together as a couple, on and off, for over fifteen years. As husband and wife, however, they were not going to make it. Says Shuster, "Basically, I wasn't ready to be married to anyone." So in 1974, Lorne Michaels moved to Los Angeles alone and rented a room in the Chateau Marmont Hotel, a bohemian enclave located just off the Sunset Strip in Hollywood. "I had to begin again," he says. "I was getting divorced and living in one room in a hotel and starting all over again. Which I did."

In Los Angeles, Lorne's experience in Canada counted for very little, and his work on *Laugh-In* was mostly a memory. Michaels spent time at the Marmont stewing. His break finally arrived in the form of a job working for comedian Lily Tomlin. Tomlin had been a fixture on *Laugh-In* and had gone on to carve out a large chunk of the comedy market for herself. She specialized in character comedy, playing everything from a little girl to a gabby telephone operator. Michaels was hired on to help write Tomlin's television specials. Lorne made his time with her pay off. He had a knack for writing character material and rose up in the show's ranks quickly. Tomlin made him a co-producer. In 1974, he won an Emmy award for his writing on her show. His cachet in Hollywood was on the rise.

In 1975, NBC was looking for a new comedy series. They had planned to do forty pilots and hoped for one credible hit. Dick Ebersol, NBC's West Coast head, went to Michaels, who pitched a show tentatively entitled *NBC's Saturday Night*. It would be aired live and be reminiscent of Sid Caesar's fifties series *Your Show of Shows*. Ebersol came back to Michaels with a go. The other pilots had been junked. Since *Saturday Night* was going to be live, there would be no pilot, which pleased Michaels, who was tired of explaining his concepts to network suits. Michaels' agent secured him a seventeen-show deal. This did not guarantee that Michaels' show would air seventeen times; it merely meant that regardless of how this experiment played out, Michaels would get paid for seventeen episodes.

There was one catch. The show had to be New York-based. There was no artistic reason for this. It was just that NBC had a free studio in the Big Apple to fill. "I didn't want to leave California," Michaels recalls. "I had to be dragged [to New York]." In retrospect, Michaels' reluctance is ironic. Twenty years later his name would be as closely associated with New York City as is the Statue of Liberty.

If you had visited the seventeenth floor in 1975, when *NBC's Saturday Night* was about to launch, you would have noticed very few assistants, few security guards, and a strong whiff of cannabis. The atmosphere was loose. "It was like a professional office," says Rosie's younger brother, Steve Shuster, who used to hang out there, "except everyone smoked a lot of dope." Drugs were part of being counter-culture. Drugs hadn't yet been demonized. They were, in fact, a badge of hipness. This in itself spoke volumes about the generation Michaels was trying to appeal to with *Saturday Night*. For the baby boomers, it wasn't enough to use a drug just to get high. There had to be some greater meaning and purpose to it. Drugs were an ingredient in the early *Saturday Night* recipe, primarily marijuana but also other hallucinogens, such as magic mushrooms. Cocaine was still in the future — most of the cast could not afford it.

The show's inaugural episode aired on October 11, 1975. Stand-up George Carlin was the host. Valri Bromfield, who was not a member of the cast, nevertheless did a two-minute monologue. Aykroyd performed a sketch he'd written while still in Toronto, in which two security-alarm salesmen rob a house to prove it needs protection. Frank Shuster attended the taping, "My wife, Ruth, and I went to the first show, naturally. George Carlin was the host, and he couldn't act very well. He kept looking at the audience after every line. I didn't get it. I see the set and what I see is a cellar, garbage cans, and a cat going by. It was a whole new world. Lorne said to me, 'I'm trying to go counter to what you did. I'll do anything that's different, anything to wake people up.'"

"It was a joke that he was given midnight on Saturday night," says Bromfield. "It was like being given three in the morning on a Wednesday. Nobody thought the slot could work."

The original cast was a team of anti-television comic minds that had been force-fed television from their days in diapers. They were guerrilla comedians. From Canada Michaels imported Dan Aykroyd, whom he'd worked with at the CBC; Toronto-trained American Gilda Radner; musical director Howard Shore; and Michaels' now ex-wife, Rosie Shuster, who came on as a writer. The cast was completed by Chevy Chase, a writer who'd worked for the Smothers Brothers; loose cannon

John Belushi, a *National Lampoon* magazine and Second City graduate from Chicago; Laraine Newman from Los Angeles; Garrett Morris; and Jane Curtin. Michaels called them the Not Ready for Prime Time Players. Michaels' writing crew was also decidedly anti-TV. Michael O'Donoghue was a *National Lampoon* writer who loathed television. Only Herb Sergeant had any real TV experience.

NBC's Saturday Night became *Saturday Night Live,* the comedic tornado. Lorne Michaels' dream became a comic institution that eclipsed all the programs that had inspired its creator. *Saturday Night Live* launched a cornucopia of careers — stars like Dan Aykroyd, John Belushi, Chevy Chase, Eddie Murphy, as well as supporting players such as Dana Carvey, Jan Hooks, and Phil Hartman.

The story of *Saturday Night Live,* however, is not the stars, the backstage action, nor the big-business angle. The story of *Saturday Night Live* is how a Toronto-born producer found the recipe that changed the way American viewers looked for laughs when they turned on their television sets. Lorne Michaels was a first in Canadian comedy's pedigree. Before Lorne Michaels, Canadian comedians had been subject to two cultural influences: British theatre and American radio and movies. Lorne Michaels added a Canadian ingredient. He was influenced by American popular culture, British television and films, and Canadian television, in the form of Wayne and Shuster and Aylesworth and Peppiatt. This eclectic mix made him a unique talent. He could extract the best from each field and combine them to create a superior hybrid. "Canada is a much more sophisticated place to experience comedy," he told me on the seventeenth floor. "There's more of it around. We get British and American comedy. In America, you just get American."

British comedy has never been fully accepted by American audiences. American audiences are unwilling to digest British comedy because English comedians tend to create comic anti-heroes. The stars of British comedies are petty, selfish, troubled weaklings who struggle to survive the world that surrounds them. They are characters like Basil Fawlty, of British comedian John Cleese's hit series *Fawlty Towers,* or Alf Garnett in *'Til Death Do Us Part.* Canadian audiences savour these characters because we share the British taste for irony. We don't expect

202 • STAND AND DELIVER

perfection from comic characters. Americans, by contrast, demand comic heroes. Every sitcom character, no matter how repugnant, must have a heart of gold. Towards that end, Hollywood has converted British hits by attaching halos to what were originally flawed, often bigoted, characters. The working-class Tory in *'Til Death Do Us Part* was cosmetically altered to become Archie Bunker in *All in the Family,* the racist with a kind soul inside. The warring father-and-son Cockney garbage collectors of *Steptoe and Son* became the salt-of-the-earth African–American father and son in *Sanford and Son.*

In the mid-sixties, the stage show *Beyond the Fringe,* which featured Dudley Moore and Peter Cook, had revolutionized British humour. Their sketches were wicked and unbridled. They lacerated British society, particularly its class system. In 1970, following fast on their footsteps, *Monty Python's Flying Circus* aired on the BBC and pushed the British sensibility further to the edge. *Monty Python* was the biggest British influence on Lorne Michaels. The show intentionally broke every rule of comedy. *Monty Python* made full use of television's new technology. They employed animated cartoon skits, and fast- and slow-motion film. They used the speed of film editing to make lightning-fast scene changes. Their sketches often had no real endings. When a scene ran out of laughs, it ended, and no conventional conclusion was necessary. An artificial segue such as "and now for something completely different" was sufficient. The troupe didn't throw out every rule. They performed most of their sketches before a live audience. They also used the British music-hall tradition of drag. The Pythons were an all-male group that played many female characters. They weren't above cheesecake. In fact, scantily clad nubile women were a staple of their sketches. The Pythons, however, used them in an ironic way. They made it clear to their audience that they knew they were using a cheap Benny Hill gag.

Saturday Night Live owes more to *Monty Python* than has ever been acknowledged, particularly its early seasons. Michaels borrowed heavily. Like *Python, SNL* exploited the clash between reality and surrealism. The *Python* gang would create a realistic scene, for example a military training class, and interpose a surreal element, like fighting off a Bengal tiger with a handful of berries. *Python* would dedicate seven minutes to "Pantomime Horse 007," a sketch in which two pantomime horses (costume horses used in children's plays, in which one man plays the front legs and the other the back) play secret service agents. With all the other elements of a James Bond film intact, the incongruity of two cloth horses driving cars and shooting guns made for a hilarious sketch. *SNL* picked up on this formula. All the elements of the sketch would be "normal," and then a surreal comedic element would intrude. In the sketch "Land Shark," a vicious white shark attacks New York women by posing as a variety of door-to-door professions, from flower delivery man to telegram boy. A completely realistic apartment is disrupted by an obviously fake shark, parodying the spectacular movie hit of the period, *Jaws.* Like *Python, SNL* used animation segments to get laughs. "Mr. Bill," a claymation spoof of a children's TV program, was a huge hit. Mr. Bill was a punching bag for the bully, Mr. Sluggo. It was a direct descendent of the animated shorts that Terry Gilliam had done for the Pythons.

The Canadian influence in Michaels' comedy manifested itself in two ways: the creative and the practical. Creatively, Lorne absorbed the literate slapstick of Wayne and Shuster. He had a fondness for classical structure and clean comedic pay-offs. Practically, he saw the limits and the advantages of the CBC school of production. "At the CBC, a one-hour show took four months to make and you were working the whole time — I mean, it's not a feature, it's an hour of television. The Los Angeles production style was too much factory style. When I first got to L.A., I did ten shows in eight weeks."

One reason the CBC spent more time producing less programming was that CBC producers were afraid of creating flops. A bad CBC show cost the taxpayers money. Everything they shot they felt obliged to use. "The CBC was trying to avoid the perception of wastefulness," Michaels says. "In American television, it's either a hit or it's off the air. So wastefulness is tolerated, because if it's successful, and a hit, it makes a lot of money. Then it doesn't matter if the sketch didn't work and you have to cut it, or the star gets paid millions. That's having two hundred million people as an audience versus fifteen million."

In 1975, Michaels' generation, the first to "grow up" with television, found little on American TV that represented its point of view. "I felt I sprang from the audience," said Michaels. "I was no different than the people who would be watching the show. I was certain that if I could just get the show through to the audience unmolested, it would work."

Many Canadian journalists have stressed the importance of ironic distance when discussing Canadian comedy. As far as *SNL* is concerned, the ironic distance was between the two great cataclysms of late twentieth-century American life: Vietnam and Watergate. Both had concluded by 1974. The unthinkable had happened. America had lost a war. The president had lied. It was so calamitous that baby-boomer parents made their kids stay up and watch Nixon resign. Everything that the Woodstock generation had feared was proven true. You couldn't trust anyone over thirty, and the war was unwinnable. These were bitter truths. Had *SNL* debuted in 1973, it likely would have failed. It would have been too soon. America wasn't ready to laugh at itself. The humiliation and pain were too close. By 1975, enough time had passed. The political disgrace of Vietnam and Watergate was history. The anguish that America endured would never fade, but because time had elapsed, humour could begin to weave its way into public discourse.

The result? Chevy Chase scored in sketches such as his portrayal of President Gerald Ford, who pardoned Nixon. Chase played him, without make-up, as an utter bumbling buffoon who pardoned his staff for having sex with his dog. *SNL,* especially in the early years, was extremely political, far more so than most American programs. Television executives considered political humour a death sentence for ratings. Michaels realized that the *SNL* generation wanted political figures to be fair game. The key lay in the presentation. They didn't want to watch a snappy political revue, with tongue-in-cheek jabs at Democrats and Republicans. The *SNL* generation wanted a more abstract approach. Says Rosie Shuster, "We'd start with logic, and then there would be a surreal lift-off. It was what we called a comic quantum leap. The logic was A, B, C — Q."

"When I came to NBC there was this curiosity as to why I would want to do political comedy, because it was a sure ratings killer," Michaels told the New York *Times* in 1993. "America was founded on the distrust of authority. In Canada, you don't feel secure in that right, so you exercise it. Defying authority in a small way is a big Canadian thing."

Saturday Night Live was as modern and hip as you could get. Its creative team relied on its instincts. It had a hyped yet casual approach to comedy. Recalls Michaels, "You did something on the seventeenth floor that made you laugh, and then you took it down and put it on television." Work and personal life often overlapped. For example, Rosie Shuster began living with Dan Aykroyd. Such soap-opera antics kept the creative atmosphere sparking. *SNL*'s satirists combined the infantile with the insightful. Guerrilla comedians such as Andy Kaufman deconstructed comedy by pulling stunts like singing along to Mighty Mouse records; Michael O'Donoghue did his impression of Elvis getting a knitting needle stuck in his eye by simply holding a needle to his eye and screaming. And yet, its formula was extremely retro. Like the programs Michaels had grown up watching, it was live and it broadcast from New York. *Saturday Night Live* brought the magic back to television by bringing the audience back to the point of creation. You could stay home on Saturday night and go to New York City. The show was at the same time very much a seventies occasion. It was an electronic happening. It was a get-together for enlightenment, where the hip traded quips. *SNL* was the counter-culture adopting the trappings of the past so it could turn them on to the future. *SNL* was comfort food for grown-up children. On a pragmatic level, by doing a live-broadcast show, Michaels cut out interference from network heads. The suits couldn't meddle with what they hadn't seen. Essentially, the creative team consisted of baby boomers who'd grown up watching television and then stopped, because television was not reflecting their values or aesthetic. Says Shuster, "We were TV snobs doing TV. It was like a big love affair, an adventure. We didn't know where it was going to go."

SNL resuscitated American TV comedy clichés by twisting them. The clearest example of this technique was Chevy Chase's pratfalls, which were an essential element of the 1975 season. A pratfall is vintage comic schtick. Dick Van Dyke had stamped it on the American Zeitgeist with his own television show, which began with the comedian tripping over an ottoman. It is the classic, man-slipping-on-a-banana-peel equation. Someone falls and we laugh. Chase transformed this old comic trick into a chic comedic statement. The old became new. He routinely sprawled in and out of sketches. Chase even opened a show by arguing with Michaels, saying he refused to do "another fall," since he'd been offered a spot on the TV series *McMillan and Wife*. Of course, Chase then proceeds to do a series of over-the-top pratfalls beyond anything he'd ever done on a previous show.

The next twenty years for *SNL* saw a mass of changes, all along a familiar pattern. Michaels left the show in 1980 and embarked on a series of projects, including *The New Show,* a prime-time version of *SNL*. The series bombed abysmally. Michaels worked on a few feature films, including *The Three Amigos,* which starred Chevy Chase, Steve Martin, and Martin Short. In 1985, he returned to *SNL* and revamped the show, which had been faltering. The head of NBC, Brandon Tartikoff, called Michaels and offered him a chance to save the show, which Tartikoff was preparing to cancel. Discussing the future of *SNL* became somewhat of a pastime during the eighties and nineties. Countless articles were published pondering this dilemma. Can it be saved? they wondered. The attention, no matter how negative, was proof that *SNL* had risen above being a mere TV show. It had become a part of the North American audience's consciousness, and as such they felt they had a right to criticize it. Viewers had a proprietary relationship with *SNL*. They felt like shareholders. When it was bad, their feelings were hurt.

The criticism of the writing, cast, and even the ideas behind the show took its toll on Michaels. "I'm very tired of the show and my role in it being judged as if I'm a Clinton appointee," he told the New York *Daily News* in 1995. "We are a comedy show. We try to put on the funniest people we can." Each time the critics called for its termination, Michaels succeeded in saving the show, with new casts, which included talents like Dana Carvey, Jan Hooks, and Canadian Phil Hartman. But the bad followed the good. By 1995, critics were again calling for *SNL*'s execution. The New York *Times* reviewed the 1996 opening episode, saying, "The *Saturday Night Live* format is tired . . .

The time has arrived for devising something entirely different."

Michaels' second contribution to North American comedy had already come and gone by 1996. It was the Kids in the Hall, a quintet from Toronto that Michaels had plucked from obscurity in the late eighties. By then, the comedy landscape had changed considerably since the early days of *SNL*. Things that were hip when *SNL* debuted were now old-hat. Stand-up had gone from being an avant-garde experiment to a money-spinning business. Like most timely bits of counter-culture, it had been embraced by the mainstream. Just as punk had gone commercial, so too had stand-up. Television was now saturated with stand-up shows, from *Evening at the Improv* to *Caroline's Comedy Hour*.

In Canada, Yuk Yuk's had its own TV series, which ran for thirteen episodes on the CBC in 1985. These programs ultimately hurt the industry. The comedy they offered was mundane. To succeed on these shows, stand-ups had to appeal to millions of viewers. The only way they could achieve this was by picking reference points they felt everyone could relate to — in other words, generic subjects like airline travel and fast food. The result? Stand-up itself became fast food. The crowd that had lined up outside Yuk Yuk's Church Street basement, the hipsters, were no longer lining up outside the Yonge and Eglinton club. Instead, they gravitated towards a new comedy movement that was beginning to muster in rock-and-roll venues and coffee houses. This shift was powered by comics who wanted to work but disliked both Yuk Yuk's-style stand-up and Second City revues.

Out of this dissatisfaction a new wave of comedians emerged. They too had been reared on television, but their reference points were more recent. Michaels had been inspired by *Your Show of Shows*. The new wave were inspired by *SNL*. These were the alternative comedians, a group that defined itself primarily by the things it was not. CBC comedy, like *Wayne and Shuster* or *The Royal Canadian Air Farce,* was square and provincial. According to proponents of the alternative, Yuk Yuk's stand-up was sexist, racist, homophobic, and misogynist. Second City was tacky and suburban. These new comedians drove hard the other way. They worked to be funny without resorting to hack put-down humour. They didn't want to insult the woman sitting in the front row in order to get a laugh. Alternative comedians did material that was gay-positive, woman-positive, ethno-positive. Even more important than ideology was creativity. Their motto was: Try something new.

The latest wave didn't know it, but, of course, there was nothing particularly new about being new. Since the seventies, Canadian comedy had always had an outside wing. These alternative acts had strong ties to the theatre and their work was very visual, incorporating costumes and props. In the seventies, Michael Rappaport and Paul K. Willis, who together made up La Troupe Grotesque, had staged similar shows with elaborate costume changes and musical interludes. Nip and Tuck Tubb Rag, another seventies troupe, had pushed the envelope and played on the edges of mainstream comedy.

In Canada, the new alternative comedy found a home at the Rivoli, a nightclub-cum-restaurant on Toronto's trendy Queen Street West. In fact, it's fair to say that the alternative movement was epitomized by the Rivoli, known to its regulars as the Riv. Prior to the advent of the Riv, there had been clubs that were borderline alternative, like the Flamingo which the Frantics had run for a year on Sherbourne Street. The Rivoli, which was stripped of glitz, willfully pretentious, and heavy with youthful attitude, became the home base for alternative comedy.

The Rivoli's theatre is located behind the restaurant and bar. It is a long rectangular black-box theatre with pipes and heating units exposed for all to see. The walls are modestly decorated with crude murals. The stage is a small twelve-by-eighteen-foot proscenium arch, which has a small dressing room off to one side. A few theatre lights are hung to offer bare-bones lighting. At the back is a small bar and a lighting board. There is a battery of mirrors on one wall which give the place a little space. There are three kinds of seating available, plastic chairs, stools, or a row of benches. The air is thick with cigarette smoke. The room is freezing in the winter and hot in the summer.

The Riv's patrons are eighteen to twenty-nine years old, often still in university or college. They dress up, or down, for the occasion. The look is young and well put together. Rivoli crowds are famously enthusiastic, often because three-quarters of the audience knows someone onstage. They're generous because they're at the Riv, and if they're at the Riv, then the comedy must be good. They won't attack the comedians, the worst they'll do is withhold applause.

In 1985, the kings of the Rivoli were a quintet from Toronto called the Kids in the Hall. The troupe — Kevin McDonald, Bruce McCulloch, Mark McKinney (older brother of Nick McKinney of Vacant Lot), Scott Thompson, and Dave Foley — formed in 1984. McCulloch and McKinney had moved from Calgary to Toronto with their sketch troupe, the Audience. As a sideline, McCulloch began doing stand-up at Yuk Yuk's. Foley and McDonald were already entrenched in the Toronto scene as the original Kids in the Hall. The comedians met while doing Theatresports, a form of improvisational comedy in which teams "compete" by improvising sketches. The four comics decided to form a troupe. Thompson, who was working with a group called the Love Cats, was brought in a few months later. Their name was taken from *The Jack Benny Show*. When he would try out bits from wannabe writers, Benny would say, "That's one from the kids in the hall."

The Kids weren't sure what they wanted their comedy to be, but, McDonald once told me, "We knew what we hated."

The Kids had a quick apprenticeship. They spent a year working every Monday night at the Rivoli. They pushed themselves to come up with a new show each week and quickly honed their natural ability into polished comedy. At the same time, the Kids began to draw a following. Word spread, and they became a Toronto phenomenon. They were the darlings of Toronto's hip scene. The Kids' material was unlike most of the Canadian sketch comedy that had gone before it. Unlike established sketch groups, like the Royal Canadian Air Farce, they weren't political or topical. They did not draw laughs from Canadianisms. There were no impressions of the prime minister, no references to Newfoundland, no soiled-politician-of-the-day material. Nor were the Kids American. Their sketches were closer to *Monty Python* than they were to *SNL*.

In December 1985, the troupe played a sold-out show at the Rivoli. A talent scout named Pam Thomas (*SCTV* comic Dave Thomas's ex-wife) was there. She was impressed, and told CBC executive Ivan Fecan about the Kids. He told Michaels. McCulloch and McKinney were hired to write for *SNL*. The group temporarily disbanded. Foley went to the West Coast to star in a low-budget movie, while McDonald and Thompson cooled their heels in Toronto. Michaels may have been based in New York, but his connection to the Canadian comedy scene remained strong. He had formed a production company, Broadway Video, and was looking for new acts to break in. After flying to Toronto to see the Kids perform, Michaels was hooked. "They're the first of the next wave," Michaels told *GQ* magazine in 1990, "for the generation that will follow the baby boomers who watched *Saturday Night Live*."

In 1987, Michaels brought the Kids to New York for a six-month "boot camp." Camp consisted of daily shows and marathon writing sessions. Out of this melting pot came the Kids' first one-hour special. Michaels secured a deal with the CBC and American cable channel Comedy Central to produce a series, *The Kids in the Hall*. It debuted in November of 1987.

The Kids in the Hall became a cult hit. Just as he had with the baby boomers, Michaels had tapped into the twenty-something generation. Their humour dealt with suburban life and parental strife, viewed with a surreal eye. They created characters like the Chicken Lady, an oversexed half woman, half chicken, and the Head Crusher, a maniac who got his kicks squeezing people's heads with the aid of his thumb, forefinger, and perspective. Each Kid, according to Thompson, had "father issues," and these played themselves out in their sketches. McKinney, on the other hand, told the New York *Times* in 1994 that the Kids "were a five-man troupe who wanted to write about the social and personal relationships we had with women." Regardless, the Kids delighted in drag comedy and made a mark as possibly the best Canadian drag comics since the Dumbells.

The formula worked for seven years. During that time, the Kids graduated to American networks like HBO and CBS. In Canada, they became the most popular sketch troupe among the so-called Generation X. Yet some knocked the Kids for being too American. They didn't say "eh," or make fun of the prime minister. In America, they were knocked for being too Canadian, and had to fight to keep Canadian references in their shows. John Blanchard, the show's director, told the New York

Times that the Kids often had to shoot two versions of each sketch: one untampered version for Canadian audiences and one cleaned-up version for Americans.

But the fighting was not confined to the networks. As a troupe, the Kids frequently fought among themselves. Foley once told me, "I hate Bruce." It was hard to tell if he was joking. This friction may have contributed to their overall creativity. In 1994, they ended their series and tried a feature film, *Brain Candy*. The film, which had a $7.5 million budget, told the story of the creation of a drug that cures depression. In it, the Kids played a total of fifty different characters. Paramount, the studio behind it, had a lot of confidence in the Kids. They were the first sketch troupe since Monty Python to be given a blessing to write and star in their own feature film. Unfortunately for the Kids in the Hall, the production was plagued by tension, much of it apparently between Dave Foley, who was starring in a successful NBC sitcom called *News Radio,* and the other Kids. In June 1995, shortly before filming was to begin, Foley told Paramount that he did not wish to do the movie, citing "family reasons." Foley was asked to honour his contract or face possible legal action. He showed up for shooting in July.

McDonald told me that everyone in the troupe considered quitting, with the exception of McKinney. "We were all going through our own hell to get the movie done. The smallest things seemed bigger. Scott was unhappy with some of the cuts we'd made to the script. While he considered quitting, I went to the bathroom and almost threw up. I thought, It's not worth it. Wives are leaving you, friends are yelling at each other. I should quit."

The Kids had always had a fiery relationship, and the friction had never hurt the quality of their television series. It's possible that it harmed their first shot at movies. *Brain Candy* opened in March of 1996 and was an immediate flop. After the failure, the Kids took an unlimited hiatus as a group.

Michaels' biggest transfer of Canadian talent occurred in the early nineties, when he took a twenty-six-year-old Second City alumnus named Mike Myers and moved him over to *Saturday Night Live*. Myers had been a fan of *SNL* since he was a kid. He'd watched the first episode in 1975, when he was only eleven. Myers had been raised in the Toronto suburb of Scarborough and was well versed in the lingo and habits of Wayne Campbell, the slacker heavy-metal anti-hero he had created. Wayne was another low-status Canadian comic character in the Alan Young vein. He was non-confrontational, lived in his parents' basement, and hosted a cable talk show with his friend Garth (played by Dana Carvey). Wayne just wanted to "party on." The comic twist came from Wayne's finely tuned intellect. He'd mix his head-banging mentality with references to obscure philosophers and works of literature. "Wayne's sort of like everybody I grew up with in Scarborough," Myers told *Maclean's* in July of 1993. "It's just the suburban adolescent experience as I knew it."

Michaels saw the potential in the character, which became a hit on *SNL*. He then produced a film around Wayne's exploits, titled *Wayne's World,* which opened in 1992. The movie was a smash, making Myers a huge star and Michaels a genius reborn. The creator of *SNL* had realized that Wayne, who was essentially a wholly Canadian character, would translate into America. The movie worked not because Americans were more open to Canadian culture, but because Canadian culture had become almost completely American. The responsibility for this change lay squarely with television. Americans and Canadians had watched the same programs for the last thirty years. Television was a bridge into America for Canadian comedians, and Michaels was not alone in identifying it. Another troupe had clued in back in 1975. They called themselves SCTV.

T W E L V E

■

Second City

What goes out must come back. What goes up must come down. That includes culture. A dominant (what used to be called imperial) culture sends its signal to its subordinate nations (once known as colonies). That is how it dominates. By enticing secondary nations to embrace its culture, and to see benefits in embracing this culture, the primary nation makes the process of being subjugated more palatable. Acquiescence to the centre is no longer a surrender, it is a beneficial exchange. When a subordinate nation's population receives signals from the dominant culture, it incorporates them and meshes them with its own cultural experience. The lesser nation then sends the cultural signal back to the centre in a new form that is specific to the subordinate nation.

The British Empire brought cricket to India and Pakistan. These countries identified strongly with the sport. They absorbed it and incorporated into it their own cultural identity, philosophies, and athletics. Today these two nations boast the world's best cricketers. This incorporation was a non-confrontational means of expressing animosity towards Britain (the centre). India was asserting its national identity by surpassing Britain at its own game. During the fifties and sixties, the world's new dominant culture, America, sent its signal to Britain in the form of rock and roll. Britain's youth embraced the new musical form. They grew up on it. To these kids, rock and roll equalled America. When they came of age, their generation appropriated the music. They transformed it by adding British influences and the experience of growing up British. Then groups like the Beatles and the Rolling Stones became part of the "British Invasion." Britain, the lesser nation, had bettered America at its own musical creation. The British intangible in British rock and roll made it superior to most of its American equivalents. Through Rock and roll, the culturally subordinate Britain expressed non-confrontational aggression against the dominant America.

In 1976, Canada was also preparing to send a signal back to America. The Canadian signal was a searing attack on the American television networks. It was a four-letter word: *SCTV*.

The SC in *SCTV* stands for Second City. Second City was an American invention, created in Chicago in 1959. Its name was a tongue-in-cheek jab at the notion of Chicago coming a close second to New York. Second City, a theatre with a repertory cast, featured sketch comedy revues created collectively by the actors. It quickly became an institution. Such American greats as Mike Nichols, Elaine May, Allan Arkin, Joan Rivers, and Ed Asner had come through its program. The content was topical. Politics and pop culture were the prime targets. The comedians would improvise scenes during rehearsal and scribble down the best lines. After each performance, they'd improvise some more in a late night "jam session." Out of these jams a new show would form. By 1973, they were ready to expand north.

Bernie Sahlins, Second City's owner, opened a Second City revue on Adelaide Street in Toronto. It was housed in the Factory Theatre, a small and rather grungy venue for experimental theatre. In the first cast were Canadians Dan Aykroyd, Valri Bromfield, Brian Murray, and Jayne Eastwood; and Americans Jeff Salsberg and Gilda Radner. Aykroyd and Bromfield met as kids in Ottawa. They each had a penchant for performing funny voices and quickly became a makeshift comedy team. According to Bromfield, Aykroyd was an oddball who hung out with the misfits, smoked dope, and would come over to her house after school to eat fish sticks. Aykroyd was a bit of a rebel. He had moved out of his parents' home while still in high school and decorated his new apartment in an eclectic style that included Madonnas with bras on them. Both Aykroyd and Bromfield had worked on the CBC sitcom *Coming Up Rosie* before moving to Second City. Aykroyd had an obsession with the dark side of life and with law enforcement institutions. These interests led Bromfield to comment that Aykroyd's biggest fantasy would be to break the law and then arrest himself.

The fledgling theatre immediately ran into trouble. Cheques bounced, the roof leaked, morale sank. The show lasted a short three months and went bankrupt. The cast was notified when they arrived for rehearsal and found the theatre padlocked from the outside (by bailiffs).

Near the end of 1974, a young American named Andrew Alexander stepped in to save Toronto's Second City. Alexander had been living in Toronto since the late sixties and had organized rock concerts, run a few "bottle clubs" (after-hours joints), and helped book a late-night theatrical revue in which both Aykroyd and Bromfield had performed. Alexander had spent 1971 in Chicago, working across the street from Second City and had developed a liking for the theatre's edgy brand of comedy. In 1974, after the Toronto Second City's demise, he found himself sharing a drink with the show's troubled producer. "One night at the bar," Alexander recalls, "Bernie said, 'I'm closing it.' I said, 'Why don't you give me the rights for a dollar, and I'll pay you a royalty if I can make a success of it?'"

Sahlins took his offer, and Alexander set about trying to pull Second City from oblivion. He moved the theatre to a beer hall called the Old Firehall. The stage was located upstairs on a floor with no air conditioning. Before each show, Alexander's actors would have to clear the stage of music equipment. In short, it was worse than the Adelaide Street venue. Alexander managed to lure a young comedian named John Candy, who had moved to Second City Chicago, back to Toronto. Along with Candy, Alexander convinced former Toronto cast members Eugene Levy and Gilda Radner (who had been appearing in the musical *Godspell*), Rosemary Radcliffe, and Joe Flaherty to give Toronto Second City one more try. The new and improved Second City's first revue, *You're Gonna Be All Right, You Creep, Leaving Home and All, Eh?*

debuted in 1974. The show, which satirized popular plays and Toronto's starchy attitude, snagged positive reviews. With some marketing pushes such as telephone soliciting by Alexander, it managed to stay afloat. Says Levy: "It was really fun. Improvisation as a means to an end. There were nights when we were brilliant and nights when we weren't. It was tremendous for establishing material."

In 1975, Sahlins opened a Second City in Pasadena, and Candy, Flaherty, and Levy moved to California to be part of the cast. The California theatre closed in six months. "I guess they didn't take into account the fact that no one goes to Pasadena," says Levy. Their departure was not without its positive side. It opened the gate for new Toronto cast members. In came Dave Thomas, Martin Short, and Catherine O'Hara. Thomas, who had been working as a copywriter at the advertising firm McCann-Erickson, had been looking for a chance to join the troupe. He had been a particular fan of Aykroyd's work with the Adelaide Street company. Says Thomas: "I saw this guy Aykroyd blow into town with this new type of comedy that has no previous model, and I was a student of comedy. I knew what was out there, and I knew Dan was doing something that nobody had seen before. He had a kind of blue-collar, techno-rap style. Long raps about the jobs of blue-collar workers, giving the audience rich details about their lives and their work. Instead of a plumber being an idiot, a plumber in a sketch with Danny Aykroyd was a hero."

Second City began to turn the corner as a business in 1976. The Old Firehall began to sell out regularly. The cast became a close-knit pseudo family. "It was my life," says Thomas. "It was what I did in the day, at night, and after the show at night. When I wasn't working, I was researching by going to movies and that sort of thing." Alexander grew to fear raids from down south, specifically from *Saturday Night Live,* which had debuted in 1975 and spawned a host of copy-cat shows, like ABC's *Fridays.* By this time he'd lost Aykroyd and Radner, who had been part of *SNL*'s original cast. Michaels had also plucked John Belushi and would eventually take Bill Murray from the Chicago company. Alexander feared another round of pillaging. He and Sahlins decided it was time to go TV. "I thought, 'Oh my God, they're going to steal my cast. Some network is going to come and take everybody.' It was self-preservation that got me into television."

But what to do? The cast — Candy, Flaherty, Levy, Martin, O'Hara, and Chicago players Harold Ramis, Sheldon Patinkin, and Del Close — held a meeting at the Old Firehall to bounce ideas around. Somebody mentioned parody. Somebody mentioned a mock station. The concept developed loosely. Meanwhile, Alexander made a deal with a southern Ontario television station, Global Television. Global agreed to produce seven episodes, and gave the show a $5,000-per-episode budget. The show's concept was deceptively simple. They'd present a day in the life of the Second City Television network (SCTV), an imaginary television station broadcasting from the make-believe town of Melonville. The show would parody American television and also have a backstage, behind-the-scenes plot that circled around regular, recurring characters. *SCTV* would attack the very medium they were about to enter. They would bite the hand that was feeding them. The show's opening sequence said everything that needed to be said about the *SCTV* mind-set: it showed a series of irate viewers hurling their television sets out windows. In 1976, Global Television broadcast the first episode of *SCTV* to an Ontario audience.

Initially, *SCTV*'s cast incorporated much of the best material from their stage shows. For example, a stage skit called "Big News, Little News" became the "SCTV News with Floyd Robertson and Earl Camembert." In the scene, Floyd (Flaherty) gets all the top news stories, and Earl (Levy) gets puny local stories. The two newscasters hate each other and take pot shots throughout their segments. Flaherty and Levy added a twist by making Floyd an alcoholic who moonlights as Count Floyd, the host of a kiddy horror-movie program. In one sketch, the realities collide when the pompous newscaster gets drunk at a cast party and arrives to deliver the news still wearing his Count Floyd vampire make-up.

SCTV limped along for two years, gaining little notice. By 1979, Alexander had managed to get syndication in 48 American markets. Its Canadian ratings were mediocre. The *SCTV* cast was once flown to New York for a press conference, and no one except a few student newspapers showed up to interview them. In its second season, *SCTV*'s syndication market grew to sixty stations, many of them NBC affiliates. In its third season, *SCTV* continued in syndication. It was a difficult show to find. Its time slot was bounced from Global to CBC. In 1980, Alexander made a deal with an Edmonton doctor named Charles Allard, who owned the giant Allarco Development company. Production of the show was moved to Edmonton. In 1981, its fifth season, *SCTV* was picked up by NBC, in the hope that it would bolster the network's ailing Friday night schedule. Better to have *SCTV* running at the same network as *SNL,* NBC executives thought, than running against it. *SCTV Network 90* aired from 12:30 A.M. to 2:00 A.M. John Candy and Catherine O'Hara, who had left the series, returned for the American run. Candy had tried an unsuccessful season hosting a CTV series called *Big City Comedy*. O'Hara had done some work directing at the Old Firehall. *SCTV Network 90* was essentially the same show that had run up north but with an added segment for musical guests, like John Cougar Mellencamp and Levon Helm of The Band. The isolation and cold in Edmonton made for fertile comedic ground. Levy says, "There was nothing to do but work." The show debuted in the late summer of 1981.

"*SCTV Network 90* should be registered with the police as a deadly weapon," wrote Los Angeles *Times* critic Howard Rosenberg. "What else can you call a show that makes you laugh hard enough to choke? . . . Levy, John Candy, Joe Flaherty, Andrea Martin, Rick Moranis, Catherine O'Hara and Dave Thomas — eat your hearts out, *Fridays* and *Saturday Night Live* — There are enough laughs in one episode of *SCTV Network 90* to sustain *Fridays* or *Saturday Night Live* for an entire season." Rosenberg's raves were echoed in newspapers and magazines around America. *SCTV* was an unqualified success.

One of *SCTV*'s top scorers was Dave Thomas. In March of 1996, I was in the Studio City parking lot in Los Angeles helping Thomas load the trunk of his car. He had long since left *SCTV* and was now a regular character on the CBS sitcom *Grace Under Fire*. Thomas had just wrapped for the day and was going to give me an hour-long interview and then hit the links for a round of golf. He looked every inch the

American Canadian with his even tan and tasteful, although conservative, clothes. He sported a white golf shirt, slacks and a navy blue blazer. The ensemble was topped off with running shoes. I commented on the sunshine, and Thomas quipped, "That's why I moved here. I couldn't fucking stand the cold weather up there. I always hated it."

We navigated a few office corridors and strolled by a few doors. Thomas's office was standard Hollywood. It had the obligatory couch, mint condition computer, television, VCR, and a scattering of books. It didn't take me long to discover that Thomas, like his SCTV character Bill Needle, was an argumentative guy who liked to match wits and wasn't about to let clumsy questions and surface answers go by unchastised. Thomas was in the process of writing a behind-the-scenes book on *SCTV*. I suggested that the fact a publisher was interested in a book on *SCTV* proved the show had made a significant impact. Thomas reclined in his chair, put his feet on his desk and countered: "They have books on gardening too, you know . . . There is a real consumer culture, not just in America and Canada, but in the entire world. There are pockets of loyal fans for virtually everything that exists. It's not surprising that there is a pocket of loyal *SCTV* fans."

SCTV targeted American television. It was not a topical show. The cast didn't chase headlines the way *SNL* did. It was apolitical. This was a savvy strategy. More people watched American TV than voted or read the newspaper. It was the great leveller. More importantly, television irritated and disappointed many — who watched it nonetheless. It was a self-important, pompous, ludicrous medium, and therefore a bottomless pit of comic possibilities. *SCTV* mocked television by creating solid comedic characters. John Candy didn't walk out as John Candy and talk about how silly TV westerns were; he appeared in a mock-western called "Yellow Belly," about a cowardly gun-poke. Although some of the celebrity parodies were painfully realistic, the show was not malicious. It did not go for the jugular. Says Levy: "The show did what people wished they could see happen on TV. That's still the basis for the stuff I do: What if?"

When *SCTV* attacked television, it was attacking America. To Canadians, American television was America in the same way that rock and roll was America to British musicians. By parodying it, *SCTV* also allowed Americans to enjoy their own disenchantment with America without feeling traitorous. The target was a good reflection of the generation from which *SCTV* sprang, which was also Lorne Michaels' generation. The entire cast had been raised on American television. They had absorbed America through the box. Thomas spent sixty hours a week as a kid watching American westerns like *Rawhide, Lawman, and Cheyenne.* O'Hara had been a *Captain Kangaroo* fan. Moranis was a *Dick Van Dyke* aficionado. Candy was partial to Jack Parr, *The Honeymooners,* and *Howdy Doody.* "We were all students of television," says Thomas. "We'd been raised on the boob tube, warming our hands before the blue glow of the electric hearth. Suddenly, we had an opportunity to take some pot shots at it, and we found out we weren't alone. There were a lot of other people who shared our cynicism, shared our comedy and our sense of what was silly and stupid about television. It provided a nice common ground for a joke."

That a Canadian comedy troupe could satirize American television so effectively demonstrated that the differences between the two countries were steadily shrinking. In 1920, the Dumbells had brought a foreign art, British music hall, to Broadway. Sixty years later, Canadian comedians (*SCTV*) were skewing an American art form for Americans. In the fifties, most Canadians would have considered themselves more British than American. By the eighties, Canadians were unquestionably more American. We watched American sports, followed American politics, and consumed American entertainment, all via television. We got the prepackaged American experience. There was no downside. By contrast, Americans watched American TV, but they also lived American lives. They suffered the disillusionment of Vietnam, Watergate, and George Bush's War on Drugs. We watched these events as if they were just another episode of *Happy Days.* Canadians watched American TV, with all its violence, sex, and hype and then went outside to play road hockey or went to the doctor for some government-subsidized health care.

SCTV was not without its Canadian content. In fact, the most arguably famous Canadian comic characters in TV history were born on that show. They were inspired by our country's most popular form of earnest neurosis, our insecurity about what it means to be Canadian. Two Canadian "hosers," brothers named Bob and Doug McKenzie, demonstrated this phenomenon. Bob (Moranis) and Doug (Thomas) had their own show on SCTV, called *The Great White North*. On it, they discussed such topics as "How to get a mouse in your beer so you can get a free case of beer." They were an answer to CBC's request for more Canadian content.

Says Thomas: "When the CBC picked up the show, they asked us to create two extra minutes of material, because CBC programs ran two minutes longer since they had fewer commercials. The CBC asked if the two minutes could be Canadian. We were insulted. The cast was more than half Canadian, it was shot in Canada, the crew was Canadian, and these whiners at the CBC wanted more Canadian content. I've always thought it was lame to make comedy an issue of nationalism. It's very neurotic the way Canadians go about trying to get their identity. Bob and Doug were an insult to the CBC. We said, 'What do you want us to do? Put up a big map of Canada? Is that Canadian enough for you? And sit there in toques and parkas and fry back bacon?' The CBC said, 'Yeah, that would be great.' Our producer said, 'If you could put a Mountie in there, that would be good.'"

Bob and Doug would have remained a Canadian segment, but Flaherty took time off in the 1982 season and the two hosers were inserted into the show. American viewers loved them. Bob and Doug were stereotypical Canadians in the most crass sense. They were two moronic hicks whose only goal in life was a beer buzz and a smoke, and maybe to fry some back bacon. They played games like "Beer Hunter." The game was a boozy descendent of Russian roulette and was a send-up of the hit movie *The Deer Hunter*. It was played with a six-pack. A single can of beer was shaken, then placed back in the beer case. Players would take turns placing beer cans next to their heads and opening them.

"The joke was that Canadians didn't embrace it first," says Thomas. "Americans embraced Bob and Doug first. When Canadians saw that Americans liked Bob and Doug, then Canadians decided they liked Bob and Doug. I have record sales that prove this. [Bob and Doug became an album that went double platinum.] It was 'Gee, you really put us on the map, eh?' Better to be on the map as nerds than nothing at all. I don't think the Australians have the same neurosis that Canadians do about presenting their entertainment. And it's the *maudits Anglais,* not the Québécois. A bunch of Scottish Nazi tight-asses who don't understand that excellence itself is proof that Canada has made a mark."

Despite its successes, *SCTV*'s poor time slot eventually killed the series. By 1984, the cast, which had grown to include Rick Moranis and Martin Short, had burnt out and could no longer sustain the creative pressure. Even the support of the critics and millions of viewers was unable to save it. "We'd run out of steam," says Alexander. "The last year we were running on empty."

"There was pressure to make *SCTV* a franchise," says Thomas, "so that the network could run it like *SNL* and just drop new cast members into it. [But] we weren't trying to create something that would last without us."

As I sat there, listening to Thomas discuss the end of *SCTV*, I began to realize that this was one of the most difficult interviews I'd ever done. Difficult, because, as hard as I tried to concentrate on Thomas, my mind kept wandering back to his portrayal of "The Cruising Gourmet" on *SCTV*. In the sketch, Thomas, clad in leather bondage gear, hooks up a half-frozen turkey to a set of chains suspended from the ceiling. As pounding rock music plays, he fists stuffing into the spread-eagled bird's cavity. The first time I saw the bit I found it so hilarious that more than twelve years later I can still bring myself to hysterics just by remembering it. The look of fury and determination on Thomas's face as he "stuffs" the poultry is sublime. He is so totally committed to his act of insanity. As far as I'm concerned, it remains one of the most accurate caricatures of modern media that exists.

I don't think I'm alone in my attachment to *SCTV*'s characters. That was the show's greatest strength. You grew to love the grotesque collection of misfits and miscreants *SCTV*'s cast concocted. John Candy's creation, Johnny LaRue, was a reprehensible, drunken, lascivious, paranoid, egomaniac cliché, and you loved him for it.

These characters were no accident. They were the result of sharp writing. Unlike its competitors, *SCTV* was a cast-written show. Like Wayne and Shuster before them, the cast did not surrender writing duties to a slew of hired Hollywood guns. By retaining scribbling responsibilities, *SCTV*'s cast took the path of most resistance. Each cast member pulled double duty for a single paycheque. On top of this, the network was constantly pushing them to open up. Here again *SCTV* resembles Wayne and Shuster. The American network couldn't intimidate them; NBC couldn't play the money card. The *SCTV* cast had been through the grinder. They'd earned almost nothing onstage at Second City and went on to earn very little on Canadian TV. Through this process, they grew to realize that the most important thing in comedy was artistic freedom, which meant maintaining artistic control. You don't suffer abuse in Canada so you can go down to Los Angeles and have some executives tell you how to run your show. Struggling teaches comedians that they only ever own one thing, and that's the work. So the smart ones never give it up.

Generally, Thomas was in charge of giving the network directions. In a way, being Canadian gave the *SCTV* cast an advantage. To American comics, America was everything. The Canadians had that tiny out: they knew they could always go back to Canada and work, albeit for considerably less money. "When the network came to tell us what they wanted for the show, I had the cast mandate to tell them to go fuck themselves. And I did. They were very shocked. Their attitude was, 'How can you say this to us? We're the network.' I said, 'Here's your choice. We respect that you're paying for the show and we understand that. And if you want to pull the show, that's your call. But if you want us to do what you want, we would rather quit.'"

Of course, it was easier to forget Hollywood when you were in Edmonton. It was easier to forget everything except freezing. Like Wayne and Shuster and the Kids in the Hall, the *SCTV* crew stayed in Canada. With the exception of one season of writing, *SCTV* was always based north of the border. This kept the cast free of the sycophants and hangers-on that pollute the Hollywood system. *SCTV* was never co-opted by the industry that it was satirizing.

SCTV kept its ironic distance. In 1981, Levy told *Playboy* magazine,

"We dictate what our show is. Nobody comes down and tells us what to do. We do it ourselves. I don't think we'll ever have this power again. You get an idea, you write it, you tape it, you edit it, you follow it through in post-production. This just won't happen again."

He was right. After Second City, the cast went Hollywood. John Candy became the most successful of the troupe. He had a stellar movie career, starring in pictures like *Planes, Trains and Automobiles* that made him one of the biggest stars in America. He maintained his Canadian connection. He was a part-owner of the CFL's Toronto Argonauts. Candy died of a stroke in 1994 while shooting a film in Mexico. The Los Angeles Police Department closed the entire 405 Highway, possibly the longest freeway in America, to make way for his funeral procession. O'Hara became a respected character actress, appearing in films such as *Beetlejuice* and *Home Alone*. Short joined *SNL* and then appeared in various Hollywood pictures. Moranis pulled duty in various comedy flicks, such as *Ghostbusters*. Thomas found work in sitcoms. Levy and Flaherty worked on the kids' show *Maniac Mansion*. Martin became a regular on Broadway and in Canadian TV commercials. They all went on to lucrative and rewarding careers. But they never came close to achieving the satiric energy and weight they had as the cast of *SCTV*. That's probably best. In comedy, nothing should last forever. A show is pertinent for a while, then it loses its edge. *SCTV* bowed out at the right time, maybe even a little late. The cast had said what it had to say about television. Their priorities had changed since the seventies, once again reflecting the mood of many of their generation. Thomas probably sums it up best: "I can't be a comedy guerrilla and take care of three kids. And besides, I don't want to be a comedy guerrilla anymore."

Not all Canadian comedians want to go south, of course. Canada's proximity to America gives some Canadians all the motivation they need to direct their attention homeward. They react to American culture by looking more closely at what makes Canada Canadian.

In December 1973, the Royal Canadian Air Farce, *Spring Thaw*'s heir, broadcast its first radio comedy special. The troupe consisted of

Spring Thaw alumnus Dave Broadfoot, British comic John Morgan, Montrealers Don Ferguson and Roger Abbott, who had worked with a cabaret troupe called the Jest Society in Montreal during the early seventies, and Luba Goy, a comedian who'd also started out in Montreal. The Air Farce took *Spring Thaw*'s Rosedale appeal and broadened it. They were astute observers of the Canadian political scene and sharp mimics. The Air Farce were particularly adroit at fixing on politicians' speech patterns. Perhaps more importantly, however, the Air Farce had a keen awareness of the code of Canadian politeness and how it applied to comedy. They were fond of lampooning public figures but tended to keep their attacks general. The Air Farce mocked groups rather than specific individuals. "The Hudson's Bay Company has decided it no longer will be involved in fur trading," Broadfoot declared during one skit. "That leaves all the trapping and skinning to the federal government." Their sketches were designed to prick but not puncture the powers that be. They knew how to go right to the line but never cross it. As such, they were a perfect fit for the CBC.

The Royal Canadian Air Farce ran for twenty-three proud years on CBC Radio. In 1980, CBC Television offered the troupe a series. It was a fiasco. It reflected none of Air Farce's strength's and accentuated its weaknesses. For example, it was shot on location without a studio audience. The group had always performed before live audiences, even when taping for radio. The Air Farce came out of the cabaret tradition and had been trained to react to and thrive on the energy exchanged between audience and actors. After this failure, the Air Farce was branded "death for television" and sent back to radio purgatory. But in 1992, Ivan Fecan, CBC's entertainment head, gave them another shot. This show was to be a low-budget topical revue, taped in the new Broadcast Centre. The set would be removable, to make room for another Fecan venture, a late-night talk show called *Friday Night with Ralph Benmergui,* which would tape in the same studio.

In the autumn of 1993, both programs premiered. Benmergui's was launched with a media blitz. Its star, Ralph Benmergui, had found viewer approval as host on the CBC's lunch-time current affairs show, *Midday*. He looked like a good bet to make late-night television work.

Unfortunately for Benmergui, his show started poorly and went downhill fast. Benmergui was grilled by the press. His show was held up as an example of CBC incompetence and waste. Benmergui became the subject of personal attacks as well, particularly in the satiric bi-weekly publication *Frank* magazine, which ran a "Benmergui Death Watch," and a contest to see which job Benmergui should take once his show was cancelled.

The Air Farce show, by contrast, took off. It was stripped down and relied on solid writing combined with well-crafted characterizations. In fact, the show became the CBC's number-one draw, pulling over a million viewers a week. This turn of events seemed to indicate a Canadian preference for characters over stars. They liked modest, moderate folk. The reaction to Benmergui, by the media, at least, was, "Who do you think you are?" The Air Farce, with their cheap sets and stock costumes, were unassuming. The Air Farce became a success story at a time when most of the news that was coming out of the CBC was bad.

In 1996, as a reward for their achievement, the CBC neglected to renew the Air Farce's contract. The CBC literally forgot to sign their biggest show. Just as they had before with Aylesworth and Peppiatt, the CBC just assumed that the Air Farce would sit and wait. The oversight was callous treatment of a troupe that had created the network's flagship entertainment program for more than twenty years. Baton Broadcasting was ready with a bid, but at the last minute, the Air Farce signed on again with the CBC, for a substantial increase in budget and salaries, and with considerably more control over the final product. The CBC had missed the boat but managed to avoid the public relations disaster that would have ensued had they lost the show.

The most scathing sketch comedy to find its way into Canadian television sprang from Newfoundland. Codco had formed in 1973, at the same time the Canadian Second City was being born. Like other Canadian comedians, they were reacting to the signal from a dominant culture. However, that signal came not from America but from central Canada. Codco was the Yin to central Canada's Yang. It was a reaction to the primary culture, Canadian federalism, from a subordinate culture, Newfoundland.

CODCO was a product of Newfoundland's amateur theatrical tradition. Of all the provinces, Newfoundland has the most vibrant semi-professional theatre scene. Plays and performing are bred in the Newfoundland psyche. CODCO's members had each separately learned his or her craft acting in small productions in Newfoundland, but employment opportunities were limited. The troupe's members would have to come to Toronto to meet. Theatre Passe Muraille, at the time one of Toronto's top alternative theatre companies, was the womb that nurtured Newfoundland's *enfant terrible*. In 1973, Cathy Jones, Mary Walsh, Tommy Sexton, Greg Malone, Diane Olsen, Bob Joy, and Paul Sametz produced their first play, *Cod On a Stick,* for Passe Muraille. The play was a surprise hit. It created such a sensation that CBC Radio asked them to return to Newfoundland and do a recording of the show. That was followed by a taping for CBC Television. CODCO's play, which was considered theatre, received an eight-thousand-dollar grant from the provincial government, which was celebrating the twenty-fifth anniversary of Newfoundland's joining Confederation, and they toured the province. Olsen, Joy, and Sametz left the troupe, and Andy Jones, Cathy's brother, joined the cast.

"CODCO was less a troupe than it was a lifestyle. We were in each other's pockets and up each other's holes," Mary Walsh reflected in 1996. "CODCO appealed to the marginalized. We felt we were marginalized. We were Newfoundlanders in Canada, and Canadians in North America. We felt we were renegades. We were angry. We felt shut out. That's where comedy comes from. It comes from anger, from the intrinsic unfairness of life."

The intrinsic unfairness of life and its comic manifestations were the building blocks CODCO used to construct their sketches. They pinpointed the most uncomfortable and painful experiences and twisted them until they bled laughter. In *Sickness, Death and Beyond the Grave,* their 1974 follow-up to *Cod on a Stick,* CODCO introduced audiences to Morton the Dying Child Molester. In this sketch, the pedophile is planted in a pediatrics ward as a result of hospital overcrowding. CODCO took the same giddy pleasure in exposing life's grim iniquities that the Dumbells had displayed mocking the atrocities of World War I.

In 1978, two of CODCO's members, Tommy Sexton and Greg Malone, made the leap to television, becoming part of a Newfoundland regional show, *The Wonderful Grand Band*. The program used a weak premise — a rock-band family — to showcase variety acts and comic sketches. In 1983, the show was broadcast nationally, featuring the rest of the CODCO group. The show flopped, but it managed to expose the outstanding talents of its cast members. Producer Michael Donovan, who headed up a Maritime company called Salter Street Films, sold the CBC on a CODCO series. CODCO shifted its base from St. John's to Halifax, and in 1987, the show, *CODCO,* aired its first season.

Television gave the cast the opportunity to lash out on a grand scale. They redirected their aim towards high-profile international figures such as George Bush, Ronald Reagan, and the British Royal Family. CODCO took particular delight in harpooning Canadian icons like newscaster Barbara Frum. Sexton, in an eerie impersonation of the CBC personality, presented his version of "The Jugular." They also created original comic monsters, like Andy Jones's sycophantic daytime talk-show host, Frank Arsenpuffen. Arsenpuffen, as his name suggests, relentlessly fawned over his guests in a binge of self-debasement. At the same time, the troupe continued to keep its Newfoundland roots. They ran almost weekly sketches about the "Budgell" family, a brood of alcoholic welfare recipients who saw life from the bottom. *CODCO* was revolutionary in the vigour with which they assailed Canadian culture. They were traditional, however, in their approach. *CODCO* used comic masks as had all the satirists who preceded them. This stemmed in part from their theatrical background: CODCO's members were trained actors before they became comedians. It was also a by-product of the Canadian aversion to direct confrontation and criticism. Says Walsh, "I'm not that comfortable as myself. I need someone with me. As myself, I just kind of wither."

Frequently, *CODCO*'s sketches drew outcries of condemnation. The troupe routinely stepped over the restricting and unwritten code of Canadian politeness. "It used to drive some people crazy," George Anthony, the head of the CBC's variety department, told John Haslett Cuff of the *Globe and Mail*. "We'd get these letters telling us to take them off the air and put them to death." Which the CBC did, in a way. The corporation censored sketches. This finally cost the troupe one of its key members. In 1991, Andy Jones quit the series after the CBC refused to air a sketch called "Pleasant Irish Priests in Conversation." The sketch suggested that Irish priests enjoyed drunkenness, sodomy, masturbation, and homosexuality. Like many of their sketches that drew fire, "Irish Priests" was later revealed to be prophetic. As Peter Gard, a writer for *Arts Atlantic,* pointed out in a 1993 essay, CODCO satirized the future. They actually lampooned events that had not yet come to light.

Three years after banning "Irish Priests," the CBC fought and won the right to air *The Boys of St. Vincent,* a miniseries that chronicled the unmitigated evil of priests who ritually abused young boys in that orphanage. Tommy Sexton's mother had taught at Mount Cashel, a Catholic school where there was to be a similar scandal. CODCO knew the truth before the rest of the country.

The CBC was willing to fight for a drama, like *The Boys of St. Vincent,* but chose to censor CODCO. It was a graphic example of the CBC's contempt for comedy. "Pleasant Irish Priests in Conversation" was just as pertinent as the dramatic film, but because its form was comedy, it was canned. On behalf of a drama, the CBC was willing to fight a court order that banned any comment on the ongoing trial of the pedophile priests. In refusing to stand by CODCO, the CBC was shooting the messenger. Their censorship killed the golden goose. After Andy Jones's departure, the troupe never managed to achieve the same level of quality or pertinence. The final two seasons of CODCO lacked satiric focus.

In October of 1992, I interviewed Cathy Jones, Mary Walsh, and Tommy Sexton in a posh Toronto hotel room, and I saw first-hand evidence of the group's disintegration. I was one of many reporters shuttled in to conduct a series of half-hour interviews. Mine was the last of the day. Jones, Walsh, and Sexton were ordering room service and unwinding by this time, which meant dining on salmon, drinking wine, and smoking hash. There was a palpable gloom over the entire proceeding. "They treat us like pigs," Sexton screamed, in a combination of mock outrage and actual distress. "Like pigs!" Jones and Walsh got in on the joke. Walsh began to pantomime crawling around like a pig. They were referring to the CBC. Ironically, in 1993, the CBC ran a special show titled *CODCO: Uncensored*. It featured the "Irish Priests" sketch as well as the sketches "Blaming Africa for AIDS," "Madonna — Penis Teaser, Media Pleaser," "Anne of Green Gut," and "Lucky Margarine." The CBC ran the program at 11 P.M. and received few complaints. "Our perception of how things were was closer to the truth than people wanted to admit," Walsh later said. "It wasn't the glossy idea of family they wanted to see."

After CODCO's demise in 1993, Mary Walsh set about work on a new creation. She enlisted Cathy Jones and an actor from St. John's named Greg Thomey. She also enlisted Rick Mercer, a kid from Newfoundland who'd had success doing one-man shows. The result was *This Hour Has 22 Minutes,* a pun on CBC's current affairs show of the seventies, *This Hour Has Seven Days.* Unlike *CODCO, This Hour Has 22 Minutes* is a purely topical show, in keeping with the tempo for Canadian comedy broadcasting in the nineties. The program pulls all its gags from the headlines and is presented as a news broadcast with recurring characters and location scenes. The heart of the show, like *CODCO,* is still passionate. Canadian society and politics obliged by providing plenty of fodder. Walsh cites as an example television's "Heritage Minutes," which profile proud moments in Canadian history: "Every time you see that 'Heritage Minute' where the Canadian peacekeeper stops two Cypriots from fighting, you see that photo of those Canadian peacekeepers in Somalia beating that child to death. But we accept it. We defer to authority because we have the United States to hold ourselves up against and make ourselves feel better."

This Hour's big discovery was Mercer. He represents an important new step in Canadian satire. His influences are entirely Canadian. He grew up in Newfoundland watching *The Wonderful Grand Band*. Mercer did not set foot in a stand-up club until he was already well established as a comedian. He came to the public's attention at the young age of eighteen. In the early nineties, he had launched a series of one-man shows, such as *Charles Lynch Must Die* and *I've Killed Before and I'll Kill Again,* all of which focused on Mercer's venomous rage against political figures. Unlike his predecessors, Mercer wore no mask. His attacks came directly from Rick Mercer.

I first met Mercer in July of 1995 at Montreal's Just For Laughs Festival. Mercer, who was then twenty-four years old, and his agent were visiting to decide whether or not the festival would be an appropriate showcase for one of his plays. We met in a bar for a couple of drinks. Mercer displayed none of the bile he practised on stage. He smiled frequently, chain-smoked, and seemed to take great pleasure in observing the Hollywood-loving comedians who were circling the bar. What remained of his stage attitude, however, was his intensity. Mercer thoughtfully mulled over each question. He formed his responses carefully.

"In my shows," he said, "I yelled at the audience for an hour. It surprised people. They thought, What's this eighteen-year-old kid doing yelling at us? For me, it was nothing new. In my family, watching the news was a spectator sport. I had grown up that way. You were free to make snide remarks."

In this respect, Mercer was not unique. Mocking the news and making snide remarks are as Canadian as back bacon. They are national pastimes played out in living rooms across the country as often as *Hockey Night in Canada*. What was remarkable, however, was that Mercer felt comfortable going public with his criticisms. It was an evolutionary step. After years of hiding behind characters and masks, a Canadian satirist felt free to show his discontent as himself. Rick Mercer, as Rick Mercer — not as some aged MP from an imaginary rural constituency or some aw-shucks hayseed — was lashing out.

As I sat listening to Mercer, I couldn't help wondering what had happened in the Canadian psyche to enable such a leap. If Mercer had grown up in Toronto or Vancouver, you could chalk it up to the growing Americanization of Canada. As a country we were becoming more American and the new comedy reflected this change. But Mercer had grown up in Newfoundland. He was as clean of American influences as a comedian could be. He had virtually no exposure to stand-up comedy, and very little to American TV. I raised the question with him, and he suggested that the secret lay not in the satirist but in the target. When circumstances get desperate, politeness flies out the window. In Canada, circa 1995, circumstances were dire. Recession, unemployment, crime — things weren't like the good old days. It was impossible to claim everything was all right. Canadian satirists had always been held back by the notion that Canada, by and large, was healthy. It was a country that needed improvement, not salvation. Now, with the economy in tatters and Quebec promising to leave Confederation, there seemed like little to lose.

Mercer's step was also the product of a generation gap. Like the rest of those born in the sixties and seventies, Mercer had only known Canada as a country in decline. Each year it had deteriorated. Even during the eighties, the economy worsened, health care crumbled, public education shrank, libraries closed, children starved. The old guard's solutions had failed, yet they were not willing to alter them. The Liberals kept chanting the benefits of big government, the NDP kept extolling the virtues of socialism, and the Tories kept singing about the good old days before income tax. They fiddled while the rest of Canada burned. The young, like Mercer, who were destined to inherit this mess, had grown understandably concerned. Desperate times had finally demanded desperate measures. So Rick Mercer, as Rick Mercer, could step forward and point a finger. Things could not possibly get worse. And as an audience, we were ready to accept political satirists confronting us with the ugly reality.

Said Mercer, "I just have an inborn desire to say the bad thing."

■

THIRTEEN

The Next Big Thing

It is the world's largest vacuum, located at the Lyndon Johnson Space Center in Houston. The vacuum is 359,000 cubic feet in volume, 120 feet high, with a circular door that is 44 feet in diameter. The door, which looks like a gigantic safe door, is so well calibrated and balanced that one person could close it using only an index finger. The vacuum's floor is movable and rotates 360 degrees. The vacuum can be used to replicate outer space. In special isolation chambers, which are located on the base of the vacuum, temperatures can be dropped to between $-300°F$ and $-450°F$. The vacuum was built in 1968. NASA used it to test astronauts for the first Apollo space mission. They had put entire space capsules, complete with crews, in the vacuum for months.

Now Hollywood was going to put Canadian comic Harland Williams in there. They were going to make him a star. A sixty-two-member film crew toiled furiously to set up what would eventually be ten seconds of screen time, a shot in which Williams strolled into the vast chamber. They spun around the towering vacuum with a solemn determination that made them seem more like medieval masons building a church than movie makers trying to capture a few moments on film.

Williams stood beside me, dressed in a bright orange space suit and matching boots. He'd been working since seven in the morning and it was now eleven o'clock at night. Williams didn't mind. "If things weren't going well, I'd be upset," he said. "But we're doing well, so I'm happy." He had good reason to be happy. Williams had been in the comedy business for eleven years. Along with *Space Cadet* (its working title), he had another movie deal, to star in the screen version of the cartoon strip "Beetle Bailey," and he had a deal with CBS to develop and produce a sitcom based on his stand-up routine. Williams was ready. He was the next big thing.

Harland Williams was about to enter the isolation chamber known as fame. I recalled a conversation we'd had back in March in Los Angeles. While other Canadian comedians were scrambling through pilot season, Williams had just signed his first feature film deal. Over dinner, Williams had discussed the big leap forward. He'd said, "I know this is the best part, when you're just making it. I know that. I'm trying to enjoy it." That "part" is the fleeting string of months in which a comedian transforms himself from a top-flight comic earning an upper-class living into full-fledge comedy star.

It was a daunting feat. More human beings have literally flown to outer space than become comedy stars. It is easier to hurl yourself into black space, to deny gravity, to travel 385,000 kilometres to the moon, to exist in an oxygen-deprived void, than it is to join the ranks of Richard Pryor, John Candy, Steve Martin, Eddie Murphy, Robin Williams, and Jim Carrey. They had the right stuff.

To reach such heights a comedian not only had to be talented, he also had to touch a nerve in the public's mood. These individuals must give the public a completely new and unique product — themselves — but that product must mesh with the temper of the time. If they don't strike a chord in the Zeitgeist, they can forget rising to the top. George Carlin's hippie persona was right for the sixties. Steve Martin's Wild and Crazy Guy was right for the mid-seventies. John Candy's vulnerability was a perfect fit for the avaricious eighties. He expressed in comic terms the public's discomfort with the dog-eat-dog ethic of that era. Jim Carrey hit in the late nineties because his physical, adolescent mania reflected the desire of the movie-going public (mostly kids in their early teens) to see man and computer meld. Jim Carrey was a human cartoon. Harland Williams looked poised to dominate the last few years of the millennium. He was a comic Janus, the two-faced Roman god of beginnings. Harland's comic character was a blend of childlike innocence and seething rebellion. Williams had a gentle, friendly delivery which he laced with a simmering anger. I remember the first time I saw Williams perform a feature set, in 1992. I was impressed by the creative approach he took to stand-up. Williams broke every rule and scored big laughs doing it. He mocked the genial style of television comedians, with their "Hi sir, where you from, ma'am" patter. For no particular reason, Williams would select an audience member and christen him "my little strawberry shortcake prince." I had the epiphany that many writers pray for. I knew I was watching a major talent. He was a natural with all the engines necessary to hit the stratosphere. When I left the club, I was prepared to bet a week's pay that he would be bigger than Jim Carrey. For the next four years I followed his career, seeing his act a total of six times. Each time that I saw him reinforced my belief in his comic prowess.

I was in Houston because, after following his career, I wanted to see Harland Williams' lift off, to witness the "best part" turn into the next part. If I waited until after he'd made it, I might still get access, but it would never be the same. That's how it was with comedians headed for the top. If you got them before the metamorphosis, you saw them at their peak, burning with desire, talent and need. Once they were airborne, they were unreachable in any real terms. How do you ask Icarus for an interview? There is too much to lose by coming down to earth.

Jim Carrey, for example, was so elevated that he talked to no one. He'd walk the grounds of his Californian estate with his best friend Wayne Flemming and point at objects of luxury, like his swimming pool, and say, "Jokes. It's all jokes." In 1994, Carrey had made $350,000 to star in his first movie, *Ace Ventura: Pet Detective.* The film made more than $120 million. His next film, *The Mask,* was already shot and in post-production. It too eventually made over $120 million. Carrey next got $7 million for *Dumb and Dumber.* To savvy producers, Carrey's

Dumb and Dumber fee was a bargain. Mike De Luca, CEO and president of production for New Line Cinema, the company that produced the film, told the Hollywood *Reporter,* "*Ace Ventura* had already opened, so we knew that he worked at the box office. We'd seen a rough cut of *The Mask* and knew it was going to be a success. The offers Jim had on the table after *Ace* had opened at around five million. So we did the math and said, 'Pay him seven million to lock the slot,' and that would give us *Dumb and Dumber* for Christmas for a budget of sixteen million. It was probably the easiest decision we ever made." The film grossed more than $200 million.

After *Dumb and Dumber,* Carrey made headlines by turning down an $18 million offer to make *The Thief of Santa Monica.* He co-starred in *Batman Forever,* and again the film grossed over $200 million. Carrey had never made a box office dog. Then *The Cable Guy* came along and he became the $20-million-dollar man.

Carrey's publicist, Marleah Leslie, told me, when I asked for an interview, "He is in filming now and not giving interviews," as well as, "He is resting from filming and not giving interviews." I was never given an outright no. I suppose they wanted to keep me living in hope. Finally, Carrey's publicist spelled it out. "He doesn't do anything," she said. "He lets *ET* [*Entertainment Tonight*] come on the set and that's it. Then he does press junket interviews when the movie comes out. I can put you on the list for that if you want." A press junket interview consists of fifteen minutes with the star, in which a reporter is expected to ask questions that have been approved, to a degree, by the publicist in charge.

At a certain point, the press, which is often instrumental in creating a star, becomes a threat. The only thing that matters is what gets kids and teenagers into movie theatres, and serious journalism is seldom responsible for that. If *The Cable Guy* worked, it would do so because of what was on the screen. There was little to be gained from talking to a writer.

Then *The Cable Guy* opened and flopped at the box office. The worm turned. When I rode the subway I overheard thirteen-year-old schoolgirls talking about how they liked "Jim Carrey's old stuff." In the post–*Cable Guy* era, Jim Carrey wasn't giving interviews because he was "concentrating on his next movie." Carrey was undoubtedly concentrating pretty hard. One *Cable Guy* was forgivable and would not damage his career, but another one? Well, that would mean Carrey was subject to gravity like the rest of us, and that wasn't good for stardom.

Back in 1992, Carrey had come to Toronto to appear in the People's Comedy Festival, Toronto's answer to Montreal's Just For Laughs extravaganza. Carrey was there to host a televised "Gala." I interviewed him for *eye WEEKLY*. Carrey was in the "best part" stage of his career. His rags-to-riches story had not yet become a comedy legend.

Jim described how he'd first tried stand-up in 1976 at age fourteen, bombed, and stayed away from the business for two years. During that time he'd practised at home, then returned in 1978. Carrey had jumped into comedy not for fame but for affection. "I didn't have a friend in the world until about grade three," Carrey admitted. "Then I broke out of my shell. I started to realize, Hey, I can act goofy and people actually respond. It was a means to an end. It was just a natural thing. I used to watch *The Ed Sullivan Show* and I'd laugh at the comedians because my parents were laughing. That's what told me it was funny."

The two years away served Carrey well. When he returned, he was no longer a lame act. At sixteen he was already one of Canada's best. Wayne Flemming met Carrey in 1979. Flemming was fifteen years older than Carrey, but like the young comedian he had a young heart and a love of devilment. The two soon became best friends. Flemming acted as a combination mentor, father figure, and older brother. "I'd heard about him before I met him," Flemming recalls. "The word was, he was a destroyer. They said, 'He blows the doors off any room.' Then I saw him and said, Holy shit. This guy's going to be a star."

Money was always an issue for Carrey. During his early teens, his family had been homeless, but, he said in a later joke, "we were from Canada, so I thought we had just gone camping." In his late teens, Carrey supported his family by doing stand-up comedy on the Yuk Yuk's circuit. There he kept to himself and eschewed the drinking and drugs that permeated the business. He spent hours in front of the mirror perfecting his impressions. He and Flemming were inseparable. At night, they would head out on long walks, sometimes ten miles, just talking and spinning jokes. The pair would break into the University of Toronto's Varsity

Arena and run the track, pretending to shatter world records. Then they would sit in the stands and talk comedy until the sun rose.

Jim displayed an uncanny comedic wisdom. When he was only seventeen, Flemming recalls, he was giving the older comedian pointers. "He'd say, 'Comb your hair back; it will make your face funnier.' Then one day he told me, 'You've got to have the voice, the face, and the joke. They all have to be strong.' I asked him, 'How do you know that?' He said, 'I just know it.'"

Carrey never let anything block his path. Leatrice Spevack says Carrey always took the fastest route. If that meant dumping a few managers, so be it. He had had three managers by the time he was twenty, in an era when Canadian comedians did not have their own managers. Success started to sprout in the early eighties. Carrey liked the feeling that minor fame brought. He won a part in a Lottario advertisement in which he was photographed dressed as a pharaoh. The ads were placed in subway cars. Carrey would find his ad, sit directly under it, and wait until somebody recognized him.

In the mid-eighties, Carrey won his shot. He went to Hollywood and starred in a television series called *The Duck Factory*. In it, he played a cartoonist working in an animated world of various comic characters. The series was an unmitigated failure. It looked for a while like Carrey's chance had passed. "He was told he would never work again in Hollywood," says Flemming. The let-down must have been devastating for a person whose entire life had been steered towards comedy fame. According to Joel Axler, Carrey descended into a black period during which he performed dark, brooding stand-up. He began to hang out with Sam Kinison, who, along with being recognized as a comic genius, was legendary for his penchant for drugs and booze. Rumours swirled about Carrey's dabbling in substance abuse. Axler met Carrey at a West Hollywood party in 1988 and thought the comedian looked "washed out and beaten. He was quiet."

The Fox TV series *In Living Color* saved his career. "I'm going to be the funniest guy on the show," Carrey told Flemming when he won a spot as the only white member of the African American comedy show. Carrey's *In Living Color* characters, such as Fireman Bill, made him a semi-famous property. "I don't mind being recognized," he admitted at the time. "I don't sign autographs when I'm with my family [he was still married to his first wife]. I try to be nice. I like people. I enjoy meeting people. It's a strange thing. In the last few years it's gotten to the point where now, when I go out, everyone knows who I am." He had no idea what was to come.

In 1992, it was time for Carrey to go to the next level. Towards that end he and his management team, the American whiz kids Eric Gold and Jimmy Miller, were planning their campaign. "I'm turning down a lot of films," he said. "I haven't found the one I want to do yet. I've turned down about five films. I just want to step into something that I'm really excited about. I could work. There's been a couple that would have been pretty good jobs, but they would have been just work."

Carrey was in top form for the People's Festival Gala that year. He tore up the stage with impersonations and jokes. Carrey possessed an irresistible magnetism, that came, perhaps, from the knowledge that he was ascending and there was little that could stop him. He was a skilled host and introduced a stream of comedians. One of them was Harland Williams. Dressed in red pants, a red shirt, and cowboy boots, with a plastic phone in his back pocket, Williams hit the stage and proceeded to burn up the audience:

> I went into a variety store the other day and ripped off a Mars bar. Then I went right home and called Crime Stoppers and turned myself in. I made a thousand bucks. Wouldn't it be great if you could walk up to these punk-rocker skin-head idiots out on the street and rip the rings out of their noses, and ten seconds later they'd blow up? Then I got in my standard automobile and I drove all the way home. I killed four hundred pedestrians. That night the police came to my door. They said, "Son, you won a free game."

Eric Gold, who was there to watch Carrey perform, approached Williams as he walked off the stage. Gold told Harland that he wanted to sign him as a client. Says Gold, "I told him that in three years he'd have his own television series, and in another three he'd be a major motion picture star."

A year and a half later, Carrey, Flemming, and Williams were in an Atlanta hotel. The comedy gods had played a strange trick, and by some serendipitous twist, the three Canadians were booked into Atlanta for the same big-money club gig. It was also *Ace Ventura: Pet Detective*'s opening weekend. That Friday evening the three Canucks sat in front of the television and watched the ticket results roll in. "It was like waiting for the scores," remembers Flemming. "The numbers flashed up and all of a sudden it's 'We beat Costner!' Jim was floored. We went onto the balcony and were looking out over Atlanta, and he said, 'Do you believe this? Do you fucking believe this? When you're young you dream of reaching a certain point, but when you attain it and go past . . . It's a long way from Canada, isn't it? You were the only one who believed in me man, the *only* one.'"

Even before Harland Williams was set for his own lift-off, the young comedian had seen firsthand what it was like to go nuclear in the Hollywood comedy game. This fact stuck in my mind. To Harland Williams, blasting into Hollywood's firmament was not a dream, it was a reality he'd witnessed with his own eyes. He knew he could hit Carrey's altitude. It was all a matter of how and when. It was, however, the *what* in Harland Williams that was most interesting.

Williams was a walking example of many of the Canadian forces that helped the best of its comedians hit sublime comedic heights. Williams pulled against the repressive push of Canadian collectivist society. He was a keen observer, particularly of the American experience. His talent had been fired in the brutal crucible of the Canadian stand-up world. Finally, along with being a performer, Williams was a writer, and he defended his right to control his own material with a determination and vigour that would have made forerunners like Johnny Wayne and Frank Shuster proud. You could chart all these elements, like stars in a solar system, right through Williams' life story.

Born in North York, Ontario, Harland Williams is the son of former Ontario solicitor general John Williams and Lorraine Williams. He has four older sisters and grew up a self-described "scrawny little freak." Even as a young kid he had a reverential regard for his intellect and protected it as a valuable resource. At age twelve, Williams decide that he was going to get rich from his imagination. "My theory," he told me in 1994, "used to be that my brain was a giant Alka Seltzer tablet, and every time I took a drink of alcohol, or if I were to do drugs, it would be melted away a little. I thought of my brain as chambers full of doors, and every time I took a drink, one of those doors would slam shut forever. But behind that door could have been a novel or a new kids' book or an idea for a movie."

The more Williams indulged his imagination, the more his marks began to slip. His parents believed that he was being influenced by "the wrong crowd" at his high school. According to Williams, they had dreams of their son becoming a priest or a member of the American military (a wish Harland has never understood), and decided he would fare better at a private school. They sent Williams to a Quaker-run boarding school. To Williams, it was a catastrophic shift. He remembers the school as a rough, intimidating place inhabited by a collection of surly sociopaths and misfits. Humour was a survival technique. "They fought to see who was dominant," he says. "My humour was my insulation. If I could be funny, the guys would like me and leave me alone."

Williams' grades improved, but he felt abandoned and betrayed by his parents. When he discovered that boys who scored poor grades were denied weekend visits home, he saw his opportunity to take revenge on them. He let his grades drop, and as a result saw his parents only sporadically for two years. During these years, Williams adopted a healthy revulsion for authority. The young North York kid learned to resist teachers, parents, and anyone else who tried to dictate his actions. Teachers liked short hair on nice boys. Williams kept his long and wild. "When the Queen Mother was over on a visit and my whole family was set to have lunch with her," he says, "my father saw an opportunity to try to get me to cut it. He said, 'If you get your hair cut, you can have lunch with the Queen Mother.' I didn't get my hair cut and I didn't go to lunch with the Queen Mother. I didn't regret it then, and I don't regret it now."

Williams never lost his distaste for authority figures. To him they were malicious killjoys bent on subordinating his right to express himself. Williams is fiercely individualistic. He loathes people who try to lump him into a group or squash his creativity. Out of this ferocious independence, Harland developed a very accessible comic personality. Fifteen years after his boarding school traumas, Williams had turned his contempt for rule makers into a merry, yet sinister, comic persona. As a comedian, Williams refused to allow society's rules to damage his optimistic view of the world. He denied authority the respect it demanded and instead blew it a contemptuous kiss. When Williams first appeared on *Late Night with David Letterman,* for instance, he wore shoes covered in peanut butter. This fashion statement had been a dream of his since he was in his late teens. He did it, he told me, to keep fresh. I think I know the real reason: by committing this seemingly insane act, he was reinforcing his own identity. It was as if he were saying: "Yes, you are a powerful American television show, but I'm still me, and I've got peanut butter on my shoes."

"My attitude," he told me, "is that I'm going to operate in the system but not give in to it. I'll play the rules but not give in to them."

By the time he was twenty-one, Williams had decided to make play his profession. He enrolled in the animation course at Sheridan College in Oakville, Ontario. Williams moved into an apartment with his cousin, Kevin Hearn, who was a musician and a kindred free spirit. The Williams-Hearn household was a fun-house of bizarre behaviour. The pair fed their imaginations and indulged in every impulse. Williams nailed raw turkey legs to the wall and called it art. The pair placed a colour TV on the balcony, turned it on, and left it running for three years — so that tenants in the building a hundred feet away would have something to watch. He and Hearn also rigged a fishing rod so that they could fling skimpy female lingerie onto their superintendent's balcony for his wife to find.

Williams' talent for observation flourished during these years. His study of animation disciplined him in the science of absorbing visual nuances. He developed a catalogue of movements and sounds, such as the sound of a tyrannosaurus, which he would incorporate into his act.

He fed himself on American pop culture and television. Williams used his bizarre decorating choices (turkey legs) and his penchant for practical jokes to alter reality. Rather than turning his imagination inward and away from reality, Williams turned it outward and used it like a paintbrush to colour the world to fit his perception of it. This extroverted energy was ideally suited to stand-up comedy, and in 1984, while still at Sheridan, Williams took his first shot at amateur night. He went down to Yuk Yuk's' Downtown club and performed a bizarre set. Williams got the response he was looking for: laughs and perplexed stares. He continued to appear each week. Williams tried to incorporate his love of animation's freedom into his comedy. He made stand-up a cartoon creation. This meant tearing down conventions. For example, he developed a "very big visual closer" involving his roommate's Hugo Man of a Thousand Faces doll. He gave his impression of the ravages of leukemia by shaking the doll's wig off. Williams then "cured" Hugo by dipping his head into a giant bucket of his "Billy Idol Peanut Butter."

Mark Breslin recalls the crowd's reaction to Williams as "Look at the freak, look at the weirdo," but he saw potential. Breslin saw another ground breaker. He began to give the young comedian more stage time and tried to help cultivate his act. At the same time, Williams began to write and illustrate *Lickity Split* and *Crazy Creatures,* his own series of children's books, which were published in North America and Europe. The books followed the adventures of a baby brontosaurus as it "learned about life."

By 1991, Williams had paid his dues on the Canadian comedy circuit. He had spent time as a road warrior out on the Prairies. The arduous nature of the stand-up game toughened Williams up, as it had his predecessors, like Carrey and Mike MacDonald. It did not break his creative determination. Williams refused to make his act generic, even when playing one-night road gigs in beer parlours. On one three-week tour, he had Colin Campbell's friend, stand-up Harry Doupe, keep a record of all the insults club owners had made about his act. Williams wanted Doupe to chronicle all the nasty and stupid remarks he'd hear about Harland when he was onstage. Entries ranged from: "If I have to watch this, so do you" to "You have done professional comedy before, right?" Williams tired of the grind. He referred to road gigs as "career stoppers" and began to turn them down. Williams dabbled in creative stunts, simply to remain interested in his own work. He spent the first six months of 1991 performing in a French chef's costume. Unfortunately for Williams, his work had not drummed up any interest at the CBC. Canada's public broadcaster missed the boat once again.

"I wanted nothing more than to advance my career with my people, so to speak. The CBC had a casting office that was across the street from Yuk Yuk's' Downtown club. I never heard of anyone from that office calling to tap into the new talent. In the six years I was at Yuk Yuk's no one came to see what was going on. No agents, no one. So I never got invited to the dance."

Like so many before him, Williams packed up and moved to Los Angeles. He saw immediate results. One month after arriving, he landed a spot at the Laugh Factory, a west Hollywood club. Williams did six minutes and was offered a spot on the cable-TV show *Comedy on the Road* promptly after leaving the stage. Six years in Canada had amounted to nothing. Six minutes in Hollywood and he was on TV. The first time I saw him, I said, 'This guy is going to be a major star,'" recalls Jamie Masada, owner of the Laugh Factory. "Onstage he is like lightning. His delivery is vibrating. He plays out the laugh like a master. He'll be bigger than Jim Carrey."

Masada signed on as Williams' manager and began hounding his friend Eric Gold. He kept pressuring Gold to see Williams perform. Masada wanted Gold and his partner Jimmy Miller to sign a three-way deal to back Harland Williams. Masada knew that talent on its own could not win in Hollywood. Williams needed powerful backing if he was going to realize his potential. In 1992, Gold saw Williams in Toronto. The deal was signed and Williams was on his way. It was not an overnight transformation. Gold decided that Harland's Canadian approach needed some acclimatizing. For starters, Gold thought Canadian humour was drier than the American alternative and had more room for nonsequiturs. Williams worked out each night at the Laugh Factory. He kept his act's spontaneity but used planned links between bits. It became more classically American, with a flow marked by set-ups and pay-off.

"In the beginning," Gold told me in the summer of 1995, "everyone dismissed Harland as simply being weird. But as his talent grew, Harland's potential became undeniable."

Williams' career rose in a steady arc. He had a small role in *Dumb and Dumber,* in which he played a police officer who accidentally drinks Jim Carrey's urine. The first major deal came from Garth Ancier, the head of programming at WB Network. WB was not a full-fledged network. It produced five hours of original programming every week and sold them to superstations like WGN. Unlike his network, Ancier had a quality track record. While he was at Fox he had given the green light to such commercial hits as *Married with Children* and *Beverly Hills 90210.* Ancier wanted to launch a sitcom called *Simon.* It had been created by producer Danny Jacobson, who had created the hit series *Mad About You.* The main character, Simon, was an innocent *faux naïf* who stumbles through life but somehow always lands on his feet. Ancier and Jacobson thought Williams fit the bill. They signed the show for thirteen episodes and went into production in the summer of 1995. Williams worked twelve hours a day on the show.

Simon premiered in September and immediately fell to the bottom of the ratings. It was one-hundredth in a field of one hundred. The show was flat, poorly written, and a misuse of Williams' talents. It was his *Duck Factory.* The young comedian found himself hemmed in creatively by the Hollywood system. Williams had hoped for more creative input, but instead he was ignored. The set for Simon's apartment, for example, was in Williams' opinion a bad fit for the character. He made repeated attempts to talk to the producers and story editors about it, but his suggestions were pushed aside. Then one night, after a rehearsal, a frustrated Williams got himself a hammer and a crowbar and dismantled the set. He placed the broken pieces on a trolley and shoved it off to the side of the stage.

"The producers wanted to fine me,' he said of the incident. "They were furious. They didn't understand the character. I was ready to put my integrity on the line. All the while I was doing it, I was thinking of all those guys in Canada who would kill to get the shot I was getting."

The best thing that could be said for *Simon* was that since it was not on a major network, few people saw the failure of Williams' first shot. Despite its poor showing, the WB was still willing to give it another shot. "They could have forced me to come back," he said. "I let it be known that I wasn't interested in doing any more shows." That was it for *Simon*. Next came a role in the film *Down Periscope*. The movie was a "submarine comedy" built around Kelsey Grammer, the star of the hit sitcom *Frasier*. *Down Periscope* also bombed, but Williams was cited by critics, such as Siskel and Ebert, as one of the movie's only redeeming features.

"Harland has a comedy gene," says *Space Cadet*'s producer Roger Birnbaum. "You see him perform and he's so funny and different that you think to yourself, What happened to you as a kid?" Birnbaum and I were sequestered in the Lyndon B. Johnson Room, a wood panelled office in which the American President had signed historic space program policies. Birnbaum was a co-founder of Caravan Pictures, the production company that was making *Space Cadet*. In appearance he was reminiscent of the Hollywood high-rollers who came to Montreal. He was good-looking, tanned, fit, and dressed in casual, obviously expensive clothing. His most recent films had been *While You Were Sleeping, The Three Musketeers,* and *Powder*. Before starting Caravan, Birnbaum was president of worldwide production and executive vice-president of Twentieth Century Fox.

Birnbaum was candid about Williams. "I had heard of Harland and seen some film on him. I'd seen *Down Periscope,* and he was without a doubt the funniest thing in the movie. *Space Cadet* was a high-concept project, and we knew we didn't need a big star as long as he was good. We saw his stand-up and he was a lot sharper than we'd thought. He was edgy but not malicious. He's got a boldness. We had him come in and do some readings, and after that I never doubted it. I thought, Wow, this guy is it."

Stuart Gillard, *Space Cadet*'s director, equally impressed, described the first time he saw Williams perform. "I was stunned by the risks he took. It was a breast and ovarian cancer benefit, and comics were coming out and dying. Harland went into areas that had me cringing. He was edgy but not angry, so there was tension but not animosity. He's a Canadian, and Canadians are very self-effacing. That allows them to comment on themselves. They don't have that puffed-up sense of nationalism."

Gillard knew about Canadians. He was from Alberta. He'd worked as an actor and director in Canada during the seventies and had produced the sitcom *Check It Out*. In 1976, he'd moved to California. "There was no work in Canada," he said. "And there was also a feeling that if you were a success in Canada, there was something wrong with you."

Williams had big dreams of success and a lot of powerful people behind him. But even with all the managers, agents, film crew and his own talent working on his behalf, there was no guarantee he'd be successfully launched as a star. It's never a sure bet. "You go on instinct," Birnbaum said. "You go with what your gut tells you. When we were in post-production for *My Cousin Vinny,* I was so sure the movie was going to bomb that I apologized to my boss almost daily. I said, 'I'm sorry I made this movie.' Then it opened and became a smash."

If Harland did make it, his path would not be without perils. During one dinner break, I got talking to Williams and one of the film grips about the downside of fame. The grip had worked on more films than he cared to remember and had seen plenty of things he would never forget. "He'd stay in his trailer and come out for his shoots," the grip said of one mega-star. "He had his bouncer with him and a golf instructor, and that's all he'd talk to. Every day his bodyguard would bring two eighteen-year-old girls. They looked hard, like they were prostitutes. He'd disappear with them into his trailer and surface again forty minutes later. He must have gone through fifty or sixty of these girls, and on top of everything, every two or three weeks his girlfriend would show up."

The story baffled Williams. "I don't know how you get like that," he said.

"They lose their perspective," I offered, thinking I'd nailed it.

The grip gazed back incredulously. "You lose your soul, man," he said with a shrug, as if he'd just told us the sky was blue. "You *lose* your *soul*."

In 1992, Jim Carrey had recounted one of his own success stories.

Carrey loved self-help books and bought as many as he could. "I was doing a gig in Las Vegas, and after it I'd gone to my room and lay down on my bed in my underwear and put on a subliminal tape in my Walkman. It would go: *You are a success. Money grows everywhere. Everything you do is gold.* I was listening to this tape, and I fell asleep. And as I woke up later in the middle of the night, I was being robbed. There was a woman going through my wallet on the bedside table. I had left the door unlatched. *You will leave the door unlatched and a woman will go through your pockets and take your credit cards.* It freaked me out. I threw her out, and she didn't get anything, but I mean, how ironic. The tape is telling me *You are the bubble of success,* and I'm being robbed."

I didn't think Harland was in too much danger of losing his soul, should he get to that rarefied level. For him, success and fame were tools he desired because they could be used to feed his imagination. Harland's life was about indulging his brilliant imagination through comedy, which in his hands was an art. He wanted to break into stardom because he knew it would give him bigger and better means towards that end. A true artist is always striving for better resources with which to produce his or her art. Harland was like a painter who was trying to move from water colours to oils and gold-leaf. His plan, he told me, was to write, direct and star in his own movies. He was going to go as far creatively as the business would allow.

The first step towards this goal had been departure. Like the Dumbells, Wayne and Shuster, Aylesworth and Peppiatt, Alan Young, Lorne Michaels, Howie Mandel, the *SCTV* cast, Mike Myers, the Kids in the Hall, Jim Carrey, and every other Canadian comic who wanted more than a chance to do cute impressions of the prime minister, he'd left home. All comedians were outsiders, whether they were American, German, British, or Chinese. They were cynics who called attention to life's shortcomings without offering any answers. Canadian comedians, however, were doubly outcast. They were people who held close to the conviction that their individuality and its expression should take precedence over the collective good. Their country was not willing to make room for such people. From the moment Harland Williams had taken that first step towards being a Canadian comedian, he was on the path taken by everyone else who had made that uphill climb. He'd done the one thing without which all the money, power, fame, and opportunity was impossible. He'd done the one thing you had to do to become a great Canadian comedian: He'd left.

FOURTEEN

■

The Punchline

In December of 1996, there were more Canadians down south than ever before. The working Canuck contingent was as follows:

In New York: Norm MacDonald, a former Yuk Yuk's stand-up, and Mark McKinney, formerly of the Kids in the Hall, were part of the *Saturday Night Live* cast. Norm Hiscock, an ex-writer for the Kids, and Lorri Nasso, a Second City alumnus, were *SNL* writers. It was produced, of course, by Canadian Lorne Michaels. John Rogers was in New York writing for Bill Cosby's new sitcom. Ex-Vacant Lot members Vito Viscomi and Nick McKinney were producing an on-line comedy Web site for Microsoft. *SCTV* star Rick Moranis lived in New York but spent most of his time making movies. Fellow *SCTV* alumnus Andrea Martin was big on Broadway and had spent the summer of 1996 touring her one-woman show. Vancouver stand-up Ian Bagg was working the clubs; he had management and an agent.

In Los Angeles: Brian Hartt, an ex-Kids writer was head writer for the Fox-TV series *Mad TV*. Also on *Mad TV* were ex-Kids writer Garry Campbell, Martin Short's brother Mike Short and Chris Finn, a former Yuk Yuk's stand-up. Toronto stand-up Frank Van Keeken was making features and had a major role in a David Lynch film. Jeremy Hotz, a Yuk Yuk's stand-up, had landed a role in *Speed II*. Dan Redican, the ex-Frantic and former writer for the Kids, had become producer for *The Jenny McCarthy Show,* a variety show built around a former Playboy centrefold. Peter Johanson, a Montrealer, was booked into a development deal with CBS. Ex-Vacant Lot members Paul Greenberg and Rob Gfroerer were working on Redican's show. Canadian sketch comic Don Lake, another Second City alumnus, was working as a character actor. Former Kids Kevin McDonald and Scott Thompson were also in L.A.: McDonald shopping scripts and Thompson playing a recurring character on HBO's *The Larry Sanders Show*. Dave Foley was a star in the NBC sitcom *News Radio*. David Steinberg was now directing TV, his most noted work being a few episodes of *Mad About You*. Former SCTV member Dave Thomas was a regular on the sitcom *Grace Under Fire*. He and Moranis were considering more Bob and Doug McKenzie projects. SCTV alumnus Catherine O'Hara was a well-respected character actor. Dan Aykroyd continued to churn out films, between entrepreneurial projects such as his House of Blues bar chain. Harland Williams had two movies and a sitcom deal. Mike Myers had a new movie, *Austin Powers,* due for a spring 1997 release. Jim Carrey had wrapped his comeback film *Liar, Liar,* also due out in the spring. Of course, by spring these comedians would be joined by the annual pilot season migration, illegals like "Steve," and comics like Lynn Shawcroft, who had deals with American networks. It was an enormous wave of Canadian comedy talent washing up on the American shore.

The question this exodus raises is, Is it something we're doing right, or something we're doing wrong? Why are Canadians so good at being funny? To answer one has to start with the Canadian soul. Canada is a country founded on the principle that security is more important than freedom. The American West was settled first by farmers and speculators; the law came later. The Canadian West was first secured by the Mounted Police; then the farmers came. Canadians chose the security of their colonial status with Britain over a chance to rule their own destiny. This choice was spurred, in part, by a fear of America. Canada needed Britain's might to protect it from a possible American invasion.

Canadians chose to subjugate themselves to Britain in exchange for a guarantee that they could go about their daily business, just as they always had. They believed that the freedom to be won by revolution was not worth the suffering endured.

Where does this phobia of change spring from? A fatalistic nature. For better or for worse, fatalism is the Canadian axiom. There from the beginning, it has been fostered by our indomitable climate. Throughout history, Canadians have been so busy battling the elements that they have barely had time to wage war on one another. Settlers have tried to tame Canada, using the Western ideologies they brought from their homelands. It was, and remains, an impossible task. That's something that Canada's first peoples understood: no one will ever tame the land. A Canadian knows instinctively that nature is the most powerful force on earth. We cannot conquer nature, so we choose to yield to it — to fate — and accept its fickle and sometimes cruel effects. As Alan Murray watched that young Irish officer die in 1917 at Ypres, what did he identify as the cause of all the destruction? An American might say that the Germans had released poisonous gas. But to Murray, a Canadian, the most important cause of the destruction and suffering was simple: *the wind had shifted*. The omnipotent forces of nature had decided who would live and who would die. All that a soldier could do was embrace his fate as best he could. Humour was one way to do that.

Americans have a problem with losing. American culture cannot make room for those who fail; it denies their existence. That's why when you drive through an American city, you see mansions on one block and slum dwellings on the next. Losers get stuffed in a drawer and forgotten. Winning is everything. Winning is so valued that Americans believe it can rub off. If you're a winner, then you're the greatest thing on earth. Just win, baby.

Canadians have a problem with winning. We're so used to playing second-best, first to Britain and now to America, that we have created a virtue of it. Better a pure loss than a dirty victory. If you win, you must have committed some sort of sin along the way. If you come second, well, that's still pretty good, and you can feel superior because you didn't resort to whatever crime the person who came first did. We don't like winners. We don't like them because they elevate themselves above the group. They think they're better than everyone else.

Canadians like to feel good about themselves and their country. What nation doesn't? One way we feel good is by comparing ourselves to the evil empire. Circumstances here may be dire, but hey, look down south. It's always worse in America. Judging by the Canadian media and public, you'd think the United States was populated entirely by gun-toting, bigoted, drug addicted, money-mad, rude, crass, fornicating, tasteless boors. Shortly before he won a gold medal in the 1996 Atlanta Olympics, Canadian sprinter Donovan Bailey was quoted in *Sports Illustrated* as saying that Canada was as racist as America. No way! outraged Canadians cried. It's a very Canadian notion that there is nobility in "not being" something. Why should the idea of not being as racist as America give us satisfaction? What does America have to do with it? The question is: Is Canada racist? But that question would require some soul searching. Asserting that Canada is not as racist as America, on the other hand, allows for a bout of self-congratulation. Maybe even a beer, eh?

That is where the comedians step in.

A comedian taps us on the shoulder and laughs in our faces. Laughter is the elixir that he or she uses to help us swallow the truth. Canadians are a nervous, second-guessing people, and that's why so many of our comics use comedic masks. The mask gives the comedian an enormous amount of freedom. He or she can say anything, assail anything, and blame it on the mask. But because the mask relieves the comic of ultimate responsibility, it can remove the sting from the barbs that are delivered.

What kind of people like to tap us on the shoulder, to draw attention to themselves and their comic views of the world? People who are so hungry for approval and love that they will sacrifice everything for the euphoria of the audience's applause. People who feel like outsiders, who have been excluded by society and want, if only for five minutes onstage, to be elevated above it. They are show-offs who don't want to be swallowed by the group, and that's why comedy clubs are filled week after week. Ordinary Canadians appreciate their courage.

Canada's cultural elite — the media, the critics, the culturecrats, the governments, the champagne socialists who preach the joys of the classless society from their Rosedale mansions, the rich who like to think of the rest of the country as a mob of deferential hicks — do not. Often the comedians are very gentle people. Their victims are almost always themselves, as was the case with Colin Campbell. That gentleness, too, is a Canadian characteristic. There is a stillness in the Canadian psyche that comes from being part of such a vast and, for the most part, sparsely populated country.

Once the need is there, a Canadian comedian enters the system. What he or she finds is a gruelling, merciless, impoverishing grind. Comedy is an American-style business, totally free market. The government supports the other arts, to some extent, but not comedy. Why? For one thing, government funding for the arts is based on the idea that art benefits and enriches society. Comedy, especially stand-up comedy — with its crudeness, vulgarity, sexuality, ridicule, and criticism of everything politicians are likely to hold dear — is not what the culturecrats have in mind. Ironically, though, this lack of government involvement has helped make Canadian comedy strong. Stand-up, for example, started weak with Starvin' Marvin's, but it grew on a solid, natural foundation, not an artificial podium erected on government largesse.

But trying to advance in the business is always extremely tough. In the early years, as a comic hones his or her craft working the clubs, it's not so bad, and there are even some advantages for Canadians. Not having a Hollywood pot of gold to aim for makes Canadian comedians place more value on the art in comedy. American comics often start tailoring their acts to Hollywood early in their careers. But since Canadian producers and agents are notoriously reluctant to look for talent in comedy clubs and, should they find any, even more reluctant to employ it, comedians here have only one consolation: their art. That's why Canadian comedians from Wayne and Shuster to SCTV and onward cling so ferociously to control their writing. For years in Canada, their writing is all they own, and it is their only reward. So when they arrive in Los Angeles, they are not unformed raw materials but finished products. Hollywood loved Harland Williams, for example, because his talent was fresh; he was unique. That's because for six years he had been allowed to work without any pressure to conform to Hollywood's tastes.

It is only when a comedian is ready to make the next step, from clubs to television, that the Canadian comedy business dries up. Once the market — the public — is removed from the equation, the comedy business derails. In 1996, the CBC was the only game in town. You either worked for the CBC or you didn't work. Most comedians understood the odds. What they hated was the scale the CBC used to judge a comic's suitability. In 1995, at the Just For Laughs Festival, the CBC held a symposium on Canadian comedy. Representatives from the CBC sat behind a row of tables and spoke of the network's fine tradition of producing Canadian comedians. They weren't lying — the CBC has produced some great stuff — but history did not concern the audience, which consisted mostly of Canadian comedians and their managers. The comics were thinking about the future. After the speeches, manager Louise Parent rose and asked just what she had to do "to get a person from the CBC to come and see my guys." Parent, it turned out, had organized plenty of showcases for her talent and had always invited the CBC's people. She had even held a showcase in the CBC's Broadcast Building, and still no one had shown. "You mean to tell me one of you couldn't take an elevator down and see them? When I hold showcases in L.A., every network sends a rep," she said. The CBC panel didn't have an answer for that one.

What they were looking for, the CBC panel members said, was the "Canadian sensibility." That was the yardstick they used to decide who got to work and who didn't. But although they talked a lot about the Canadian sensibility that day, they had difficulty defining it. The Canadian sensibility was like pornography: they couldn't tell you what it was, but they knew it when they saw it. Through all the blather, they seemed to be saying that material is "Canadian" if it's set in Canada and if the comics involved make a lot of Canadian geographical and political references. Those who fit this bill, and there are not many, get put on the air. The best of them, like CODCO, are then touted as a credit to the CBC.

This leaves a whole lot of comedians out on the street. They soon realize that there is no "up" left. The math is simple. In 1996, the CBC (including radio), employed approximately twenty-five comedians and comedy writers. About fifteen of Yuk Yuk's top stand-ups made over forty thousand dollars that year. *The Red Green Show* most likely brought another two comedians in above forty thousand. That means that in 1996, a grand total of forty-two comedians earned a full-time living doing comedy. Imagine if there were only forty-two Canadian painters earning a middle-class forty grand, or forty-two Canadian actors, or forty-two Canadian pianists. There really is no decision to be made. Most comedians would rather live in Canada, but they can't. Those who like road work and corporate gigs remain. Those who dream of more money and, more importantly, more creative outlets, go to America.

"I made my home here in Toronto," Eugene Levy told me sadly. "I moved back here because I love this city and I wanted my kids to grow up Canadian. But I just can't work here. It's impossible. I think I'm finally going to have to leave." That was Eugene Levy speaking, from *SCTV,* one of the best television comedy series ever to spring from Canada — or America, for that matter. If he couldn't navigate the Canadian system, what did that say about anyone else's chances?

When they arrive in America, those comedians with talent can rise fast, provided they have the right management. They sound American, they look American. They are seasoned, yet new to the market. Canada's status as the official observer of the American experience arms Canadian comedians with the ironic distance needed to mock America until it laughs. Canadian comedians also have the British connection. They have grown up influenced by the likes of Monty Python. This added dimension gives Canadian comedy its dark irony. We can handle grey. We don't need our comic heroes to be good guys. In Canada, CODCO built a career out of this talent. Their characters were always textured in light and dark. This Canadian complexity gave comedians like *SCTV*'s John Candy, Catherine O'Hara, Dave Thomas, and Eugene Levy their bite. If their stars are aligned properly, the Canadian newcomers to America find fame, fortune, and a bigger audience.

Yet there must be something else. The rest of the world is also immersed in American culture, and they have not been able to produce the same number of Hollywood hits. There must be an intangible that separates Canadian comics from the pack.

In Canada, comedy's inherent individualism is unappreciated. In America, comedy's collective nature is unappreciated. Comedy creates consensus. It creates groups. We laugh as individuals, but when we laugh at a comedy show, we become part of a collective. Unlike the audience at a tragedy, a comedy crowd externalizes its responses. So when we are laughing, and we can hear those around us laughing, we realize that we are sharing a common take on the world. Sure, we're only sharing a joke, but that joke has powerful cultural, sexual, and political implications. We are expressing our value systems publicly. After all, what is a sense of humour, if not a reflection of our values? Each is as distinctive as a fingerprint, and yet in the hands of a master comedian, each can be forged into a single imprint. We are, therefore, during those few seconds of laughter, not entirely alone. When a comedian makes an audience laugh, he or she is helping them survive. The comedian extinguishes anxiety by exposing our weaknesses and laughing at them. The Dumbells were literally helping their audience to survive. The release those soldiers felt allowed them to endure the horrors of the war in some small way.

It's a symbiotic relationship. The comedian asks the audience to place him or her (or the troupe) above it. The comedian asks the audience to listen and submit to the comic's view. In exchange, the audience expects the comedian to place its well-being above his or her own. Audience members expect the comedian to make them feel good, to be their surrogate by voicing their fears and trepidations, while at the same time slaying them. They expect the comedian to ease their pain and help them survive.

Given this dynamic, the "why" of Canadian comedy and its success in America becomes clear. Canada's comics are individualists in a culture that values the collective good over individual freedom and expression. They grow and develop here, constantly battling against this cultural barricade. Then they depart for America, a culture that values individual expression over the collective good. There the Canadian comedian is a double threat. The Canadian comedian has all the nerve and drive of the individualist combined with all the group ethics of a collectivist. The system is as simple and seamless as the change of seasons. Maybe, just this once, we're number one.